Julie Johnson's Guide to AP* Music Theory

Julie McIntosh Johnson

J. Johnson Music Publications

5062 Siesta Lane
Yorba Linda, CA 92886
Phone: (714) 961-0257
Fax: (714) 242-9350
www.bktmusic.com
info@bktmusic.com

©2010, Julie McIntosh Johnson

*AP and Advanced Placement are trademarks registered and/or owned by the College Board, which was not involved in the production of, and does not endorse, this product.

Julie Johnson's Guide to AP* Music Theory

Published by:

J. Johnson Music Publications
5062 Siesta Lane
Yorba Linda, CA 92886 U.S.A.
(714) 961-0257
www.bktmusic.com

All rights reserved. No part of this book may be reproduced or transmitted in any form or by any means, electronic or mechanical, including photocopying, recording, or by any information storage and retrieval system without written permission from the author, except for the inclusion of brief quotations in a review.

©2010 by Julie McIntosh Johnson
Printed in United States of America

Library of Congress Cataloging in Publication Data

Johnson, Julie Anne McIntosh
Julie Johnson's Guide to AP* Music Theory

ISBN 10: 1-891757-12-1
ISBN 13: 978-1-891757-12-9

PA 1-723-351

*AP and Advanced Placement are trademarks registered and/or owned by the College Board, which was not involved in the production of, and does not endorse, this product.

TABLE OF CONTENTS

Lesson 1: Major and Minor Key Signatures ……………………..………………………….1

Lesson 2: Scales………………………………………………………………………………17

Lesson 3: Intervals……………………………………………………………………...........29

Lesson 4: Modes………………………………………………………………...……………39

Lesson 5: Triads and Inversions…..………………………………………………………….51

Lesson 6: Primary and Secondary Triads……………………………………………………63

Lesson 7: Seventh Chords…………………………………………………………………....77

Lesson 8: The Secondary Dominant and The Secondary Leading Tone Chord........................89

Lesson 9: Cadences…………………………………………………………………………..99

Review: Lessons 1-9………………………………………………………………...……….111

Lesson 10: Melodic Devices………………………………………………………………….115

Lesson 11: Phrase Structure…………………………………………………………………..127

Lesson 12: Ornaments and Nonharmonic Tones……………………………………………..139

Lesson 13: Harmonic Function………………………………………………..………………153

Lesson 14: Tonicization and Modulation……………………………………………………..167

Lesson 15: Altered Chords and Suspensions………………………..…………………………179

Lesson 16: Introduction to Four Part Harmony……………………………………………….185

Lesson 17: Doubling…………………………………………………………………………..193

Lesson 18: Harmonic Progression…………………………………………………………….203

Lesson 19: Introduction to Voice Leading…………………………………………………….213

Lesson 20: Poor Voice Leading……………………………………………………………….221

Lesson 21: Realizing Figured Bass……………………………………………………………227

Lesson 22: Four Part Writing………………………………………..…………………………235

Review: Lessons 10-22……………………………………………………………………………….241

Lesson 23: Interpreting Lead Sheets………………………………………………………………245

Lesson 24: Form and Structure……………………………………………..……………………..253

Lesson 25: The Fugue………………………………………...…...………………………………277

Lesson 26: Rhythm and Meter……………………………………………………………………..285

Lesson 27: Texture………………………………………………………………………………….299

Lesson 28: Performance Terms…………………………………………………………………….313

Lesson 29: Instrumental Terms……………………………………..……………………………..321

Lesosn 30: Genre……………………………………………………………………………………327

Lesson 31: Vocal Terms……………………………………………………………………………333

Lesson 32: Jazz and Pop Terms……………………………………………………………………341

Review: Lessons 23-32……………………………………………………………………..……..347

Answer Key……………………………………………………………………………………….353

Blank Staff Paper………………………………………………………………………………….384

References………………………………………………………………………………………...387

Index……………………………………………………………………………………………...389

Ear Training and Listening CD (MP3 Format)……………………………………….Inside Back Cover

LESSON 1
MAJOR AND MINOR KEY SIGNATURES

The **KEY SIGNATURE** for a musical composition is found at the beginning of the piece, next to the clef signs. Most music is written in major or minor keys. **CONSONANCE** refers to musical sounds that involve major or minor chords, or major, minor or perfect intervals, and have a stable sound. **DISSONANCE** refers to unstable sounds, including groups of notes that are not within the context of these chords or intervals.

The key signature identifies which notes in the music are to receive sharps or flats, and the **KEY** or **TONALITY** of the music. **TONAL** music gives preference to one tone, making this the tonal center. For example, the key of C Major has a tonal center of C.

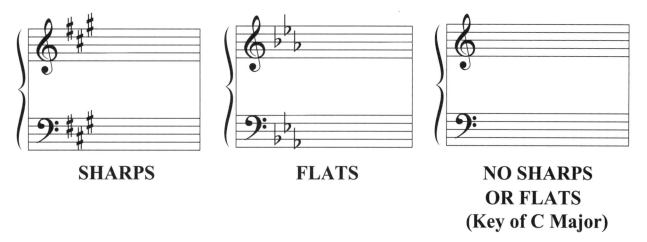

SHARPS　　　　　**FLATS**　　　　　**NO SHARPS OR FLATS**
(Key of C Major)

If the key signature has <u>SHARPS</u>, they will be written in this order, on these lines and spaces. This is called the **ORDER OF SHARPS**.

THE ORDER OF SHARPS

A saying to help you remember this order is:

Fat Cats Go Down Alleys Eating Bologna

If a key signature has one sharp, it will be F♯. If a key signature has two sharps, they will be F♯ and C♯, etc.

To determine which Major key a group of sharps represents, find and name the last sharp (the sharp furthest to the right), then go up a half step from that sharp. The note which is a half step above the last sharp is the name of the Major key.

Three sharps: F♯, C♯, G♯

Last sharp is G♯

A half step above G♯ is A

Key of A Major

To determine which sharps are in a Major key, find the sharp which is a half step below the name of the key. Name all the sharps from the Order of Sharps up to and including that sharp.

Key of D Major

A half step below D is C♯

Name all sharps, from the Order of Sharps, up to and including C♯

F♯ and C♯

If a key signature has <u>FLATS</u>, they will be in the following order, written on these lines and spaces. This is called the **ORDER OF FLATS.**

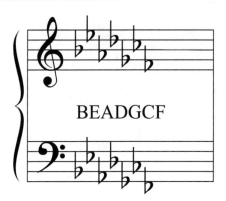

BEADGCF

THE ORDER OF FLATS

The Order of Flats can be memorized this way:

BEAD Gum Candy Fruit

If a key signature has one flat, it will be B♭. If it has two flats, they will be B♭ and E♭, etc.

To determine which Major key a group of flats represents, name the next to last flat.

Three flats: B♭, E♭, A♭

Next to last flat is E♭

Key of E♭ Major

To determine which flats are needed for a given key, name all the flats from the Order of Flats up to and including the name of the key, then add one more.

Key of E♭ Major

Name all flats from the Order of Flats up to and including E♭, then add one more.

B♭, E♭, A♭

The key signature for F Major is an exception. It has one flat: B♭.

KEY SIGNATURE FOR F MAJOR

Major keys which have sharps will be named with a letter only, or a letter and a sharp (for example, G Major, D Major, F♯ Major).

Major keys which have flats will have a flat in their name (for example, B♭ Major, D♭ Major, E♭ Major).

The two exceptions to the above rules are F Major (one flat: B♭), and C Major (no sharps or flats).

1. Name these Major keys.

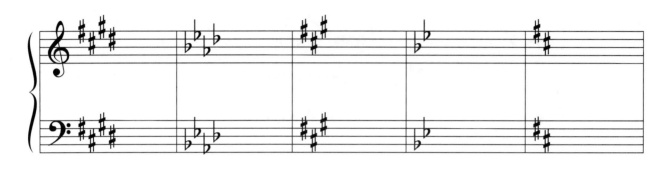

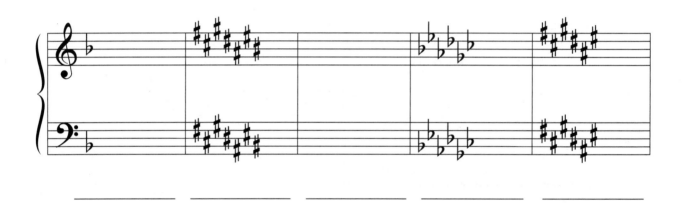

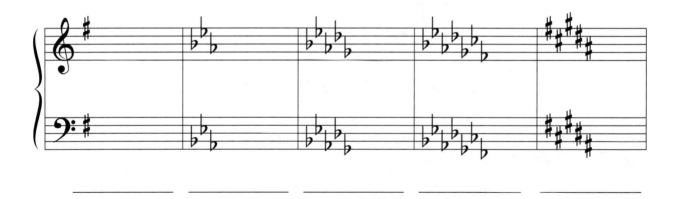

2. Write the key signatures for these Major keys.

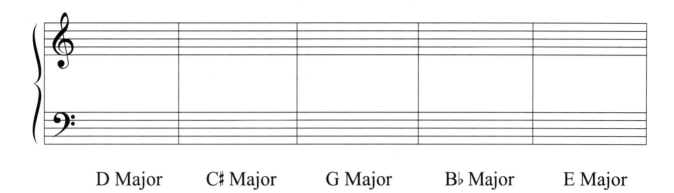

    D Major   C♯ Major   G Major   B♭ Major   E Major

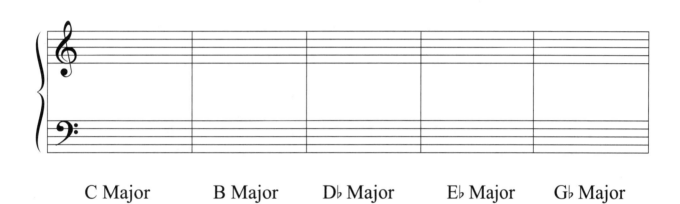

    C Major   B Major   D♭ Major   E♭ Major   G♭ Major

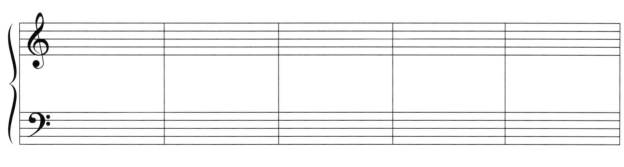

    F♯ Major   A♭ Major   A Major   F Major   C♭ Major

PARALLEL KEYS (or **PARALLEL MAJOR AND MINOR)** have the same letter names. For example, C Major and c minor are parallel keys or parallel Major and minor.

The **RELATIVE MINOR** for a Major key is found by going down three half steps from the name of the Major key. Skip one letter between the names of the keys.

KEY SIGNATURE FOR D MAJOR
THREE HALF STEPS BELOW D IS B
KEY OF B MINOR

One way to determine whether a composition is in the Major or minor key is to look at the last note of the piece. It is usually the same as the name of the key. (For example, a piece which is in the key of e minor will probably end on E.) Also, look at the music to find the note around which the music appears to be centered. This should be the tonal center, which is the same as the name of the key.

3. Name these <u>minor</u> keys. (Determine the name of the major key, then go down three half steps. Skip one letter name between the name of the major key and the name of the minor key.)

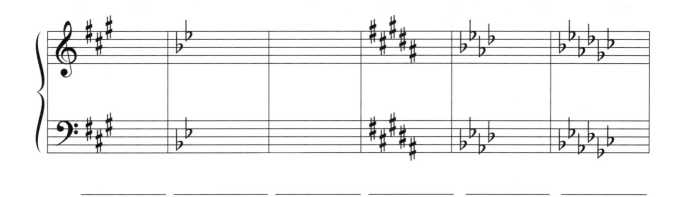

4. Write the key signatures for these minor keys.

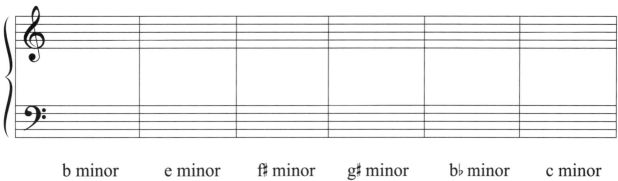

    b minor   e minor   f♯ minor   g♯ minor   b♭ minor   c minor

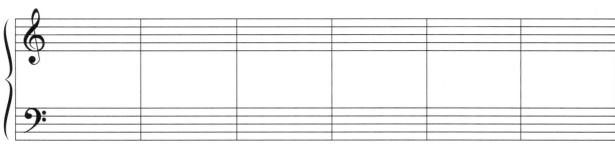

    a minor   c♯ minor   d minor   g minor   f minor   e♭ minor

5. Determine the name of the major or minor key for each of the following musical examples.

a. From *Sonata, Op. 31, No. 1,* by Beethoven. _____

b. From *Fugue, BWV 873,* by J.S. Bach. _____

c. From *Ballade, Op. 118, No. 3,* by Brahms. _____

d. From *Sonata, Op. 2, No. 1,* by Beethoven. _____

e. From *Sonata, Hob. XVI:41,* by Haydn. _____

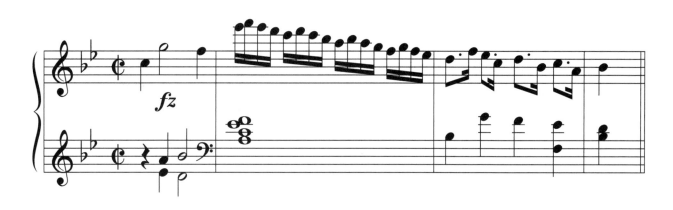

f. From *Partita No. 1, BWV 825: Allemande,* by J.S. Bach. _____

g. From *Prelude, Op. 28, No. 9,* by Chopin. _____

h. From *Sonata, Hob. XVI:46,* by Haydn. _____

i. From *Sonata, KV 533 u. 494,* by Mozart. _____

The **CIRCLE OF FIFTHS** (sometimes called the **Circle of Keys**) is a method of organizing the Major and minor keys so that when ascending by perfect fifths from key to key, one sharp is added to each new key. When the keys of B, F♯, and C♯ are reached, there is an <u>enharmonic</u> change (notes with the same pitch but different letter names, such as F♯ and G♭). Flats are then used, and as the keys ascend by perfect fifths, one flat is deleted from each key.

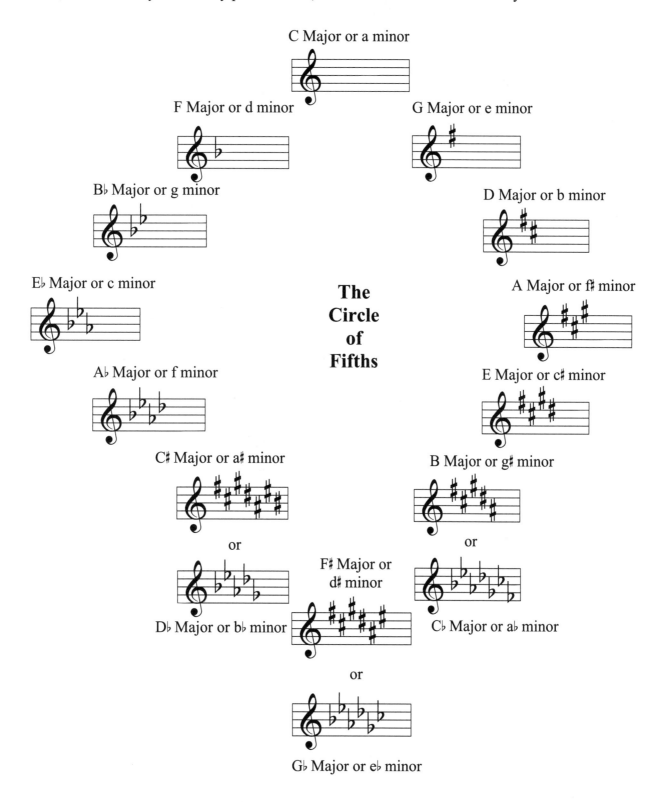

6. Fill in the Circle of Fifths (Circle of Keys) below. Include the Major and minor key names, enharmonic equivalents, and write each key signature on its staff.

Check the correct answer for each of the following questions.

7. What is the order of sharps?

   _____ a. F♯ C♯ D♯ E♯ A♯ B♯ G♯
   _____ b. F♯ C♯ G♯ D♯ A♯ E♯ B♯
   _____ c. F♯ G♯ D♯ E♯ A♯ B♯ C♯
   _____ d. F♯ C♯ D♯ B♯ A♯ G♯ E♯

8. What is the order of flats?

   _____ a. B♭ E♭ A♭ G♭ D♭ C♭ F♭
   _____ b. B♭ C♭ D♭ E♭ F♭ G♭ A♭
   _____ c. B♭ F♭ A♭ G♭ D♭ C♭ E♭
   _____ d. B♭ E♭ A♭ D♭ G♭ C♭ F♭

9. If a key signature has flats, which flat is the same as the name of the key?

   _____ a. The first flat
   _____ b. The last flat
   _____ c. The second flat
   _____ d. The next to last flat

10. What is the relative Major for the key of f♯ minor?

    _____ a. A Major
    _____ b. E Major
    _____ c. B Major
    _____ d. D Major

11. What is the parallel minor for the key of E Major?

    _____ a. c♯ minor
    _____ b. e minor
    _____ c. g minor
    _____ d. f♯ minor

12. What is the relative minor for the key of B Major?

    _____ a. c minor
    _____ b. g minor
    _____ c. g♯ minor
    _____ d. a♭ minor

13. What is the tonal center for the key of A Major?

    _____ a. E
    _____ b. A
    _____ c. A♭
    _____ d. F

14. What two things does the key signature indicate?

_____ a. How fast and loud to play

_____ b. When to start and stop

_____ c. The pulse and tempo

_____ d. The tonality and which notes receive sharps or flats

15. Which key is next in this sequence from the circle of fifths: C Major, G Major, D Major, _____ Major

_____ a. A Major

_____ b. F Major

_____ c. C♯ Major

_____ d. A♭ Major

16. Which two of these can help determine whether music is in the Major key or in the minor key? (Check two answers.)

_____ a. The first note

_____ b. The last note

_____ c. The tonal center

_____ d. The time signature

17. If a key signature has four flats, what is the name of the key?

_____ a. F♯ Major

_____ b. D♭ Major

_____ c. F Major

_____ d. A♭ Major

18. If a key signature has four sharps, what are the names of the sharps?

_____ a. A♯ B♯ C♯ D♯

_____ b. D♯ A♯ E♯ F♯

_____ c. C♯ G♯ D♯ A♯

_____ d. F♯ C♯ G♯ D♯

19. If a key signature has six sharps, what is the name of the key?

_____ a. F Major

_____ b. G♭ Major

_____ c. C♯ Major

_____ d. F♯ Major

20. What is the relative Major for the key of c♯ minor?

_____ a. D Major

_____ b. E Major

_____ c. B♭ Major

_____ d. C Major

SIGHT SINGING
MAJOR AND MINOR MELODIES

Sing each of the following examples. (Adjust the octave to fit your vocal range.)

EAR TRAINING
RECOGNIZING MAJOR AND MINOR KEYS

Listen to Examples 1-10. Each example will be played twice. Check whether each example has major tonality or minor tonality.

Example 1: _____ Major _____ Minor

Example 2: _____ Major _____ Minor

Example 3: _____ Major _____ Minor

Example 4: _____ Major _____ Minor

Example 5: _____ Major _____ Minor

Example 6: _____ Major _____ Minor

Example 7: _____ Major _____ Minor

Example 8: _____ Major _____ Minor

Example 9: _____ Major _____ Minor

Example 10: _____ Major _____ Minor

LESSON 2
SCALES

SCALES are a series of notes, which are each a step apart. They begin and end with notes of the same letter name. **DIATONIC** scales include Major scales, and all three forms of minor (natural, harmonic, and melodic).

MAJOR SCALES contain eight notes, and have all the sharps or flats from the Major key signature with the same name. Major scales are made up of two **TETRACHORDS,** which are four note patterns made up of whole step, whole step, half step. There is a whole step between the two tetrachords.

Example: D Major Scale begins and ends with the note "D," and has F♯ and C♯. (In Major scales, most of the steps are whole steps, with half steps occuring between notes 3-4 and 7-8.)

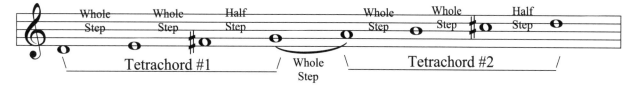

D MAJOR SCALE

There are three different forms of minor scales: **Natural Minor**, **Harmonic Minor**, and **Melodic Minor**.

NATURAL MINOR SCALES contain all the sharps or flats from the minor key signature with the same name.

Example: d natural minor scale begins and ends with the note "D," and has B♭.

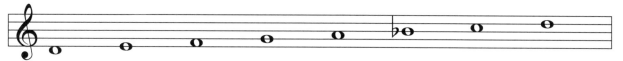

D NATURAL MINOR SCALE

HARMONIC MINOR SCALES are created by raising the seventh note of the natural minor scale a half step. This creates a half step, rather than a whole step, between the seventh and eighth notes of the scale, making the seventh a **LEADING TONE**.

D HARMONIC MINOR SCALE

MELODIC MINOR SCALES are created by raising the sixth and seventh notes of the natural minor scale while ascending, and returning them to natural minor (lowering them) while descending.

D MELODIC MINOR SCALE

The **CHROMATIC SCALE** is a series of thirteen notes. Each note is a half step away from its neighbor. Using sharps while the scale is ascending and flats while the scale is descending helps avoid the use of many naturals, but is not required.

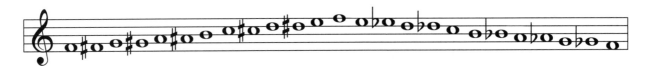

CHROMATIC SCALE BEGINNING ON F

The **WHOLE TONE SCALE** consists entirely of whole steps. There are only seven notes in the whole tone scale, so when writing the scale on the staff, one letter name will be missing.

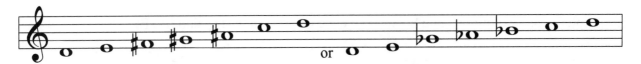

WHOLE TONE SCALE BEGINNING ON D

The **PENTATONIC SCALE** consists of five notes. There are multiple forms of pentatonic scales, but the most common uses the following pattern. This scale can be formed easily by playing only the black keys on the piano.

PENTATONIC SCALE BEGINNING ON C

1. Write these scales. Do not use a key signature. Write accidentals (sharps or flats) before the notes.

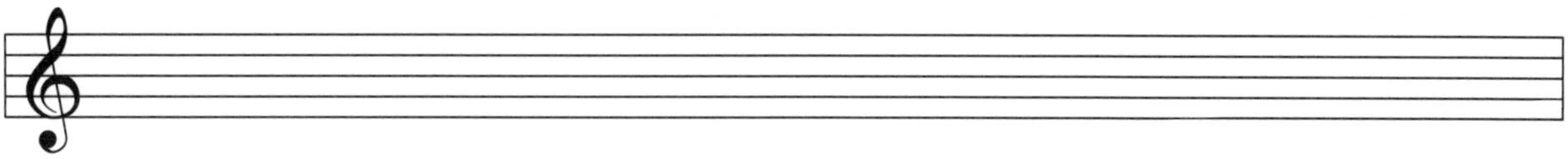

C# Major

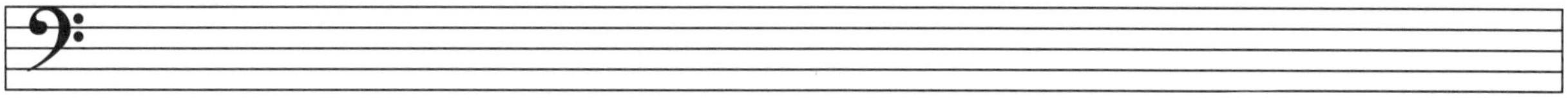

Pentatonic beginning on C

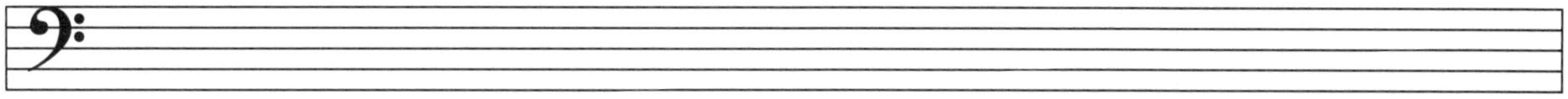

Chromatic beginning on B (ascending and descending)

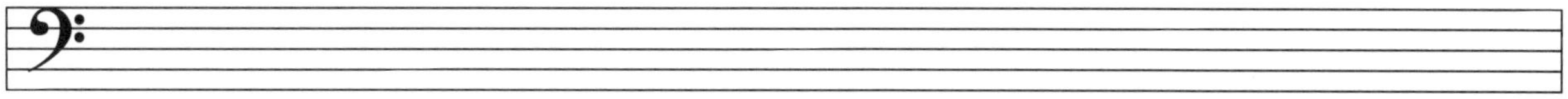

f harmonic minor

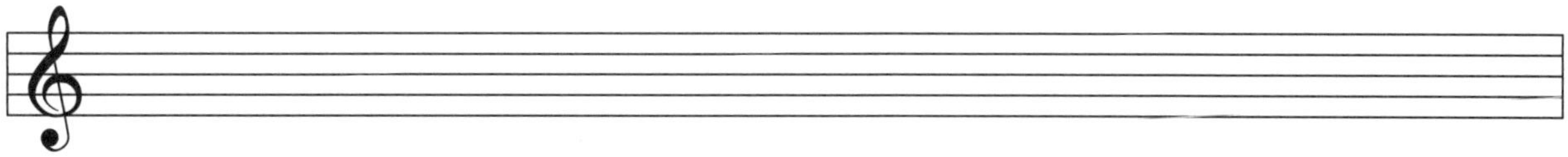

Db Major

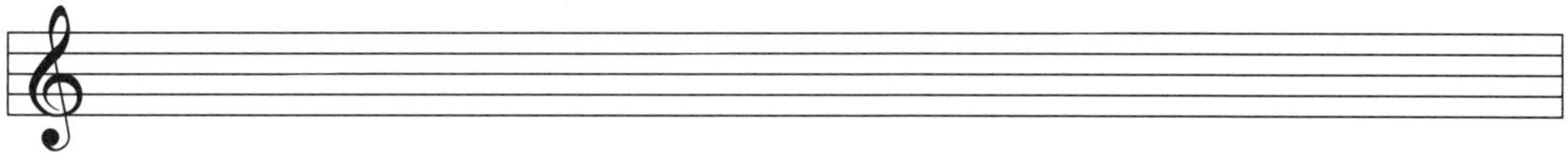

Whole Tone beginning on E

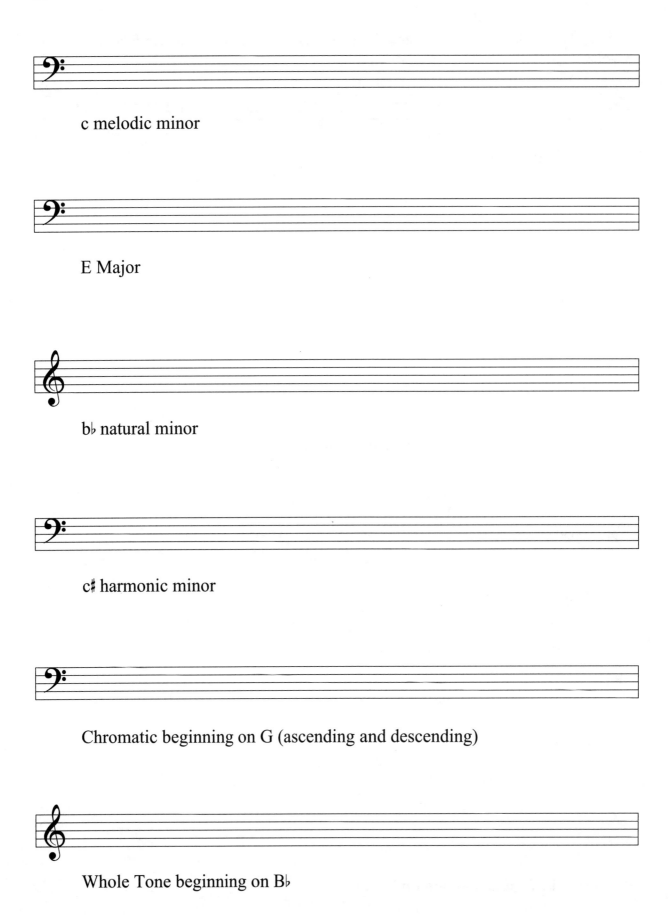

c melodic minor

E Major

b♭ natural minor

c♯ harmonic minor

Chromatic beginning on G (ascending and descending)

Whole Tone beginning on B♭

d melodic minor (ascending and descending)

f♮ natural minor

e♭ harmonic minor

g♯ melodic minor

Chromatic beginning on C♯ (ascending and descending)

Whole Tone beginning on A

2. Name the circled scale in each of the following examples. For minor scales, include the form of minor that is used (natural, harmonic or melodic).

a. From *Nocturne, Op. 48, No. 2,* by Chopin. _____ Scale

b. From *Sonata, K. 279,* by Mozart. _____ Scale

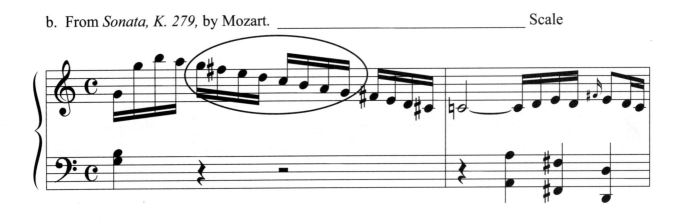

c. From *Sonata, Op. 26,* by Beethoven. _____ Scale

d. From *Sonata, K. 280,* by Mozart. _____ Scale

e. From *Nocturne, Op. 62, No. 1,* by Chopin. _____ Scale

f. From *Sonata, Op. 27, No. 1,* by Beethoven. _____ Scale

g. From *Sonata, Op. 31, No. 1,* by Beethoven. _____ Scale

h. From *Sonata, K. 281,* by Mozart. _____ Scale

i. From *Nocturne, Op. 9, No.2*, by Chopin. _____ Scale

Check the type of scale used in each example.

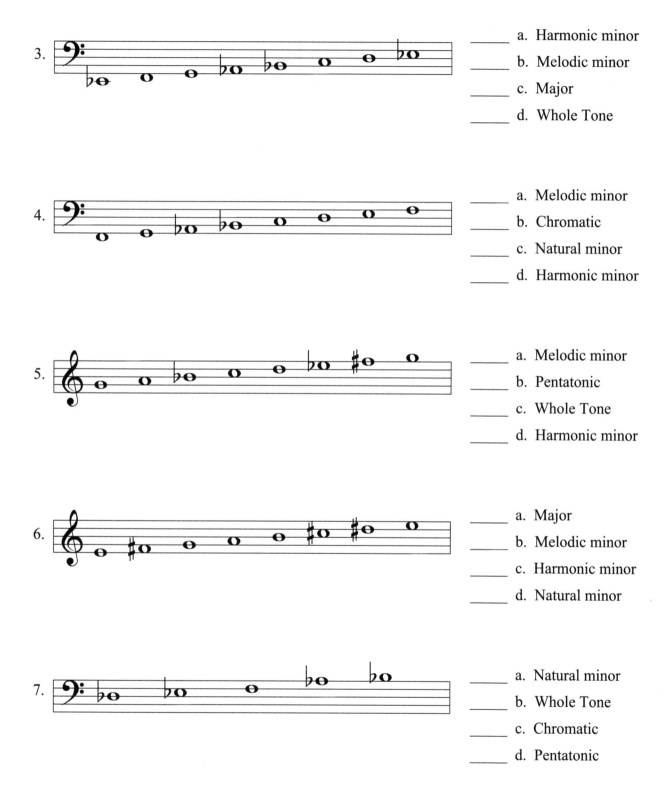

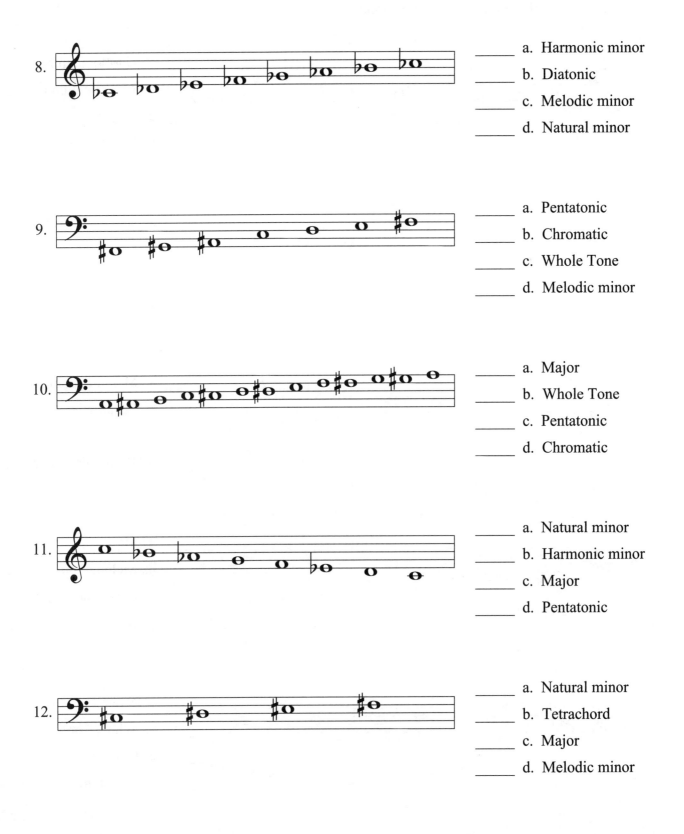

SIGHT SINGING
SCALES

Sing each of the following examples. (Adjust the octave to fit your vocal range.)

a.

b.

c.

d.

e.

f.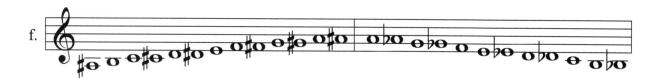

g.

h.

EAR TRAINING
RECOGNIZING SCALE TYPES

Listen to Examples 11-15. Each example will be played three times. Check the type of scale that is played.

Example 11: _____ Major _____ harmonic minor _____ melodic minor

Example 12: _____ whole tone _____ pentatonic _____ tetrachord

Example 13: _____ natural minor _____ harmonic minor _____ chromatic

Example 14: _____ natural minor _____ Major _____ melodic minor

Example 15: _____ harmonic minor _____ natural minor _____ whole tone

Listen to Examples 16-20. Each example will be played three times. Complete each scale on the appropriate staff.

LESSON 3
INTERVALS

An **INTERVAL** is the distance between two notes. In music, intervals are named with numbers. When naming intervals, count the two notes that make the interval, and all the lines and spaces, or all the letter names, between the two.

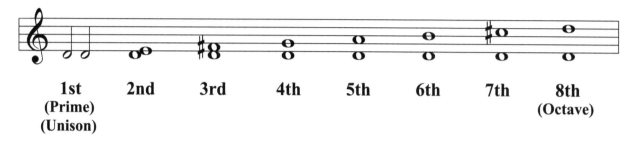

If the top note of the interval is within the key of the bottom note, the interval is **Major** or **Perfect**. 2nds, 3rds, 6ths, and 7ths are Major. 4ths, 5ths, and 8ths are Perfect.

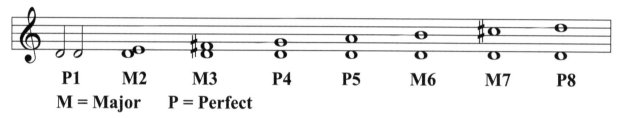

Intervals that are played at the same time are called **HARMONIC INTERVALS**. Intervals that are played one at a time are called **MELODIC INTERVALS**.

If a Major 2nd, 3rd, 6th, or 7th is made smaller by lowering the top note or raising the bottom note a half step, without changing the letter name of either note, the interval becomes **minor**.

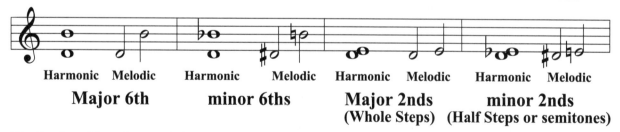

If a Perfect 4th, 5th, or 8th is made smaller by lowering the top note or raising the bottom note a half step, without changing the letter name of either note, the interval becomes **diminished**.

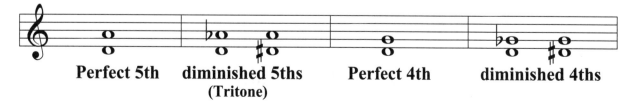

If a Major 2nd, 3rd, 6th, or 7th is made smaller by lowering the top note or raising the bottom note a whole step, without changing the letter name of either note, the interval becomes **diminished**.

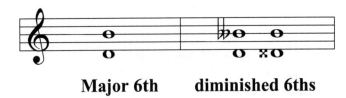

Major 6th   diminished 6ths

If a Major or Perfect interval is made larger by raising the top note or lowering the bottom note a half step, without changing the letter name of either note, the interval becomes **Augmented.**

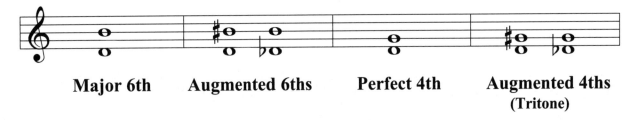

Major 6th   Augmented 6ths   Perfect 4th   Augmented 4ths
                                                              (Tritone)

To write an interval above a given note, determine the key signature for the lower note, and add any necessary accidentals. For Major or Perfect intervals, keep those accidentals. For minor, diminished, or Augmented intervals, raise or lower the top note by using accidentals and without changing the letter name.

In the example below, an Augmented 4th above F is needed. F Major has B♭. The 4th is made Augmented by removing the B♭ (raising the note a half step).

A4 up   Answer: B

To write an interval below a given note, determine all possibilities the note could be. Then, determine which of those notes is the correct one for the quality of the interval needed.

In the example below, a minor 7th below C is needed. The three possibilities are D, D♭, and D♯. A minor 7th above D♭ is C♭, a minor 7th above D♯ is C♯, and a minor 7th above D is C. The answer is D.

m7 below C   Answer: D

Intervals larger than an octave are called **COMPOUND INTERVALS.** The qualities remain the same as when the intervals were less than an octave. For example, C-G is a Perfect 5th. The compound interval C-G, which is a 12th, is a Perfect 12th. Compound intervals are altered in the same way as intervals that are less than one octave. (Subtract 7 from the number of the compound interval to find the corresponding interval that is less than one octave.)

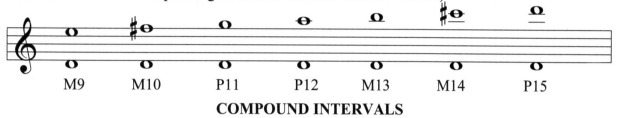

COMPOUND INTERVALS

1. Name these intervals. Give their qualities and numbers, such as M3 or P4.

2. Complete these intervals. Do note change the given note.

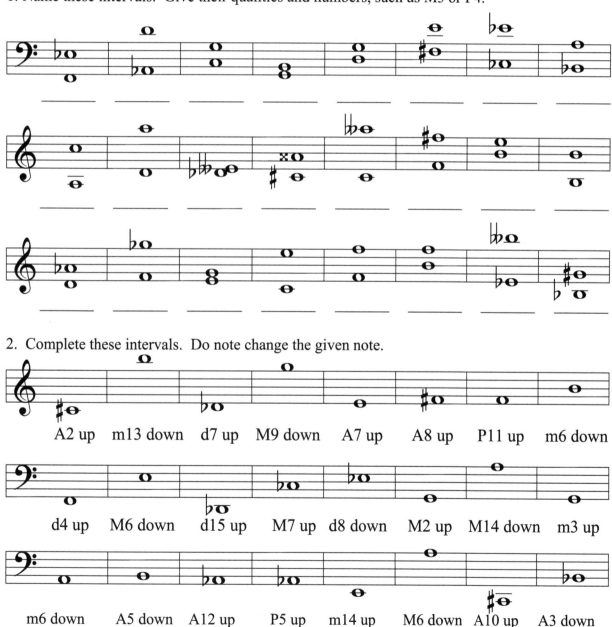

When naming intervals within music literature, follow these steps:

a. Write the sharps or flats from the key signature, or from earlier in the measure, before the notes (as reminders).

b. Determine the number for the interval (by counting the lines and spaces, or the letter names).

c. Using the key signature for the <u>lowest note of the interval</u>, find the quality (Major, minor, Perfect, diminished, or Augmented).

3. Name the circled intervals in the passages below. Follow the steps listed above for each interval.

a. From *Sonata, Op. 2, No. 1,* by Beethoven.

b. From *Nocturne, Op. 9, No. 2,* by Chopin.

c. From *Partita No. 1, BWV 825: Allemande,* by J.S. Bach.

Check the correct answer for each question.

4. How can a Major interval be changed into minor?

   _____ a. Raise the top note a half step

   _____ b. Lower the top note a half step

   _____ c. Raise the top note a whole step

   _____ d. Lower the top note a whole step

5. Which of these determines the accidentals needed for Major or Perfect intervals?

   _____ a. The Major key signature

   _____ b. The minor key signature

   _____ c. The whole tone scale

   _____ d. The chromatic scale

6. What accidental will make this an augmented 5th?

   _____ a. ♯

   _____ b. ♭

   _____ c. ×

   _____ d. ♭♭

7. What is another name for a Perfect 8th?

   _____ a. Unison

   _____ b. Semitone

   _____ c. Octave

   _____ d. Prime

8. What determines whether an interval is compound?

   _____ a. It is smaller than an octave

   _____ b. It has two accidentals

   _____ c. It uses a double sharp or double flat

   _____ d. It is larger than an octave

9. Which of these is another name for a Major second?

_____ a. Whole step

_____ b. Half step

_____ c. Unison

_____ d. Prime

10. Which two of these are other names for a Perfect 1? (Check two answers.)

_____ a. Prime

_____ b. Semitone

_____ c. Unison

_____ d. Half step

11. Which note is a Major sixth below the given note?

_____ a. B

_____ b. B♭

_____ c. A♯

_____ d. B♯

12. Which two of these are other names for a minor second? (Check two answers.)

_____ a. Prime

_____ b. Half step

_____ c. Semitone

_____ d. Octave

13. What is another name for an Augmented 4th or a diminished 5th?

_____ a. Tricep

_____ b. Triangle

_____ c. Triad

_____ d. Tritone

INVERTED INTERVALS are intervals that have been turned upside down. The top note becomes the bottom note. **The names of the notes do not change.**

When inverting intervals, the following rules apply to the numbers:

    2nds become 7ths   7ths become 2nds

    3rds become 6ths   6ths become 3rds

    4ths become 5ths   5ths become 4ths

    8ths stay 8ths

The following rules apply to the qualities:

    Perfect intervals stay Perfect

    Major intervals become minor   minor intervals become Major

    Augmented intervals become diminished   diminished intervals become Augmented

14. Write the missing note to invert each interval, and name the new interval with its number and quality. Do not change the letter of the missing note. The first one is given.

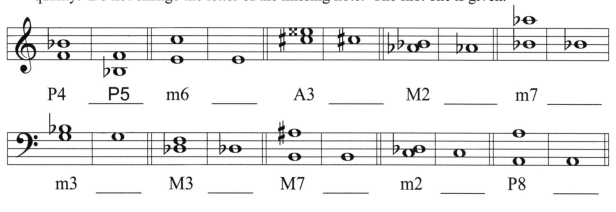

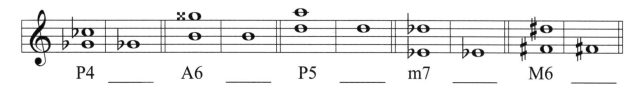

Check the correct answer for each question.

15. When inverted, Major intervals become what quality?

    _____ a. minor
    _____ b. Major
    _____ c. diminished
    _____ d. Augmented

16. What will be the name of this interval when inverted?

    _____ a. A4
    _____ b. d4
    _____ c. P4
    _____ d. d5

17. When inverted, 4ths become which interval?

    _____ a. 3rds
    _____ b. 6ths
    _____ c. 7ths
    _____ d. 5ths

18. Augmented intervals become what quality when inverted?

    _____ a. Major
    _____ b. minor
    _____ c. diminished
    _____ d. Augmented

19. When inverted, Major 6ths become what interval?

    _____ a. minor 3rds
    _____ b. Major 3rds
    _____ c. diminished 4ths
    _____ d. Augmented 2nds

SIGHT SINGING
INTERVALS

Each of the following phrases is based on one interval. Sight sing each example. (Adjust the octave to fit your vocal range.)

EAR TRAINING
RECOGNIZING INTERVALS

Listen to Examples 21-25. Each example will be played three times. Check the type of interval that is played.

Example 21: _____ M2   _____ m2   _____ m3   _____ M3

Example 22: _____ A4   _____ P4   _____ P5   _____ M3

Example 23: _____ m6   _____ M6   _____ A6   _____ P5

Example 24: _____ M2   _____ m2   _____ M3   _____ m3

Example 25: _____ m6   _____ P4   _____ P5   _____ d5

Listen to Examples 26-30. Each example will be played three times. Write the second note of each interval.

LESSON 4
MODES

The term **MODE** is used to indicate any of a number of scale formations, including Major and minor. Most commonly, the term is associated with the following scale patterns.

IONIAN MODE has the same pattern of whole and half steps as the Major scale.

IONIAN MODE ON C (C MAJOR SCALE)

DORAN MODE contains the pattern of whole and half steps that occurs when beginning and ending on the SECOND note of the Major scale. Half steps occur between notes 2-3 and 6-7. It is the same as a Major scale which has the third and seventh scale degrees lowered a half step.

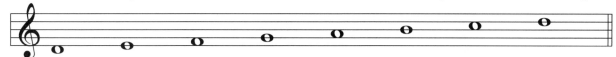

DORIAN MODE ON D

PHRYGIAN MODE contains the pattern of whole and half steps that occurs when beginning and ending on the THIRD note of the Major scale. Half steps occur between notes 1-2 and 5-6. It is the same as a Major scales with the second, third, sixth and seventh scale degrees each lowered a half step.

PHRYGIAN MODE ON E

LYDIAN MODE contains the pattern of whole and half steps that occurs when beginning and ending on the FOURTH note of the Major scale. Half steps occur between notes 4-5 and 7-8. It is the same as a Major scale which has the fourth scale degree raised a half step.

LYDIAN MODE ON F

MIXOLYDIAN MODE contains the pattern of whole and half steps that occurs when beginning and ending on the FIFTH note of the Major scale. Half steps occur between notes 3-4 and 6-7. It is the same as a Major scale with the seventh scale degree lowered a half step.

MIXOLYDIAN MODE ON G

AEOLIAN MODE contains the pattern of whole and half steps that occurs when beginning and ending on the SIXTH note of the Major scale. Half steps occur between notes 2-3 and 5-6. It is the same as the natural minor scale.

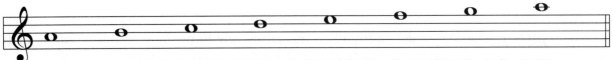

AEOLIAN MODE ON A (A NATURAL MINOR SCALE)

LOCRIAN MODE contains the pattern of whole and half steps that occurs when beginning and ending on the SEVENTH note of the Major scale. Half steps occur between notes 1-2 and 4-5. It is the same as a Major scale which has the second, third, fifth, sixth and seventh scale degrees each lowered a half step.

LOCRIAN MODE ON B

These examples show how to determine the name of a given mode.

1. Look at the accidentals in the above mode. Determine the Major key signature for those accidentals.
   The example has A♭, B♭, and E♭. The correct order for the Major key signature is B♭, E♭, A♭. The Major key for these flats is E♭ Major.

2. The first note of the mode will determine the name of the mode. G is the third scale degree of E♭ Major scale. The mode is Phrygian.

1. The accidentals in the above mode are C♯ and F♯. The correct order for the Major key signature is F♯, C♯. The Major key for these sharps is D Major.

2. A is the fifth scale degree of D Major. The mode is Mixolydian.

Fill in the blanks for each example to determine the name for each mode. The first one is given.

1. [bass clef staff with notes]

   a. Accidentals are: C♯, D♯, F♯, G♯
   b. Key signature order: F♯, C♯, G♯, D♯
   c. Name of Major key: E
   d. Count up from name of key to first note of mode: E to A: 4th note
   e. Type of mode: Lydian

2. [bass clef staff with notes]

   a. Accidentals are: ___, ___, ___
   b. Key signature order: ___, ___, ___
   c. Name of Major key: ___
   d. Count up from name of key to first note of mode: ___
   e. Name of mode: ___

3. [treble clef staff with notes]

   a. Accidentals are: ___, ___, ___, ___, ___, ___
   b. Key signature order: ___, ___, ___, ___, ___, ___
   c. Name of Major key: ___
   d. Count up from name of key to first note of mode: ___
   e. Name of mode: ___

4. [treble clef staff with notes]

   a. Accidentals are: ___, ___, ___, ___
   b. Key signature order: ___, ___, ___, ___
   c. Name of Major key: ___
   d. Count up from name of key to first note of mode: ___
   e. Name of mode: ___

41

5. Name each mode.

a. _____ mode

b. _____ mode

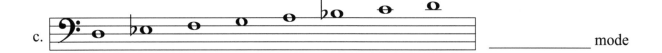

c. _____ mode

d. _____ mode

e. _____ mode

f. _____ mode

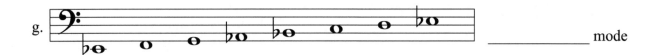

g. _____ mode

h. _____ mode

To determine which accidentals to use for a given mode, use the following intervals to find the Major key that has the sharps or flats needed:

Ionian mode: Use Major key signature

All other modes, go down the indicated interval, and use the key signature for the resulting note:

Dorian mode: M2

Phrygian mode: M3

Lydian mode: P4

Mixolydian mode: P5

Aeolian mode: M6

Locrian mode: M7

These two examples show how determine the accidentals needed for an indicated mode:

To write Phrygian mode on G:

1. Find the note that is a Major 3rd below G. A Major 3rd below G is E♭.

2. Determine the key signature for E♭ Major: B♭, E♭, A♭.

3. Write Phrygian mode beginning and ending on G, and add the accidentals B♭, E♭, and A♭.

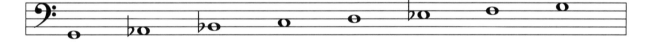

To write Mixolydian mode on A:

1. Find the note that is a Perfect 5th below A. A Perfect 5th below A is D.

2. Determine the key signature for the key of D Major: F♯, C♯.

3. Write Mixolydian mode beginning and ending on A, and add the accidentals F♯ and C♯.

Fill in the blanks for each example, then add the accidentals to complete each mode. The first one is given.

6. a. Go down the interval of a __P4__ to find key signature

   b. Major key: __E__

   c. Key signature: __F#, C#, G#, D#__

   Lydian Mode on A

7. a. Go down the interval of a ____ to find key signature

   b. Major key: ____

   c. Key signature: _____

   Phrygian Mode on D

8. a. Go down the interval of a ____ to find key signature

   b. Major key: ____

   c. Key signature: _____

   Aeolian Mode on C

9. a. Go down the interval of a ____ to find key signature

   b. Major key: ____

   c. Key signature: _____

   Mixolydian Mode on E

10. a. Go down the interval of a ____ to find key signature

    b. Major key: ____

    c. Key signature: _____

    Locrian Mode on C#

11. Write each mode.

a. (bass clef staff) Ionian Mode on B

b. (treble clef staff) Phrygian Mode on E

c. (bass clef staff) Mixolydian Mode on C♯

d. (bass clef staff) Lydian Mode on A♭

e. (treble clef staff) Dorian Mode on F♯

f. (treble clef staff) Locrian Mode on E

g. (treble clef staff) Aeolian Mode on G

h. (bass clef staff) Lydian Mode on C

12. Name the mode on which each of these musical examples is based.

a. _____ mode

b. _____ mode

c. _____ mode

Check the correct answer for each question.

13. Which sharps need to be added to make this Dorian mode?

    _____ a. F#, C#, G#

    _____ b. F#, C#

    _____ c. F#, C#, G#, D#, A#

    _____ d. F#, C#, G#, D#

14. To determine the major key with the same accidentals as Mixolydian mode, which of these intervals will you descend?

    _____ a. P4

    _____ b. M3

    _____ c. P5

    _____ d. M7

15. Ionian mode is the same as which of these scales?

    _____ a. Natural minor

    _____ b. Pentatonic

    _____ c. Harmonic minor

    _____ d. Major

16. Which flats need to be added to make this Phrygian mode?

    _____ a. B♭, E♭, A♭, D♭

    _____ b. B♭, E♭

    _____ c. B♭, E♭, A♭, D♭, G♭

    _____ d. B♭, E♭, A♭,

17. Which degree of the major scale should be the first and last note when writing Locrian mode?

    _____ a. 4th

    _____ b. 6th

    _____ c. 2nd

    _____ d. 7th

18. Which note needs to be lowered to change this scale into Mixolydian mode?

_____ a. D

_____ b. F

_____ c. G

_____ d. E♭

19. Which note needs to be raised to make this Lydian mode?

_____ a. A

_____ b. C♯

_____ c. D♯

_____ d. F♯

20. Natural minor is the same as which mode?

_____ a. Ionian

_____ b. Mixolydian

_____ c. Dorian

_____ d. Aeolian

21. On which degree of the major scale would you begin and end to create Dorian mode?

_____ a. 4th

_____ b. 5th

_____ c. 2nd

_____ d. 3rd

22. To determine the major key with the same accidentals as Aeolian mode, which of these intervals will you descend?

_____ a. M3

_____ b. P5

_____ c. M6

_____ d. M7

SIGHT SINGING
MODES

Sing each of the following modes. Adjust the octave to fit your vocal range.

a.

b.

c.

d.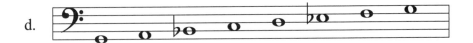

e.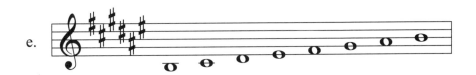

f.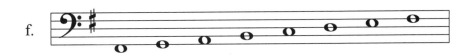

g.

EAR TRAINING
IDENTIFYING MODES

Listen to Examples 31-35. Each example will be played three times. Check the name for each mode that is played.

Example 31: _____ Lydian   _____ Dorian   _____ Aeolian   _____ Phrygian

Example 32: _____ Dorian   _____ Mixolydian   _____ Ionian   _____ Lydian

Example 33: _____ Mixolydian   _____ Locrian   _____ Aeolian   _____ Phrygian

Example 34: _____ Lydian   _____ Aeolian   _____ Locrian   _____ Dorian

Example 35: _____ Phrygian   _____ Mixolydian   _____ Ionian   _____ Lydian

Listen to examples 36-40. Each example will be played three times. Complete each mode that is played by writing the final notes on the correct staff.

Example 36:

Example 37:

Example 38:

Example 39:

Example 40:

LESSON 5
MAJOR, MINOR, AUGMENTED AND DIMINISHED TRIADS AND INVERSIONS

A **TRIAD** is a chord which contains three notes.

D Major Triad
DM

MAJOR TRIADS are made up of the first, third, and fifth notes of the Major scale with the same letter name. The lowest note of a Major triad in root position (see example) names the triad. The root and third form a Major 3rd, and the third and fifth form a minor 3rd.

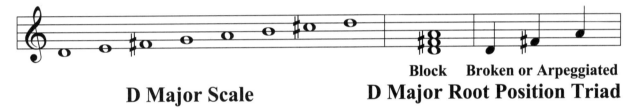

D Major Scale   Block   Broken or Arpeggiated
                       D Major Root Position Triad

To change a Major triad into a **MINOR** triad, lower the middle note (the third) a half step. Minor triads have the same sharps or flats as the minor key signature with the same letter name. The root and third form a minor 3rd, and the third and fifth form a Major 3rd.

D Major Triad   **d minor triad**
                             Dm or dm

To change a Major triad into an **AUGMENTED** triad, raise the top note (the fifth) a half step. The intervals between the root and third and between the third and fifth are both Major 3rds.

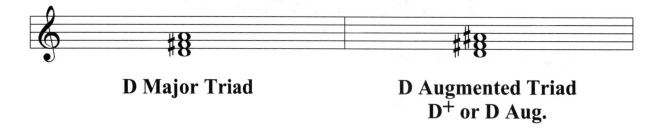

D Major Triad   D Augmented Triad
D⁺ or D Aug.

To change a Major triad into a **DIMINISHED** triad, lower the middle note (the third) and the top note (the fifth) a half step each. The intervals between the root and third and between the third and fifth are both minor 3rds.

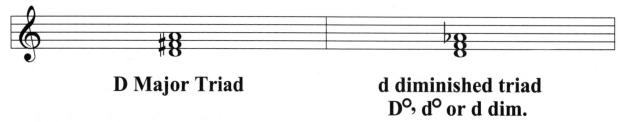

D Major Triad   d diminished triad
D°, d° or d dim.

A **ROOT POSITION TRIAD** occurs when the note which names the triad is on the bottom. The **FIGURED BASS** symbol $\frac{5}{3}$ is used for root position triads, because when the triad is in its simplest position, the intervals of a 5th and a 3rd are formed above the lowest note. When labeling a triad in root position, only the root and quality are needed, but the figured bass may be added if desired.

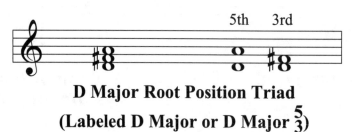

D Major Root Position Triad
(Labeled D Major or D Major $\frac{5}{3}$)

A **FIRST INVERSION TRIAD** occurs when the **third** or **middle** note of the triad is the lowest note. The figured bass symbol for first inversion triads is $^6_3$, because when they are in their simplest position the intervals of a 6th and a 3rd are formed above the lowest note.

When labeling first inversion triads, the figured bass symbol ^{6} or $^6_3$ is used.

A **SECOND INVERSION TRIAD** occurs when the **fifth** or **top** note of the triad is on the bottom. Second inversion triads are called $^6_4$ triads, because when they are in their simplest position the intervals of a 6th and a 4th are formed above the bottom note.

When labeling second inversion triads, the figured bass symbol $^6_4$ is used beside the name of the triad.

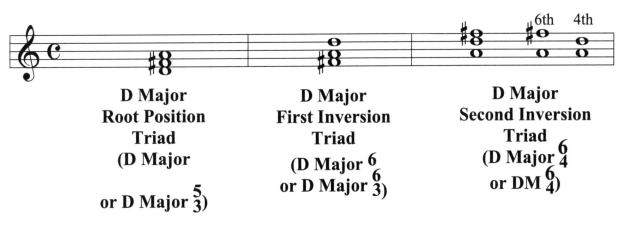

If only two notes of the triad are present, the two notes will most likely be the root and third of the chord (see example 1), or possibly the root and fifth (see example 2.)

It is less common for the two notes to be the third and fifth of the chord (see example 3).

Ex. 1. G Major Triad Root and Third — Common

Ex. 2. G Major Triad Root and Fifth — Occasional

Ex. 3. G Major Triad Third and Fifth — Rare

1. Write these triads in root position, first inversion, and second inversion.

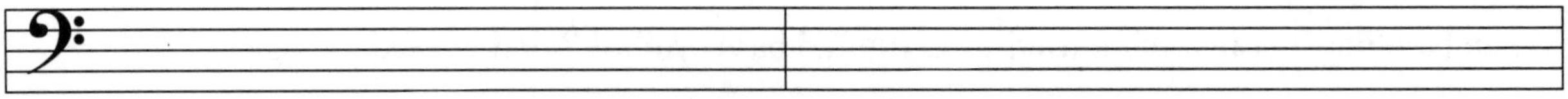

A Major   c♯ m

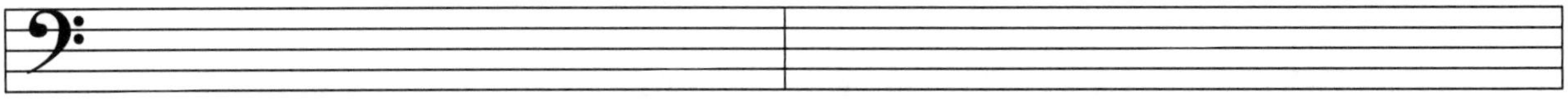

G♭ Major   e diminished

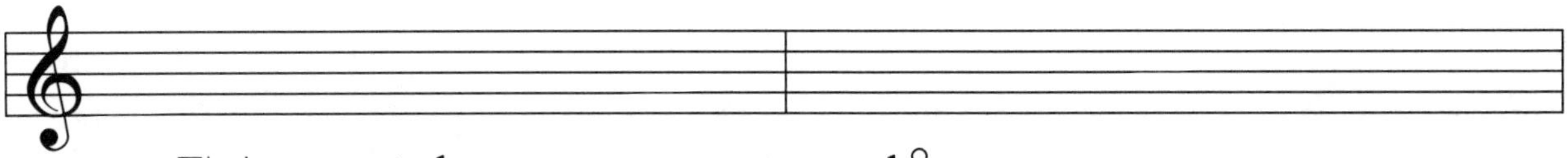

E♭ Augmented   b°

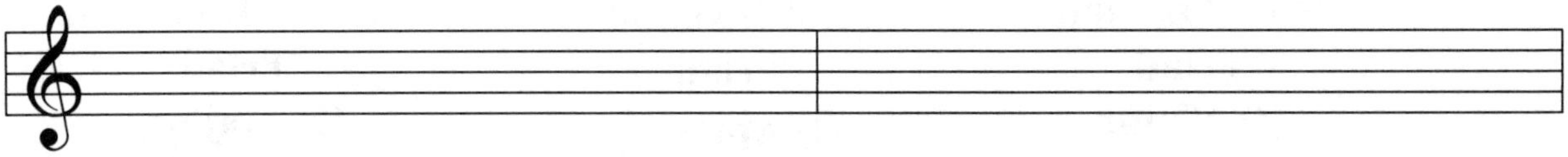

A♭ Augmented   d diminished

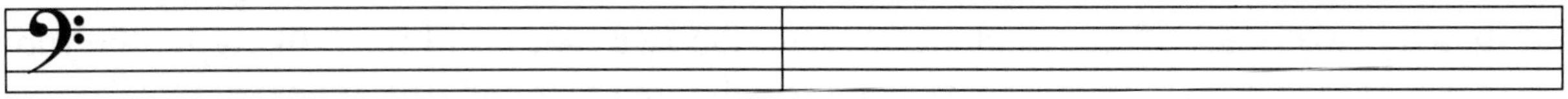

c minor   F♯ M

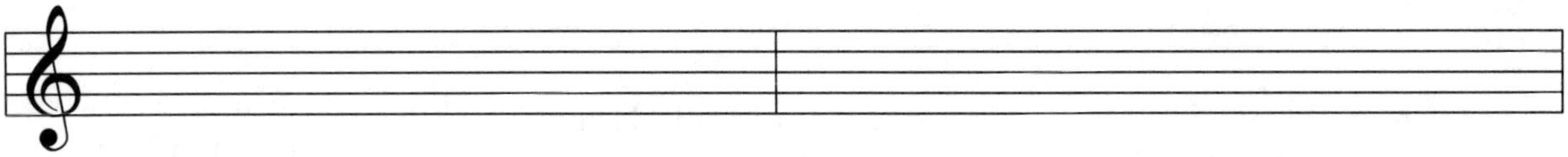

F⁺   B♭ Major

2. Name these triads with their roots, qualities, and figured bass (for example, C Major $^6_4$).

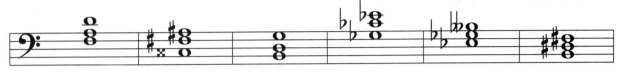

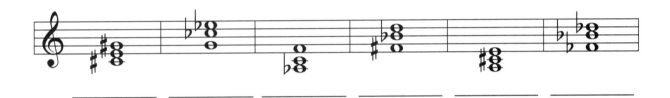

3. Write these triads.

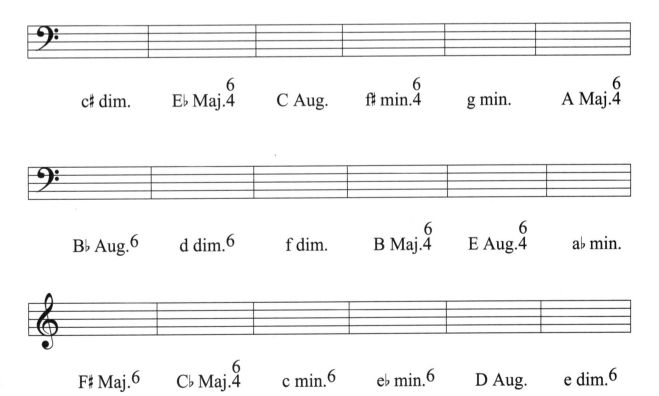

In actual music, triads are rarely in their simplest positions. To determine the root and quality of a triad within a piece, follow these steps:

a. Put the triad in its simplest root position form by placing the letter names so that there is one letter between each (for example, F-C-F-A becomes F-A-C).

b. Add all sharps or flats from the key signature, or from earlier in the measure, to the letter names.

c. Determine the root and quality of the triad.

d. Determine the inversion of the triad by looking at the lowest note on the <u>lowest</u> staff.

Example (From *Minuet in G* by Beethoven):

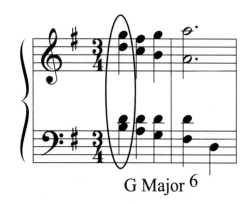

G Major 6

a. Notes are B-D-D-G.

b. Simplest root position form is G-B-D.

c. G Major Triad.

d. B is the lowest note (in the bass clef), so the triad is in first inversion ($^6_3$).

e. G Major 6 (or G Major $^6_3$)

4. Name each circled triad in the examples below by giving the root, quality, and figured bass.

a. From *Ballade, Op. 118, No. 3,* by Brahms.

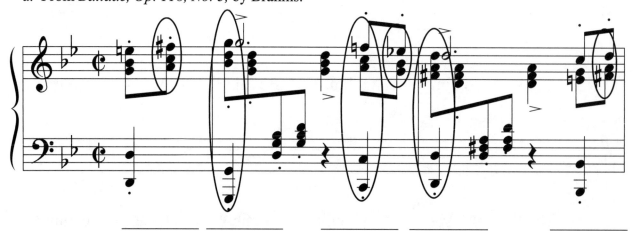

_____ _____ _____ _____ _____

b. From *Sonata, Hob. XVI:41,* by Haydn.

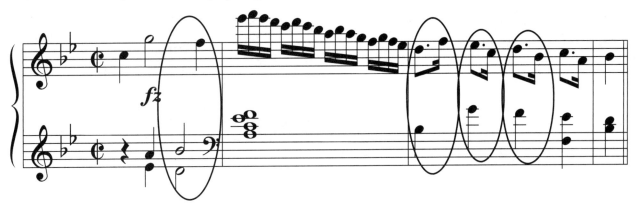

c. From *Prelude, Op. 28, No. 9,* by Chopin.

d. From *Sonata, Hob. XVI:46,* by Haydn.

e. From *Waldszenen: Jäger auf der Lauer,* by Schumann.

f. From *Impromptu, Op. 90, No. 2,* by Schubert.

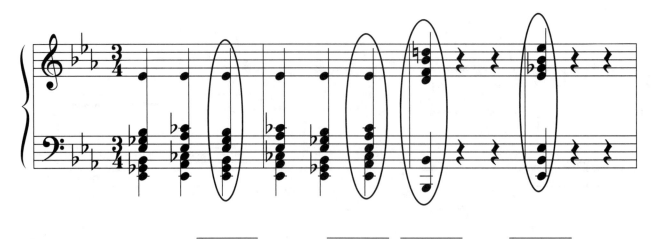

g. From *Songs Without Words: Confidence, Op. 19, No. 4,* by Mendelssohn.

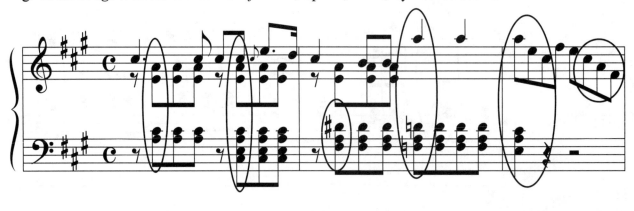

Check the correct answer for each question.

5. What is the name for the numbers that indicate inversions?

   _____ a. Figured bass

   _____ b. Augmented

   _____ c. Root

   _____ d. Diminished

6. How is a major triad changed into an augmented triad?

   _____ a. Lower the fifth

   _____ b. Raise the fifth

   _____ c. Lower the root

   _____ d. Raise the root

7. Which of these notes will make this triad diminished?

   _____ a. A♯ and C♯

   _____ b. F♯ and A♯

   _____ c. A♭ and C♭

   _____ d. F♭ and A♭

8. What is the root of this triad?

   _____ a. A

   _____ b. C

   _____ c. E

   _____ d. G

9. What term describes this triad?

   _____ a. Split

   _____ b. Block

   _____ c. Arpeggiated

   _____ d. Articulated

10. Which symbol indicates an Augmented triad?

_____ a. -

_____ b. =

_____ c. +

_____ d. ○

11. What quality does the symbol M indicate?

_____ a. Major

_____ b. Augmented

_____ c. Minor

_____ d. Musical

12. In which position is this triad?

_____ a. Root position

_____ b. Second inversion

_____ c. First inversion

_____ d. Major inversion

13. What does $\frac{6}{4}$ indicate?

_____ a. First inversion

_____ b. Augmented triad

_____ c. Second inversion

_____ d. Diminished triad

14. Which of these symbols indicates the same inversion as 6?

_____ a. +

_____ b. $\frac{6}{4}$

_____ c. M

_____ d. $\frac{6}{3}$

SIGHT SINGING
TRIADS

Sing each of the following triads. Adjust the octave to fit your vocal range.

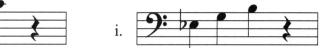

EAR TRAINING
IDENTIFYING TRIADS

Listen to Examples 41-45. Each example will be played three times. Check the quality of each triad that is played.

Example 41: _____ Major _____ minor _____ Augmented _____ diminished

Example 42: _____ Major _____ minor _____ Augmented _____ diminished

Example 43: _____ Major _____ minor _____ Augmented _____ diminished

Example 44: _____ Major _____ minor _____ Augmented _____ diminished

Example 45: _____ Major _____ minor _____ Augmented _____ diminished

Listen to Examples 46-50. Each example will be played three times. Check the inversion for each triad that is played.

Example 46: _____ 5/3 _____ 6/3 _____ 6/4

Example 47: _____ 5/3 _____ 6/3 _____ 6/4

Example 48: _____ 5/3 _____ 6/3 _____ 6/4

Example 49: _____ 5/3 _____ 6/3 _____ 6/4

Example 50: _____ 5/3 _____ 6/3 _____ 6/4

Listen to Examples 51-54. Each example will be played three times. Notate the missing notes for each triad. The root is given, and each chord is in root position.

Example 51: 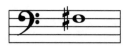 Example 52:  Example 53:  Example 54: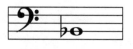

LESSON 6
PRIMARY AND SECONDARY TRIADS

Most music of the Baroque, Classical and Romantic periods of music history (appx. 1600-1900) follow certain harmonic standards. This is called **COMMON PRACTICE STYLE.** The harmonies are based on the triads and seventh chords that are created within major and minor tonalities.

A triad can be built on each note of the scale. When building triads on scale tones, all of the sharps or flats that are in the key are added to the chords which have those notes. For example, the key of D Major has F♯ and C♯. When writing the triads of D Major, every time an F or C appears in a chord, a sharp is added to it. (See example below.)

Triads of the scale are labeled using Roman numerals. Upper case Roman numerals are used for major triads, lower case Roman Nnmerals are used for minor triads, upper case Roman numerals with "+" are used for Augmented triads, and lower case Roman numerals with "o" are used for diminished triads. When handwritten, Roman numerals for major triads typically have lines above and below, such as V͟ .

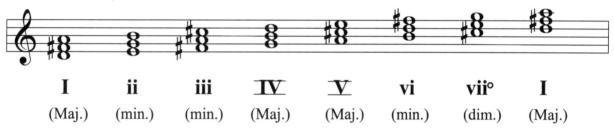

PRIMARY AND SECONDARY TRIADS IN THE KEY OF D MAJOR

I, IV, and V are the **PRIMARY TRIADS**. In Major keys, these three triads are Major, and are the most commonly used chords for harmonizing tonal melodies. The chords are labeled with upper case Roman Numerals.

ii, iii, vi, and vii° are the **SECONDARY TRIADS**. In Major keys, ii, iii, and vi are minor, and vii° is diminished. The chords are labeled with lower case Roman numerals, and the vii° chord has a small circle beside the Roman numeral.

The qualities of the triads in minor keys are different from those for Major keys. When using **harmonic minor**, the triads have the following qualities:

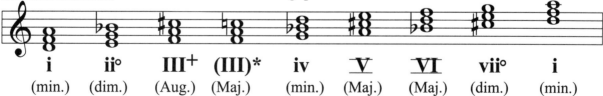

PRIMARY AND SECONDARY TRIADS IN THE KEY OF D MINOR

*Typically, the Augmented III (III⁺) chord is not used in minor keys. The III chord is usually Major, and is often found when the key is moving to the relative Major.

1. Write the Primary and Secondary Triads for these keys, and label the triads with Roman numerals. Circle each Primary Triad. Do not use a key signature. Write the sharps or flats before the notes. For minor keys, use harmonic form. (The first one is given.)

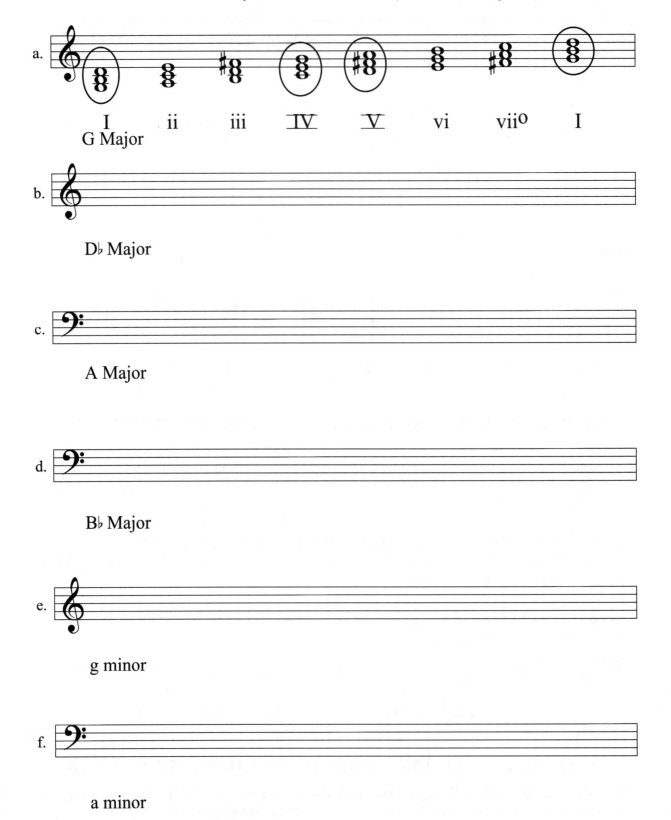

g. 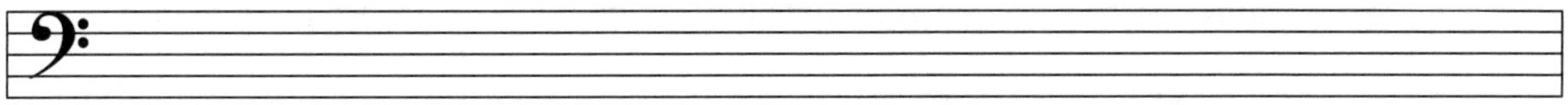 (bass clef)

g# minor

h. 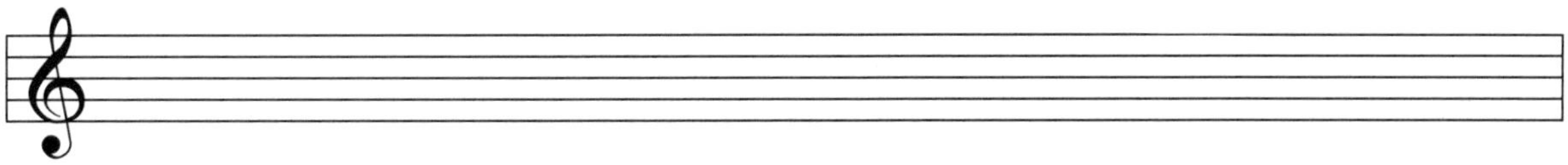 (treble clef)

F Major

i. 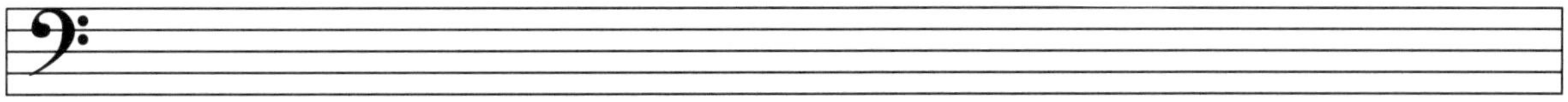 (bass clef)

b minor

j. 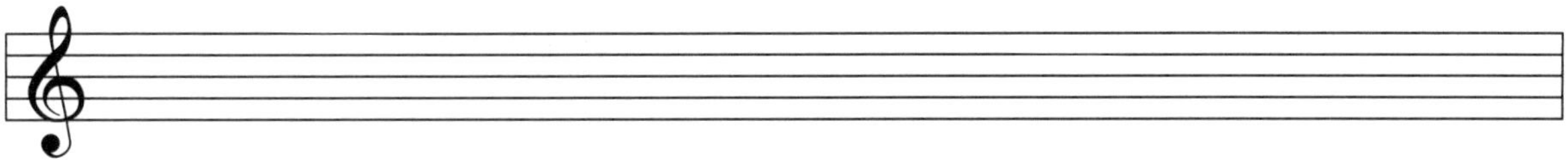 (treble clef)

G♭ Major

k. 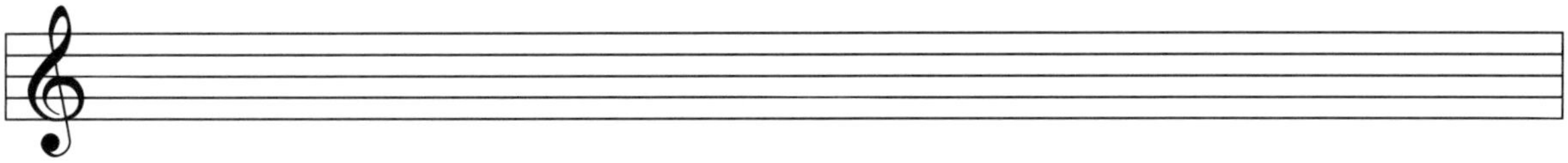 (treble clef)

f# minor

l. 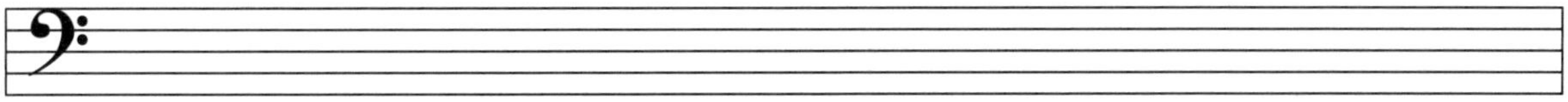 (bass clef)

C♭ Major

m. 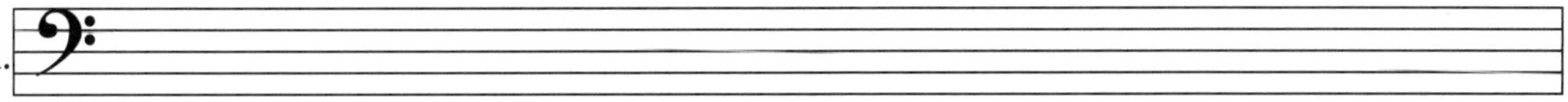 (bass clef)

C# Major

2. Write the Primary Triads for these keys, and label the triads with Roman numerals. Do not use a key signature. Write the sharps or flats before the notes. (The first one is given.)

3. Write the Secondary Triads for these keys, and label the triads with Roman Numerals. Do not use a key signature. Write the sharps or flats before the notes. (The first one is given.)

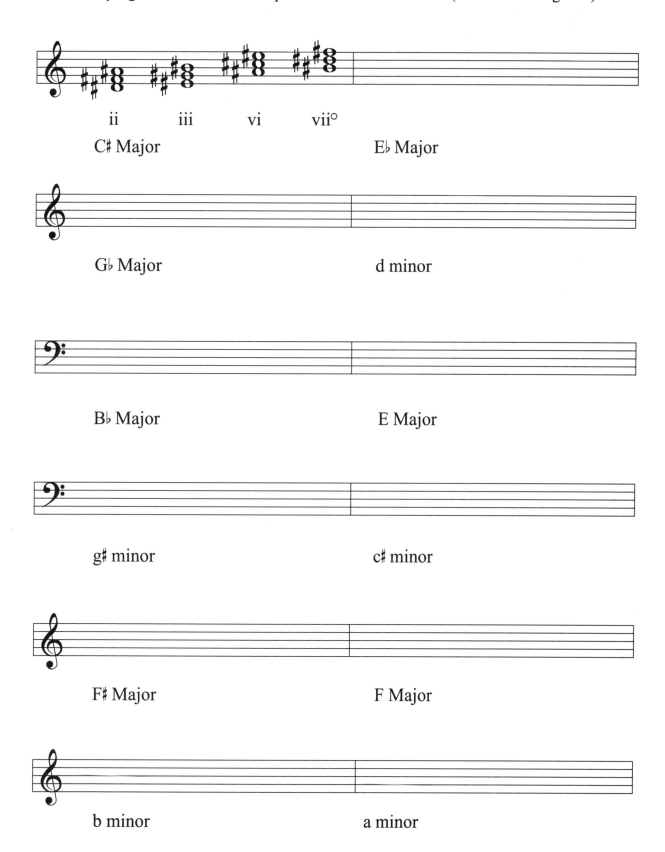

Each degree of the scale has a name. These are called the **SCALE DEGREE NAMES:**

The **I** chord is **TONIC**.

The **ii** chord is **SUPERTONIC**.

The **iii** chord is **MEDIANT**.

The **IV** chord is **SUBDOMINANT**.

The **V** chord is **DOMINANT**.

The **vi** chord is **SUBMEDIANT**.

The **vii°** chord is **LEADING TONE**.

(Note: Qualities used above are from Major keys. The names stay the same when in minor.)

4. Match these Roman numerals with their scale degree names.

a. ii _____ Submediant
b. I   _____ Dominant
c. iii _____ Supertonic
d. vii° _____ Subdominant
e. IV _____ Leading Tone
f. vi _____ Mediant
g. V   _____ Tonic

5. Write the scale degree names for these Roman numerals.

I   _____
ii   _____
iii _____
IV   _____
V   _____
vi   _____
vii° _____

In actual music, chords are rarely in their simplest position. To determine the Roman numeral of a chord within a piece, do the following:

a. Determine the Major or minor key of the piece.

b. Put the chord into its simplest root position form by placing the note names so that there is one letter between each (for example, F-C-F-A becomes F-A-C).

c. Add all sharps or flats from the key signature or from earlier in the measure to the letter names.

d. Determine the Roman numeral of the chord by counting from the letter name of the key up to the root of the chord.

e. Determine the inversion of the chord by looking at the lowest note (on the <u>lowest</u> staff).

Example (From *Minuet in G* by Beethoven):

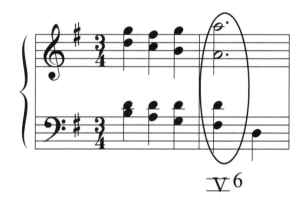

a. Key of G Major

b. Notes are: F#-D-A-A

c. Simplest form is: D-F#-A

d. D Major Triad. The piece is in the key of G Major. D is the fifth note of the G Major Scale; therefore, this is the V chord.

e. The lowest note (in the bass clef) is F#. The chord is in first inversion. Label the chord V^6_3, (or V^6).

Reminders:

In most compositions written using harmonic minor, the III chord is usually a major chord. III+ is not typically found.

Adding figured bass to root position chords is optional (I or I^5_3).

First inversion chords may be labeled with ^{6} or $^6_3$ (I^6 or I^6_3).

Second inversion chords are labeled with $^6_4$ (I^6_4).

When handwritten, lines are typically added above and below Roman numerals for major chords, to designate that they are major, such as V̲.

6. Label each circled chord with its Roman numeral and figured bass.

a. From *Sonata, Hob. XVI:41,* by Haydn. Key of: _____

b. From *Prelude, Op. 28, No. 9,* by Chopin. Key of: _____

c. From *Sonata, Hob. XVI:46,* by Haydn. Key of: _____

d. From *Waldszenen: Jäger auf der Lauer,* by Schumann. Key of: _____

e. From *Songs Without Words: Homeless, Op. 102, no. 1,* by Mendelssohn.

Key of: _____

f. From *Sonata, K. 284,* by Mozart. Key of: _____

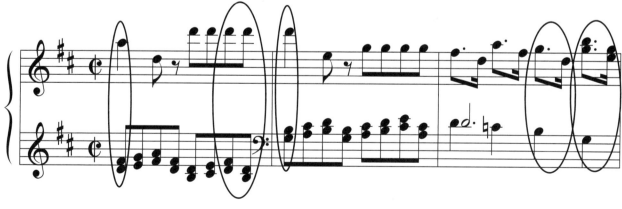

g. From *Capriccio, Op. 76, No. 2,* by Brahms. Key of: _____

7. Write the Roman numeral and figured bass for each of these chords, using the Major key for each example.

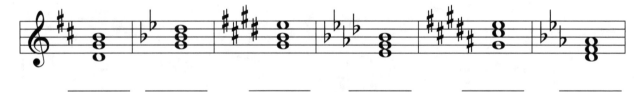

8. Write each of these chords. Determine whether to use the major or minor key by the quality of the Roman numeral, unless otherwise indicated.

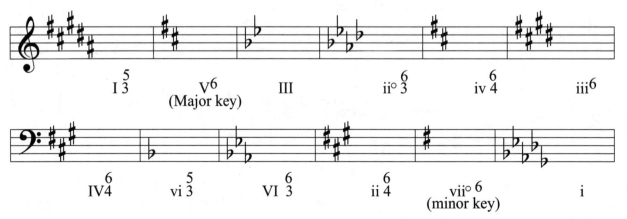

Check each correct answer.

9. What name is used for the I, IV, and V chords?

    _____ a. Primary triads

    _____ b. Perfect triads

    _____ c. Principal triads

    _____ d. Pentatonic triads

10. Which of these is a secondary triad?

    _____ a. V

    _____ b. I

    _____ c. IV

    _____ d. ii

11. Which of these Roman numerals is from a minor key?

    _____ a. I

    _____ b. iii

    _____ c. ii°

    _____ d. IV

12. What quality is this triad: ii°?

    _____ a. diminished

    _____ b. Major

    _____ c. Augmented

    _____ d. minor

13. Using the minor key, what is the Roman numeral and figured bass for this triad?

    _____ a. i$^6_4$

    _____ b. III

    _____ c. iv$^6_3$

    _____ d. V$^5_3$

14. What is the scale degree name for the IV chord?

_____ a. Submediant

_____ b. Subdominant

_____ c. Subterranian

_____ d. Submerged

15. Which Roman numeral represents the Dominant?

_____ a. IV

_____ b. V

_____ c. vi

_____ d. I

16. What is the quality of the Roman numeral VI?

_____ a. minor

_____ b. Augmented

_____ c. diminished

_____ d. Major

17. Using the major key, what is the Roman numeral and figured bass for this chord?

_____ a. iii⁶

_____ b. I⁶

_____ c. V$^6_4$

_____ d. vii°

18. What is the scale degree name for the ii chord?

_____ a. Leading tone

_____ b. Dominant

_____ c. Supertonic

_____ d. Mediant

SIGHT SINGING
PRIMARY AND SECONDARY TRIADS

Sing each of these melodies, which are based on the primary and secondary triads. (Adjust the octave to fit your vocal range.)

EAR TRAINING
RECOGNIZING PRIMARY AND SECONDARY TRIADS

Listen to Examples 55-60. Each example will be played three times. Check the chord progression that is played.

Example 55: ___ I V7 IV I   ___ I IV V7 I   ___ I IV V I   ___ I ii V I

Example 56: ___ I ii V$_5^6$ I   ___ I iii V$_5^6$ I   ___ I IV$_4^6$ V$_5^6$ I   ___ I vi V$_5^6$ I

Example 57: ___ I iii ii V7 I   ___ I vi ii V7 I   ___ I vi IV V7 I   ___ I iii IV V7 I

Example 58: ___ i ii° IV$_4^6$ V$_5^6$ i   ___ i iv$_4^6$ vi V$_5^6$ i   ___ i ii° vi V i   ___ i iv4^6 ii° V5 i^6

Example 59: ___ I iii IV vii° I   ___ I vi IV vii° I   ___ I ii IV V I   ___ I iii IV V I

Example 60: ___ I iii4^6 IV^6 V V7 I   ___ I vi^6 IV ii V7 I   ___ I iii IV ii V I   ___ I vi^6 IV ii V I

Listen to Examples 61-65. Each example will be played three times. Notate each missing chord (indicated by arrows).

LESSON 7
SEVENTH CHORDS

SEVENTH CHORDS are chords which contain four different notes, and are made up of a triad plus the interval of a 7th above the root.

The **DOMINANT SEVENTH CHORD** is created when a fourth note is added to the V chord (the Dominant chord). This fourth note is a seventh above the root of the chord, giving it the name "Dominant 7th." The chord consists of a Major triad on the bottom, with the added interval of a minor 7th.

The Dominant Seventh is so named because it is based on the V or Dominant chord, and has the interval of a 7th within the chord.

Inversions of the Dominant Seventh chord are:

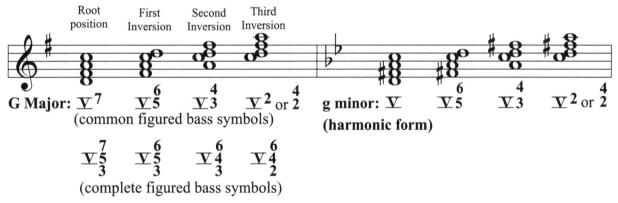

Dominant Seventh chords can be on a given note, or in a given key. When asked to write a Dominant Seventh on a given note, write a Major triad on that note, and add a minor seventh.

To write a Dominant Seventh within a given key, find the fifth note of the key (the dominant), and write a V chord. Add the note which is a minor 7th above the root of the chord. When in harmonic minor, the third of the chord (which is the leading tone or 7th of the key) must be raised a half step.

DOMINANT 7TH ON D   **DOMINANT 7TH IN THE KEY OF D MAJOR**

When this type of seventh chord is not functioning as a Dominant 7th chord within the context of the music, it is called a **Major-minor seventh chord (D Mm7)**.

1. Write Dominant Seventh chords and their inversions in the following keys, and label the chords with Roman numerals and figured bass.

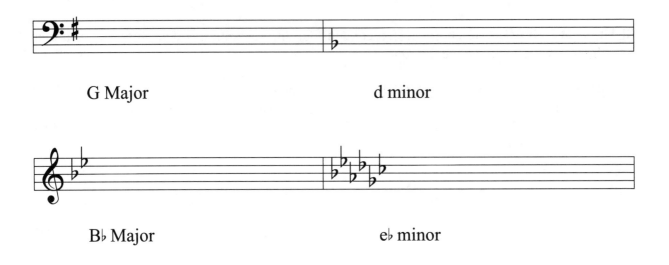

G Major   d minor

B♭ Major   e♭ minor

2. Write Major-minor Seventh chords and their inversions on these notes.

MAJOR SEVENTH CHORDS consist of a Major triad and a Major 7th above the root. These chords are also called **Major-Major seventh chords**. When writing Major Seventh chords, add all sharps or flats which are contained in the Major key signature of the root.

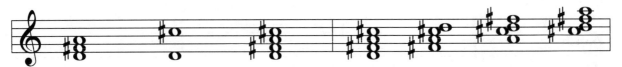

D Major Triad   Major 7th   D Major   Inversions of D Major 7th
                              Seventh Chord (DM7)

MAJOR SEVENTH CHORD ON D

3. Write these Major Seventh chords and their inversions.

      A Major 7   E♭ Major 7

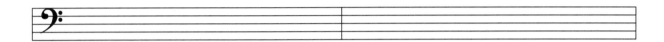

      F Major 7   B♭ Major 7

MINOR SEVENTH CHORDS contain a minor triad and the interval of a minor seventh above the root. These are also called **minor-minor seventh chords**. When writing minor seventh chords, add the sharps or flats from the natural minor key signature of the root.

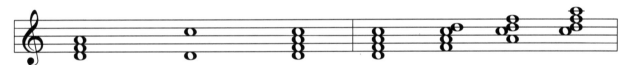

  d minor triad   **minor 7th**   **d minor**   **Inversions of d minor 7th**
                         seventh chord (dm7)

MINOR SEVENTH CHORD ON D

4. Write these minor seventh chords and their inversions.

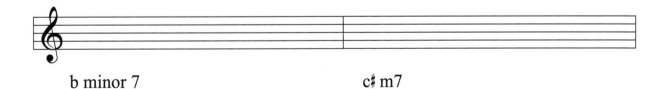

      b minor 7   c♯ m7

      g minor 7   a♭ m7

HALF-DIMINISHED SEVENTH CHORDS consist of a diminished triad, and a minor seventh above the root. These are also called **diminished-minor seventh chords**.

    d diminished   minor 7th   d half-diminished   Inversions of d half-diminished 7th
       triad   seventh chord

HALF-DIMINISHED SEVENTH CHORD ON D
(d⌀7)

5. Write these half diminished seventh chords and their inversions.

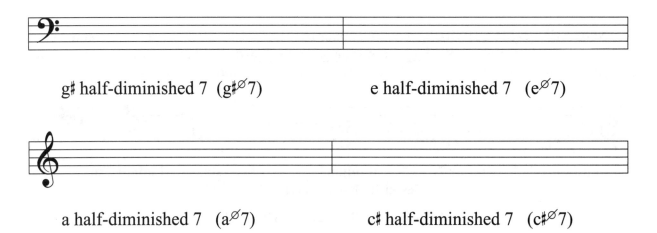

    g♯ half-diminished 7 (g♯⌀7)   e half-diminished 7   (e⌀7)

    a half-diminished 7   (a⌀7)   c♯ half-diminished 7 (c♯⌀7)

The **DIMINISHED SEVENTH CHORD** consists of a diminished triad, with the interval of a diminished seventh added to the top. These are also called **diminished-diminished seventh chords**.

    d diminished   diminished 7th   d diminished   Inversions of d diminished 7th
      triad   seventh chord

DIMINISHED SEVENTH CHORD ON D
(d°7)

6. Write these diminished 7th chords and their inversions.

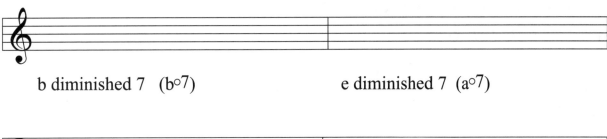

b diminished 7   (b°7)   e diminished 7   (a°7)

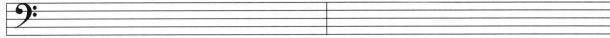

f diminished 7   (f°7)   c diminished 7   (c°7)

7. Label these seventh chords with only their roots and qualities, such as C Major 7. The first one is given.

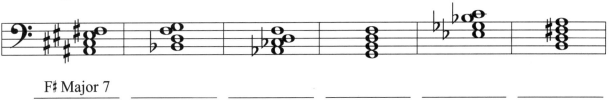

F♯ Major 7 _____ _____ _____ _____ _____

_____ _____ _____ _____ _____ _____

_____ _____ _____ _____ _____ _____

_____ _____ _____ _____ _____ _____

8. Label the circled seventh chords in the examples below with their roots, qualities, and figured bass. (The first one is given.)

a. From *Sonata, Hob. XVI:41,* by Haydn.

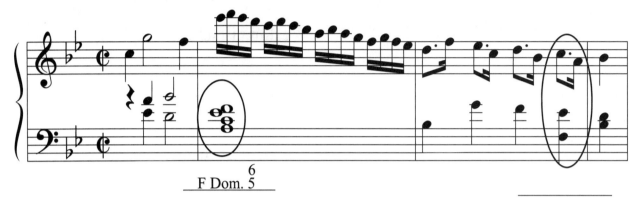

F Dom. $^6_5$

b. From *Songs Without Words: Homeless, Op. 102, no. 1,* by Mendelssohn.

c. From *Sonata, K. 284* by Mozart.

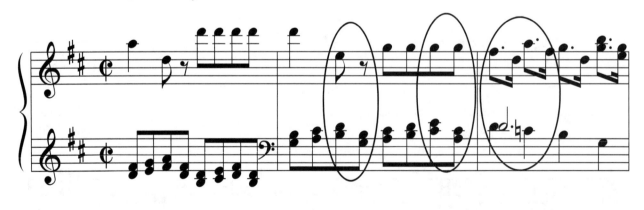

d. From *Capriccio,* Op. 76, No. 1 by Brahms.

e. From *Sonata, K. 284,* by Mozart.

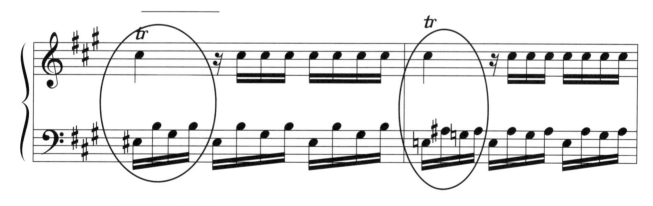

f. From *Impromptu, Op.142, No. 4,* by Schubert.

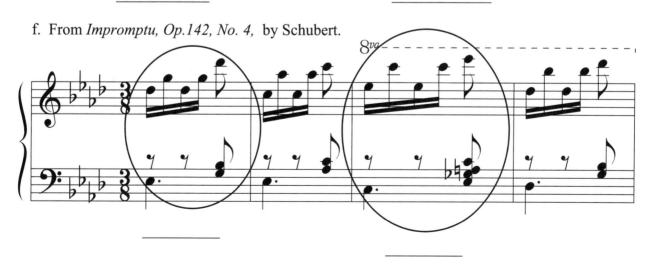

g. From *Etude Tableaux, Op. 39, No. 9,* by Rachmaninoff.

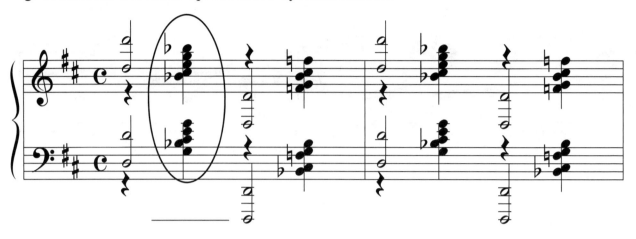

h. From *Etude Tableaux, Op. 39, No. 5,* by Rachmaninoff.

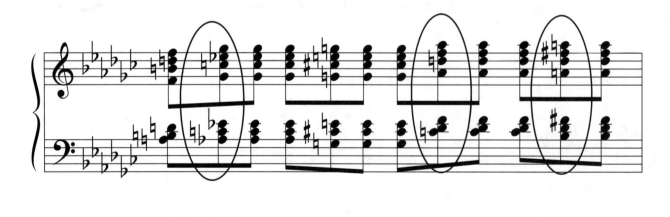

Check each correct answer.

9. What is another name for a diminished seventh chord?

   _____ a. diminished-major
   _____ b. diminished-diminished
   _____ c. minor-diminished
   _____ d. Major-diminished

10. Which of these are the qualities of the triad and the seventh that make up a Major seventh chord?

    _____ a. minor-minor
    _____ b. Major-minor
    _____ c. Major-Major
    _____ d. minor-Major

11. What quality is this chord?

    _____ a. half-diminished 7th
    _____ b. diminished 7th
    _____ c. Dominant 7th
    _____ d. Major 7th

12. Which position does the figured bass $\substack{6\\5}$ indicate?

    _____ a. root position
    _____ b. first inversion
    _____ c. second inversion
    _____ d. third inversion

13. What is the full figured bass symbol for the abbreviation "2?"

    _____ a. $\substack{6\\5\\2}$
    _____ b. $\substack{7\\5\\2}$
    _____ c. $\substack{4\\3\\2}$
    _____ d. $\substack{6\\4\\2}$

14. Which of these symbols indicates a
    a half-diminished seventh chord?

    _____ a. ⌀7

    _____ b. o7

    _____ c. +7

    _____ d. -7

15. Which accidentals need to be added
    to give this chord min. 7th quality?

    _____ a. F♯ and A♯

    _____ b. C♭ and E♭

    _____ c. A♭ and E♭

    _____ d. C♯ and E♭

16. What is the root of this diminished 7th chord?

    _____ a. E♭

    _____ b. G♭

    _____ c. B♭♭

    _____ d. C

17. Which type of seventh chord does the symbol
    "o7" indicate?

    _____ a. diminished 7th

    _____ b. Dominant 7th

    _____ c. minor 7th

    _____ d. Major 7th

18. If a seventh chord is in third inversion,
    which note is lowest?

    _____ a. root

    _____ b. third

    _____ c. fifth

    _____ d. seventh

SIGHT SINGING
SEVENTH CHORDS

Each of the following examples is based on a seventh chord. Sing each example. Adjust the octave to fit your vocal range.

EAR TRAINING
RECOGNIZING SEVENTH CHORDS

Listen to Examples 66-70. Each example will be played three times. Check the type of seventh chord that is played.

Example 66: ___ diminished 7th   ___ Major 7th   ___ minor 7th   ___ half-diminished 7th

Example 67: ___ diminished 7th   ___ minor 7th   ___ half-diminished 7th   ___ Major 7th

Example 68: ___ minor 7th   ___ Major 7th   ___ half-diminished 7th   ___ diminished 7th

Example 69: ___ minor 7th   ___ Dominant 7th   ___ half-diminished 7th   ___ Major 7th

Example 70: ___ half-diminished 7th   ___ Dominant 7th   ___ Major 7th   ___ minor 7th

Listen to Examples 71-75. Each example will be played three times. Notate the missing note for each chord.

Example 71:

Example 72:

Example 73:

Example 74:

Example 75:

LESSON 8
THE SECONDARY DOMINANT
THE SECONDARY LEADING TONE CHORD

Many times, a composer will use chords which are not within the key of the piece of music. One of the most common of these is the **SECONDARY DOMINANT**. Also common is the **SECONDARY LEADING TONE CHORD**. These add harmonic color to the music.

These chords are called "secondary" because they are either the Dominant (V) or leading tone (vii°) of a key other than Tonic (I). Each is typically followed by the chord which would be a I chord of the key to which it belongs. The qualities of secondary dominants and secondary leading tone chords are different from those of the primary and secondary triads.

Examples in the key of C Major:

Chord	Quality
I	Maj.
I^7	Maj.7
V^7/IV	Dom.7
IV	
vii°/ii	dim.7
ii	

ii	min.
ii7	min.7
V/V	Maj.
V	
V^7/V	Dom.7
V	
vii°/iii	dim.
iii	

iii	min.
iii7	min.7
V/vi	Maj.
vi	
V^7/vi	Dom.7
vi	
vii°/IV	dim.
IV	

IV	Maj.
IV7	Maj.7
V^7/♭VII	Dom.7
♭VII	
vii°/V	dim.
V	

vi	min.
vi7	min.7
V/ii	Maj.
ii	
V^7/ii	Dom.7
ii	
vii°/♭VII	dim.
♭VII	

vii°	dim.
vii⌀7	half dim.7
V/iii	Maj.
iii	
V^7/iii	Dom.7
iii	

V	Maj.
V7	Dom.7
vii°/vi	dim.
vi	

If a chord that appears to be a secondary chord leads to a change of key, the chord is not considered a secondary chord. If the music stays in the same key, the chord is secondary.

1. Write these secondary dominants. Determine whether to use the Major or minor key by the quality of the second Roman numeral. V of V examples have "Major" or "minor" written below them. Remember to use harmonic minor. Follow the steps in the example below to write each one.

a. Find the chord which represents the second Roman numeral (for example, for V of IV, find the IV chord of the given key).

b. Find the V, V7 or vii° chord for that second chord. (For example, if the IV chord is C Major, count up five notes to G Major chord.

c. Write the Secondary Dominant chord, followed by the chord represented by the second Roman numeral.

Example: V^6_5 of iii in the key of A Major.

a. Find the iii chord in A Major: c# minor chord.

b. Find the V7 chord of c# minor: G#7.

c. Write G# $^6_5$ (the inversion of G#7) followed by c# minor (the iii chord).

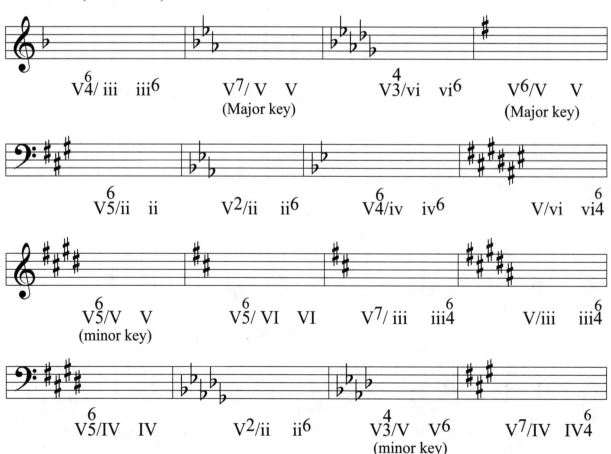

2. Write these secondary leading tone chords. Determine whether to use the Major or minor key by the quality of the second Roman numeral.

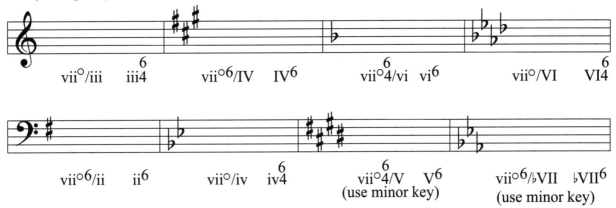

vii°/iii   iii$^6_4$ vii°^{6}/IV   IV^6 vii°$^6_4$/vi   vi^6 vii°/VI   VI$^6_4$

vii°^{6}/ii   ii^6 vii°/iv   iv$^6_4$ vii°$^6_4$/V   V^6 vii°^{6}/♭VII   ♭VII^6
                                            (use minor key)   (use minor key)

In music, secondary dominants or secondary leading tone chords have accidentals that are not in the key signatures. To analyze them in music literature:

a. Determine the Major or minor key of the piece.

b. Label the secondary chord (the first of the two chords) with the Roman Numeral V or vii°, and the figured bass (for example, V, vii°, V^6, etc.), followed by /____, using the Roman numeral for the second chord to fill the blank.

c. Label the second chord with its Roman numeral and figured bass.

d. The two chords will be labeled, for example, "V/iii   iii."

Example: From *A Little Canon* by Schumann.

a. Key of A Major.

b. The first chord is Dominant 7th on A. Label the chord V7.

c. The second chord is D Major. This is the IV chord in A Major. The chord is in second inversion. Label the chord IV $^6_4$.

d. Chords are labeled   V7/IV   IV $^6_4$. Sometimes, they are labeled (V7 of IV)   IV$^6_4$.

V7/IV   IV$^6_4$

3. Label the circled secondary chords and their resolutions using Roman numerals and figured bass in each of the following excerpts.

a. From *Romanze, Op. 118, No. 5,* by Brahms. Key of: _____ Major

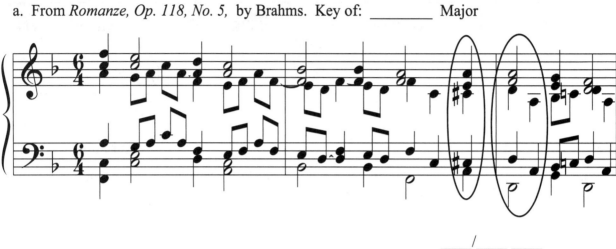

___/___ ___

b. From *Intermezzo, Op. 118, No. 2,* by Brahms. Key of: _____ Major

___/___   ___   ___/___   ___

f. From *Waltszenen: Herberge,* Op. 82, by Schumann. Key of: _____ Major

___/___ ___

g. From *Sonata, K. 280,* by Mozart. Key of _____ Major

___/___ ___

h. From *Sonata, K. 283,* by Mozart. Key of: _____ Major

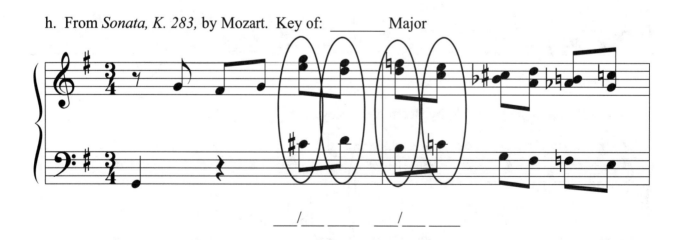

___/___ ___/___

Check the correct answer for each question.

4. What makes secondary dominants and secondary leading tone chords different from primary and secondary triads?

   _____ a. They have accidentals

   _____ b. They are minor

   _____ c. They are louder

   _____ d. They are not different

5. Which chord is most likely to follow this secondary dominant?

   _____ a. V

   _____ b. vi

   _____ c. IV

   _____ d. ii

6. Using the major key, what is the correct Roman numeral for this chord?

   _____ a. V/vii

   _____ b. V/V

   _____ c. iii

   _____ d. ii

7. What two accidentals must be added to make this a V/iii chord?

   _____ a. D♭ and F♯

   _____ b. F♯ and A♭

   _____ c. F♯ and A♮

   _____ d. D♯ and F♯

8. What is the difference between a iii chord and a V/vi chord?

   _____ a. iii is minor, V/vi is Major

   _____ b. iii is diminished, V/vi is Major

   _____ c. iii is minor, V/vi is minor

   _____ d. iii is minor, V/vi is Dominant 7

9. Using the major key, what chord is the secondary leading tone chord for this chord?

_____ a. c diminished

_____ b. F Major

_____ c. d# diminished

_____ d. B Dominant 7

10. What will typically follow a secondary chord?

_____ a. The music will end

_____ b. The key will change

_____ c. The key will stay the same

_____ d. The music will return to the beginning

11. What accidental needs to be added to make this a V7/V chord?

_____ a. B♭

_____ b. G♭

_____ c. C#

_____ d. E♮

12. What quality are secondary leading tone chords?

_____ a. Major

_____ b. minor

_____ c. diminished

_____ d. Dominant 7th

13. What quality are secondary dominant chords?

_____ a. Major or Dominant 7th

_____ b. diminished or diminished 7th

_____ c. minor or minor 7th

_____ d. half-diminished 7th

SIGHT SINGING
SECONDARY DOMINANTS

Each of the following melodies is based on a chord progression that includes a secondary dominant or secondary leading tone chord. Sing each example. Adjust the octave to fit your vocal range.

EAR TRAINING
SECONDARY DOMINANTS

Listen to Examples 76-80. Each example will be played three times. Write the Roman numerals for each missing secondary dominant and its resolution.

Example 76: I   IV   V   I   ____/____   ____   V7   I

Example 77: I   IV   V   I   ____/____   ____   V7   I

Example 78: I   IV   V   I   ____/____   ____   V7   I

Example 79: I   IV   V   I   ____/____   ____   V7   I

Example 80: I   IV   V   I   ____/____   ____   V7   I

Listen to Examples 81-85. Notate each missing secondary dominant chord, indicated by arrows.

LESSON 9
CADENCES

A **CADENCE** is a closing or ending for a musical phrase or section, made up of a combination of chords.

Cadences are either **INCONCLUSIVE**, meaning that something needs to follow the cadence, or **CONCLUSIVE**, meaning that the music could end at that point and sound finished.

An **AUTHENTIC CADENCE** consists of a V or V^7 chord followed by a I chord. Authentic cadences are considered conclusive.

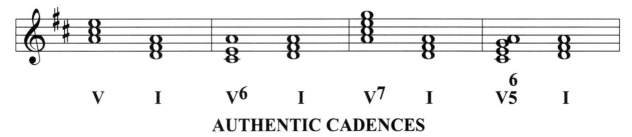

AUTHENTIC CADENCES

A **PLAGAL CADENCE** consists of a IV chord followed by a I chord. Plagal cadences are considered conclusive.

PLAGAL CADENCES

A **HALF CADENCE** is a cadence which ends with a V or V^7 chord. Half cadences are inconclusive.

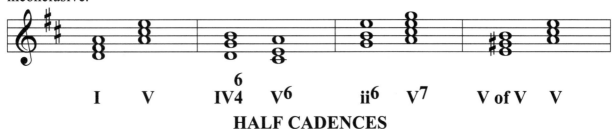

HALF CADENCES

A **DECEPTIVE CADENCE** consists of a V (or sometimes IV) chord followed by a vi chord. Deceptive cadences are inconclusive.

DECEPTIVE CADENCES

Less common is the **PHRYGIAN HALF CADENCE**, which, in minor keys, consists of the iv⁶ chord followed by a V chord.

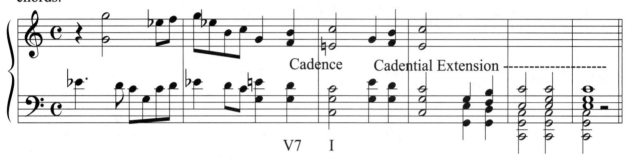

PHRYGIAN HALF CADENCE IN THE KEY OF B MINOR

A **CADENTIAL EXTENSION** is created when the cadence is lengthened. This may be accomplisehd by repeating the cadence, or by lengthening the cadence rhythmically. In this example, from *Impromptu, Op. 90, No. 1* by Schubert, the cadence is extended by repeating the chords.

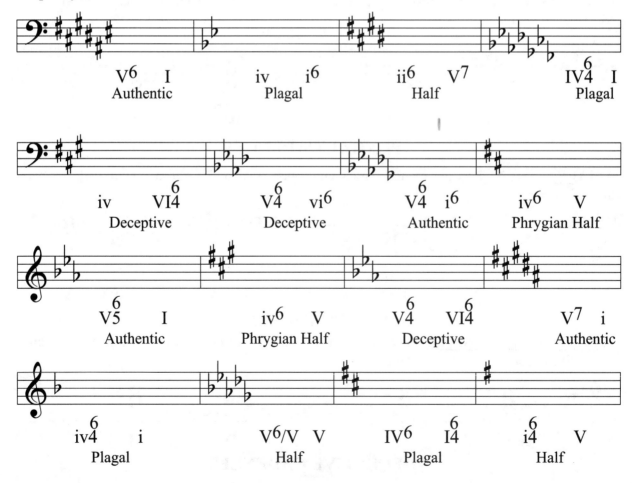

1. Write the following cadences. Determine whether to use the Major or minor key by the quality of the Roman numerals.

2. Label the chords of each of these cadences with Roman numerals and figured bass, then put the type of cadence (Authentic, Half, Plagal, Deceptive or Phrygian Half) on the line below the Roman Numerals.

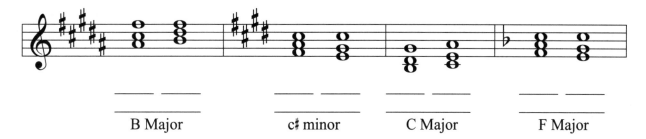

B Major   c# minor   C Major   F Major

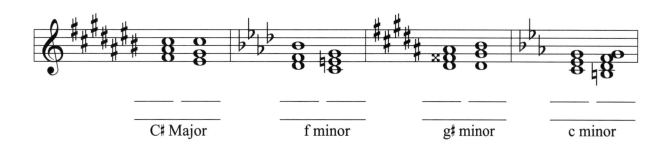

C# Major   f minor   g# minor   c minor

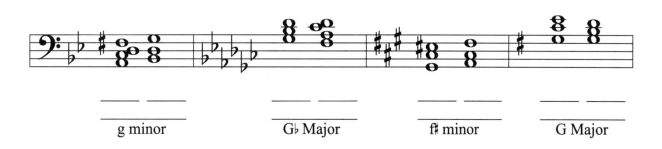

g minor   Gb Major   f# minor   G Major

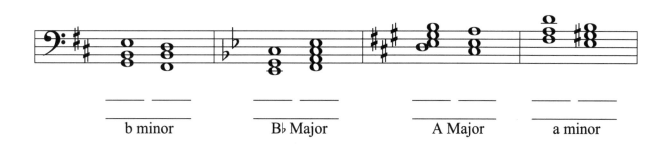

b minor   Bb Major   A Major   a minor

A **PERFECT AUTHENTIC CADENCE*** is a V-I cadence in which both chords are in root position, and the final tonic (I) chord has the root as the highest note (soprano).

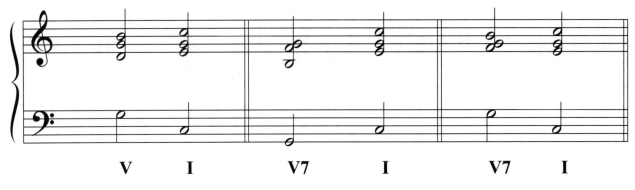

PERFECT AUTHENTIC CADENCES IN C MAJOR

If one or both of the chords in an authentic cadence are not in root position, or the I chord has a note other than tonic as the highest note, the cadence is called an **IMPERFECT AUTHENTIC CADENCE**.

IMPERFECT AUTHENTIC CADENCES IN C MAJOR

3. Identify each authentic cadence as perfect or imperfect. Use the major key for each.

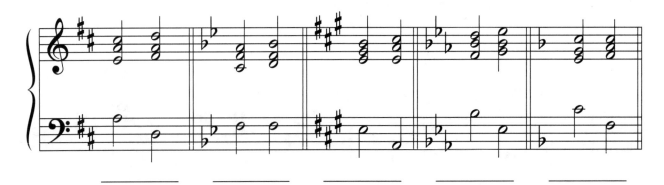

*Some theory scholars consider most V-I cadences to be perfect.

4. Label the chords for each cadence, and identify each as perfect authentic, imperfect authentic, half, plagal, deceptive, or Phrygian Half. Whether to use the major or minor key is indicated under each example.

When labeling cadences in music literature, label the last two chords of a phrase with their Roman numerals. These are the two chords which make up the cadence. Then, give the cadence its name.

Example (From *Waltz, Op. posth. 69, No. 1,* by Chopin.): Key of A♭ Major, Perfect Authentic Cadence

5. Write the name of the major or minor key for each of these examples. Write the Roman numerals for the circled two chords, and name the type of cadence (Perfect Authentic, Imperfect Authentic, Half, Plagal, Deceptive or Phrygian Half).

a. From *Prelude, Op. 28, No. 4,* by Chopin.

Key of: _____

Type of Cadence: _____

b. From *Intermezzo, Op. 118, No. 2,* by Brahms..

Key of: _____

Type of Cadence: _____

c. From *Waldszenen: Eintritt, Op. 82, No. 1,* by Schumann.

Key of: _____

Type of Cadence: _____   ____ ____

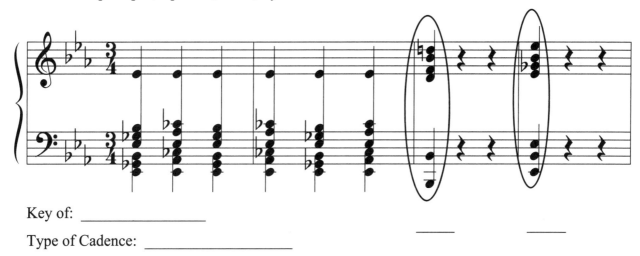

d. From *Impromptu, Opus 90, No. 2,* by Schubert.

Key of: _____

Type of Cadence: _____   ____ ____

e. From *Waldszenen* by Schumann.

Key of: _____

Type of Cadence: _____   ____ ____

f. From *Sonata, Hob. XVI:42* by Haydn.

Key of: _____

Type of Cadence: _____

g. From *Sonata, Hob. XVI:41,* by Haydn.

Key of: _____

Type of Cadence: _____

h. From *Sonata, K 545* by Mozart.

Key of: _____

Type of Cadence: _____   Circle the cadential extension on the music.

Check the correct answer for each question.

6. Which of these identifies a IV-I cadence?

   _____ a. Deceptive

   _____ b. Plagal

   _____ c. Perfect authentic

   _____ d. Half

7. Which chords create a Phrygian half cadence?

   _____ a. IV-I

   _____ b. V6-IV

   _____ c. IV6-V

   _____ d. V7-I

8. Which two are characteristics of a perfect authentic cadence? (Check two answers.)

   _____ a. root position chords

   _____ b. third on top of first chord

   _____ c. first inversion I chord

   _____ d. tonic on top of I chord

9. Using the minor key, identify this cadence.

   _____ a. Imperfect authentic

   _____ b. Half

   _____ c. Plagal

   _____ d. Deceptive

10. Which of these is a conclusive cadence?

    _____ a. Deceptive cadence

    _____ b. Half cadence

    _____ c. V-I

    _____ d. IV-vi

11. Which Roman numerals represent a deceptive cadence?

_____ a. I-V

_____ b. V-vi

_____ c. IV-V

_____ d. I-IV

12. Which two of these represent Authentic cadences? (Check two answers.)

_____ a. V-I

_____ b. V7-i

_____ c. IV-I

_____ d. V-vi

13. What is the name for a V7-I cadence?

_____ a. Plagal

_____ b. Half

_____ c. Deceptive

_____ d. Authentic

14. Which of these cadences is inconclusive?

_____ a. Plagal

_____ b. IV-1

_____ c. Perfect Authentic

_____ d. V-vi

15. What will change this imperfect authentic cadence into a perfect authentic cadence?

_____ a. Change treble clef B♮ to B♭

_____ b. Change second bass clef G to C

_____ c. Put G on top of the last chord

_____ d. Change first bass clef G to C

SIGHT SINGING
CADENCES

Sing each of the following melodies, each of which ends with a cadence. Adjust the octave to fit your vocal range.

a. (Deceptive Cadence)

b. (Phrygian Half Cadence)

c. (Plagal Cadence)

d. (Authentic Cadence)

e. (Deceptive Cadence)

f. (Authentic Cadence)

g. (Half Cadence)

h. (Plagal Cadence)

EAR TRAINING
CADENCES

Listen to Examples 86-90. Each example will be played three times. Check the cadence that is formed by the final two chords.

Example 86: _____ Authentic _____ Half _____ Plagal _____ Deceptive

Example 87: _____ Half _____ Deceptive _____ Plagal _____ Authentic

Example 88: _____ Perfect Authentic _____ Imperfect Authentic _____ Phrygian Half

Example 89: _____ Half _____ Deceptive _____ Authentic _____ Plagal

Example 90: _____ Perfect Authentic _____ Imperfect Authentic _____ Phrygian Half

Listen to Examples 91-95. Each example will be played three times. Notate the final two chords for each.

Example 91:

Example 92:

Example 93:

Example 94:

Example 95:

REVIEW
LESSONS 1-9

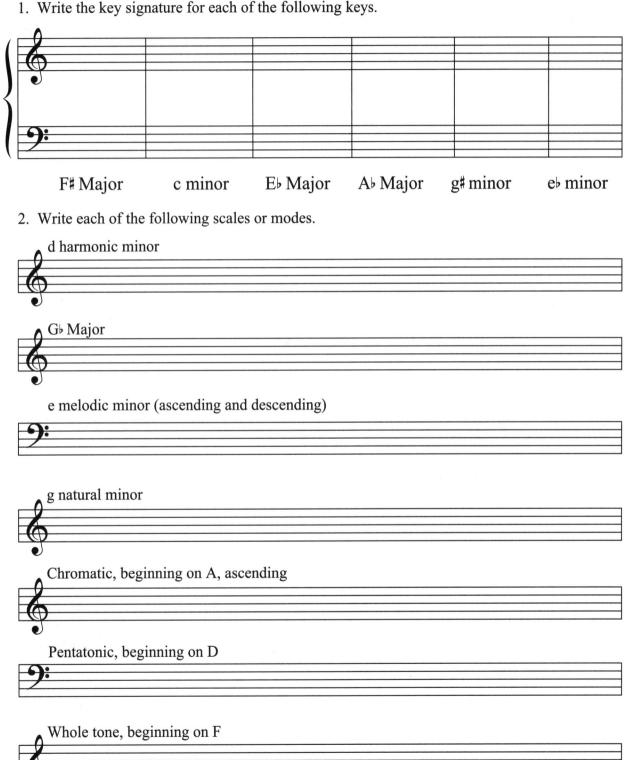

The questions on this page are based on the excerpt on page 112, which is from *Capriccio, Opus 116, No. 3,* by Brahms. Check each correct answer.

3. What is the key?

    _____ a. B♭ Major
    _____ b. E♭ Major
    _____ c. g minor
    _____ d. c minor

4. What is the name for the chord in circle 1?

    _____ a. a minor 7
    _____ b. a diminished 7
    _____ c. a dominant 7
    _____ d. a half-diminished 7

5. What is the name for the chord in circle 2?

    _____ a. g minor
    _____ b. G Major
    _____ c. g diminished
    _____ d. G Augmented

6. What is the Roman numeral for the chord in circle 3?

    _____ a. vii°7
    _____ b. V7
    _____ c. vii°
    _____ d. V

7. What is the name for the chord in circle 4?

    _____ a. C♯ Major 7
    _____ b. c♯°7
    _____ c. c♯ø7
    _____ d. c♯ minor 7

8. What is the name for the chord in circle 5?

    _____ a. E Major
    _____ b. e minor
    _____ c. e diminished
    _____ d. E Augmented

9. What is the name for the interval in circle 6?

    _____ a. Tritone
    _____ b. Unison
    _____ c. Compound
    _____ d. Octave

10. What is the name for the interval in circle 7?

    _____ a. m7
    _____ b. M7
    _____ c. A7
    _____ d. d7

11. What term best describes the relationship of the notes in circle 8?

    _____ a. whole tone
    _____ b. pentatonic
    _____ c. Dorian
    _____ d. chromatic

12. What is the name for the chord in circle 9?

    _____ a. c minor 7, third inversion
    _____ b. c half-diminished 7
    _____ c. C Dominant 7
    _____ d. C Major 7, third inversion

LESSON 10
MELODIC DEVICES

A **MOTIVE** (or **motif**) is a short melodic or rhythmic musical idea (two or more successive notes). Motives have distinct melodic, pitch, or rhythmic patterns. A motive is used throughout a piece of music as a unifying element.

A **THEME** is a longer musical idea, typically several measures. The theme may or may not contain a recurring motive. A theme may contain one or several phrases. **THEMATIC TRANSFORMATION** is the process of developing a theme by changing it in various ways. The following melodies are themes. Each theme uses a motive. The motive is circled. (A musical composition may or may not be based on a theme.)

From Beethoven *Symphony No. 5:*

From *March* by Shostakovich:

From *Minuet in G* by J.S. Bach

115

MOTIVIC TRANSFORMATION is achieved by using a variety of musical devices. The theme from *Twinkle, Twinkle, Little Star* will be used as an example.

Original theme:

REPETITION or **LITERAL REPETITION** takes place when a motive (or a theme) is repeated exactly the way it was the first time it occurred, on the same note.

Repetition

SEQUENCE or **SEQUENTIAL REPETITION** occurs when a motive is repeated immediately on a different note, usually a 2nd or 3rd higher or lower.

Sequence

IMITATION occurs when a motive is repeated immediately in another voice, such as in the bass clef following a statement of the motive in the treble clef, or by a different instrument. The term **Imitation** may also be used as a general term that includes repetition and sequence.

Imitation

FRAGMENTATION or a **FRAGMENTED MOTIVE** occurs when only a portion of the motive appears. A fragment of a motive can be broken off and developed separately.

The **CONTOUR** of a melody refers to the rise and fall by pitch. This portion of *Twinkle Twinkle* rises, then falls.

Rising   Falling

A melody is considered **CONJUNCT** when it moves in a stepwise manner, using the successive degrees of the scale, and **DISJUNCT** when the notes form intervals larger than a second. The first measure of the *Twinkle Twinkle* excerpt is disjunct, and the last three measures are conjunct.

AUGMENTATION is the exact doubling of the rhythmic value of the notes within a theme (for example, the quarter notes become half notes).

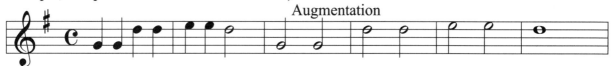

DIMINUTION occurs when the rhythmic values of a theme are divided in half (for example, quarter notes become eighth notes).

An **EXTENSION** or **EXTENDED VERSION** is created by adding to the motive.

INTERNAL EXPANSION is similar to extension, except that the added notes are place within the motive.

A theme that is written in **RETROGRADE** is written backwards, that is, the last note becomes the first, and the first becomes last.

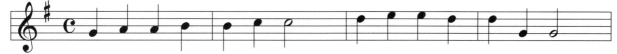

If the intervals of a melody are turned upside down, the melody has been written in **INVERSION** or **MELODIC INVERSION**.

A theme may reappear in a composition in **SHORTENED VERSION (ABBREVIATED** or **TRUNCATED)**. This means that a portion of the theme has been deleted.

The term **TRUNCATION** can refer to many different types of shortening the music: leaving out a portion of a melody, a phrase, or an entire section, for example.

TRANSPOSITION is the process of presenting the melody in a key other than the original. Transposition differs from sequence because the intervals keep the same qualities as in the original.

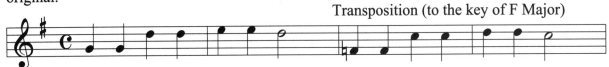

Transposition (to the key of F Major)

If a note or portion of a melody is placed in a different octave, it is referred to as **OCTAVE DISPLACEMENT**

Octave displacement

RHYTHMIC TRANSFORMATION of a melody can be achieved in many ways, by adding rests, dotted rhythms, augmentation, diminution, lengthening certain notes, etc.

A **COUNTERMELODY** is a contrasting melody which can stand on its own, but also complements the theme or original melody. The countermelody may occur at the same time as the theme, may follow it, or may begin part way through the theme.

Countermelody

Original melody:

In each question, the melody above has been changed. Check the term that indicates the type of change.

1.
_____ a. Sequence
_____ b. Imitation
_____ c. Repetition
_____ d. Retrograde

2.
_____ a. Extended version
_____ b. Melodic inversion
_____ c. Transposition
_____ d. Augmentation

3.
_____ a. Extended version
_____ b. Diminution
_____ c. Fragmentation
_____ d. Countermelody

4.
_____ a. Literal Repetition
_____ b. Inversion
_____ c. Shortened version
_____ d. Internal expansion

5.
_____ a. Retrograde
_____ b. Imitation
_____ c. Truncation
_____ d. Octave displacement

Check the motivic transformation used in each example.

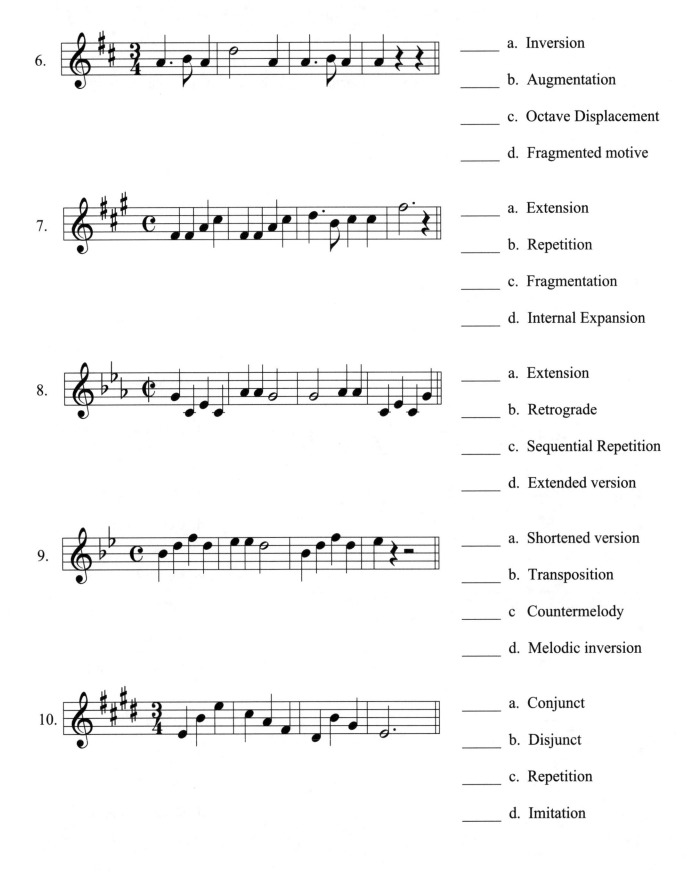

Select the musical example that describes the motivic transformation that is given.

11. Literal repetition of this motive:

_____ a.

_____ b.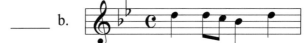

_____ c.

_____ d.

12. Fragmentation of this motive:

_____ a.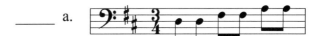

_____ b.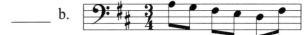

_____ c.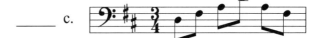

_____ d.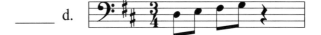

13. Melodic inversion of this motive:

_____ a.

_____ b.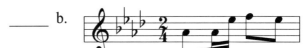

_____ c.

_____ d.

14. Transposition of this motive:

15. Rhythmic transformation of this motive:

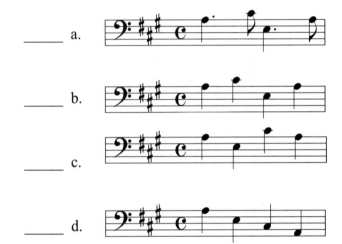

16. Check the motive that is conjunct.

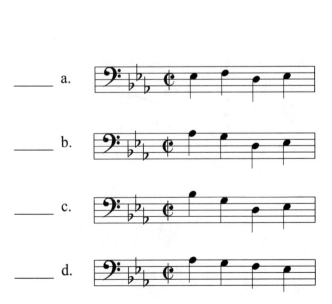

17. Write this motive in the blank measure, using repetition.

18. Write this motive using retrograde.

19. Write this motive using octave displace on the last two notes.

20. Write this motive using sequence the interval of a 2nd below the original motive.

21. Write this motive using diminution.

22. Match each term with the correct definition.

a. Motive _____ Developing a theme by changing it in various ways

b. Coutour _____ The rise and fall of a melody by pitch

c. Theme _____ A musical idea or statement, typically several measures long, which is the basis for a composition

d. Thematic transformation _____ A short melodic or rhythmic musical idea used throughout a piece of music as a unifying element.

Check the term that describes each example.

_____ a. Retrograde

_____ b. Sequence

_____ c. Imitation

_____ d. Countermelody

_____ a. Internal expansion

_____ b. Fragmentation

_____ c. Melodic inversion

_____ d. Shortened version

_____ a. Octave displacement

_____ b. Augmentation

_____ c. Transposition

_____ d. Abbreviated

_____ a. Shortened version

_____ b. Countermelody

_____ c. Extended version

_____ d. Truncation

SIGHT READING
MELODIC DEVICES

Each of the following melodies contains one of the melodic devices studied in this lesson. Sing each melody. Adjust the octave to fit your vocal range.

EAR TRAINING
IDENTIFYING MELODIC DEVICES

Listen to Examples 96-100. Each example will be played three times. Check the melodic device that is used in each example.

Example 96: _____ Retrograde _____ Rhythmic Transformation _____ Augmentation

Example 97: _____ Truncation _____ Repetition _____ Extended Version

Example 98: _____ Melodic Inversion _____ Sequence _____ Augmentation

Example 99: _____ Diminution _____ Truncation _____ Imitation

Example 100: _____ Sequence _____ Rhythmic Transformation _____ Octave Displacement

Listen to Examples 101-105. Each example will be played three times. Notate the final two measures of each melody.

LESSON 11
PHRASE STRUCTURE

A **PHRASE** is a musical statement or "sentence." Although typically four measures in length, there are many instances of phrases that are not four measures in length.

The following are examples of four measure phrases:

From *Frere Jacques*

From *Twinkle Twinkle Little Star*

A **PERIOD** consists of two or more phrases. The first phrase ends with an incomplete cadence, such as a half cadence. The second phrase ends with a complete cadence, such as an authentic cadence. Periods contain an **ANTECEDENT** or question phrase, and a **CONSEQUENT** or answer phrase, as demonstrated in this example from *Minuet in G* by J.S. Bach.

Antecedent Phrase (Question Phrase)

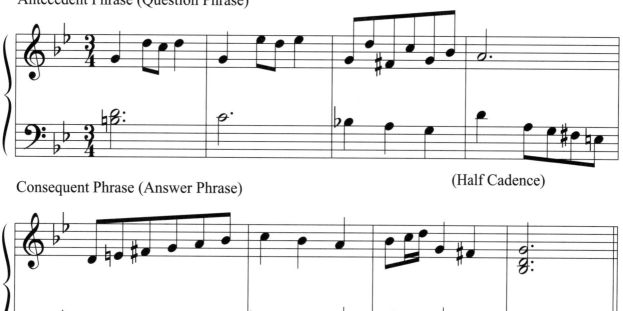

(Half Cadence)

Consequent Phrase (Answer Phrase)

(Authentic Cadence)

CONTRASTING PERIODS contain phrases with different motivic or harmonic material. The structure of the period is indicated by using the letters "a b." This example, from *Minuet in G* by J.S. Bach, is a contrasting period.

PARALLEL PERIODS consist of two phrases that begin with the same melodic material, either on the same pitch or transposed (beginning on a different note), and have similar harmonic structure. The structure of parallel periods is indicated by using the letters "a a" if the phrases are exactly the same, or "a a' " if the second phrase is modified. This example, from *Sonata K.576* by Mozart, is a parallel period.

A **DOUBLE PERIOD** consists of two consecutive periods, and contains four phrases. The structure of double periods has varying definitions. Some theory scholars describe double periods as follows: the second period closely resembles the first period, with the first and third phrases being similar melodically and harmonically. The first three phrases end with incomplete cadences, and the fourth phrase ends with a complete cadence.

Double periods have a weak cadence, such as a half cadence or an incomplete authentic cadence at the end of the first period, and have a strong cadence, such as a perfect authentic cadence, at the end of the second period. The following example, from *Minuet in G* by J.S. Bach, is an example of a double period with the structure a b a b'.

A **PHRASE GROUP** consists of phrases that occur in an irregular grouping, such as three or five phrases. The first two phrases end with incomplete cadences (such as half, deceptive, or imperfect authentic), and the third phrase ends with a complete cadence (such as perfect authentic). Theory scholars differ on the structure of phrase groups. Some state that all three phrases must be related but different, while others state that two of the phrases must be similar (aab or abb form). Those who define phrase groups as aab or abb form define groups of three phrases that are all contrasting as **PHRASE CHAINS**.

The following example, from *Musette* by J.S. Bach, illustrates a phrase group (phrase chain) with three contrasting phrases.

Phrase 1

Phrase 2

Phrase 3

An **ELISION** (or **PHRASE ELISION**) is the overlapping of two phrases, in which the last measure of the first phrase also acts as the first measure of the second phrase. The following example, from *Arabesque, Op. 100, No. 2* by Burgmuller, contains an elision.

Each of these musical examples consists of phrases and/or periods. Check the answer that applies to each example.

1. From *Sonata in c minor, KV 457,* by W.A. Mozart.

_____ a. Phrase Group

_____ b. Antecedent/Consequent Phrases

_____ c. Double Period

_____ d. Phrase Chain

2. From *Sonata in C Major, KV 545,* by W.A. Mozart

_____ a. Parallel Period

_____ b. Contrasting Period

_____ c. Double Period

_____ d. Phrase Group or Phrase Chain

3. From *Sonata in F Major, KV 457* by W.A. Mozart.

_____ a. Double Period

_____ b. Elision

_____ c. Contrasting Period

_____ d. Phrase Group (Phrase Chain)

4. From *Sonata in C Major, KV 545,* by W.A. Mozart.

_____ a. Double Period

_____ b. Phrase Group

_____ c. Contrasting Period

_____ d. Phrase Group

5. From *Sonata in D Major, K. 576,*, by Mozart.

_____ a. Phrase Group

_____ b. Phrase Chain

_____ c. Double Period

_____ d. Parallel Period

Check the correct definition for each term.

6. Anecedent/Consequent Phrases
   _____ a. Question and answer phrase
   _____ b. Phrases that are unusual lengths
   _____ c. Phrases that are always identical
   _____ d. Phrases that do not end with a cadence

7. Contrasting Period
   _____ a. Period with two identical phrases
   _____ b. Period with phrases that begin on the same pitch
   _____ c. Period with phrases that have different melodic material
   _____ d. Period with phrases that have the same cadence

8. Parallel Period
   _____ a. Period with phrases that have the same cadence
   _____ b. Period with phrases that have similar motives and harmony
   _____ c. Period with phrases that have an odd number of measures
   _____ d. Period with phrases that have different harmony

9. Phrase Group
   _____ a. A group of four phrases
   _____ b. A group of eight phrases
   _____ c. A group of three, five or other unusual grouping of phrases
   _____ d. A group of two phrases

10. Double Period
    _____ a. One period with a weak cadence
    _____ b. Two similar periods with a strong cadence at the end of the second phrase
    _____ c. Two similar periods with a weak cadence at the end of the second phrase
    _____ d. Two periods that are entirely different

11. Elision
    _____ a. Phrases that are always identical
    _____ b. Phrases that end with a weak cadence
    _____ c. Two phrases that overlap
    _____ d. Two phrases that are completely different

SIGHT SINGING
PHRASE GROUPS AND PERIODS

Sing each of the following melodies, each of which is a phrase group or period. Adjust the octave to fit your vocal range.

EAR TRAINING
PHRASE STRUCTURE

Listen to Examples 106-110. Each example will be played three times. Check the phrase structure that is used in each example.

Example 106:   _____ Contrasting Period   _____ Phrase Group   _____ Double Period

Example 107:   _____ Phrase Group   _____ Parallel Period   _____ Double Period

Example 108:   _____ Phrase Group   _____ Antecedent/Consequent   _____ Phrase Chain

Example 109:   _____ Parallel Period   _____ Phrase Chain   _____ Double Period

Example 110:   _____ Contrasting Period   _____ Phrase Group   _____ Parallel Period

LESSON 12
ORNAMENTS AND NONHARMONIC TONES

NONHARMONIC TONES are notes that do not fit with the harmony or chords with which they appear.

An **Anticipation** is a nonharmonic tone in which the presentation of a chord tone occurs immediately before the actual chord.

An **APPOGGIATURA** is a nonharmonic tone that appears with the chord on a strong beat, then resolves by step.

There are a number of different types of **NEIGHBORING TONES**. Neighboring tones are a step away from the chord tone. Neighboring tones may also be called **AUXILIARY TONES** or **EMBELLISHING TONES.**

An **ESCAPE TONE** or **ÉCHAPPÉE** is a nonharmonic tone that steps away from a chord tone, then returns by skip (3rd or larger) to a note that is in the next chord. The non-harmonic tone (the escape tone) moves in the opposite direction from the two main notes.

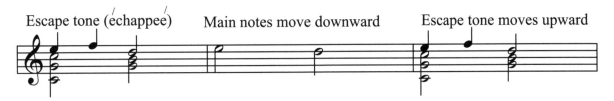

A **NEIGHBOR GROUP** is similar to an escape tone, except that the motion with the chord tones is in similar motion instead of contrary motion. Neighbor groups are also known as **CAMBIATA**, **CHANGING TONES,** or **CHANGING NOTES.**

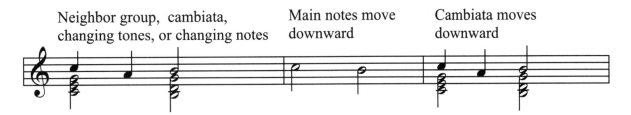

PASSING TONES pass between two chord tones in a stepwise manner. There are many types of passing tones.

UNACCENTED PASSING TONES occur on weak beats.

ACCENTED PASSING TONES occur on strong beats, with the chord. Accented passing tones are often also called Appoggiaturas.

CHROMATIC PASSING TONES are created by the use of half steps.

A **PEDAL POINT** is a note that is held, typically in the bass, for an extended time while the other voices move above it.

A persistently repeated note or pattern is called **OSTINATO.**

PREPARATION is a nonharmonic tone that is used to soften the impact of a dissonant note by first presenting it as a chord tone.

A **SUSPENSION** is a nonharmonic tone that is held beyond the next chord change, then resolves downward after the new chord appears. A **REARTICULATED SUSPENSION** occurs when the suspension is repeated rather than tied.

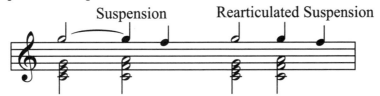

RETARDATION is similar to a suspension, except that the nonharmonic tone resolves upward.

A **SUSPENSION CHAIN** is created by combining a series of suspensions over several chord changes.

ORNAMENTS or **EMBELLISHMENTS** are another group of nonharmonic tones. Ornaments are typically indicated by symbols, but can also be indicated by small notes written between the main beats of the music. The notes of an ornament that are not the main note are called **AUXILIARY TONES**.

A **TRILL** alternates between the written note, and a neighbor note. The interpretation of the trill is dependent on the practices of the historical period in which the music was written, as well as on the context of the music.

Two symbols are used to indicate trills: Trills may begin on the note above the written note (begin on the auxiliary tone):

Trills may begin on the written note and go up to the auxiliary tone:

Trills may begin on the auxiliary tone and go down to the written note.

The **MORDENT** includes the written note, the note below the written note (the auxiliary tone), and a return to the written note:

Mordent

The **TURN** begins on the auxiliary tone a step above the written note, then steps down to the main note and to the auxiliary tone below the written note, and returns to the written note.

Turn

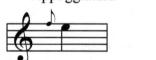 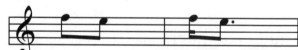

The **APPOGGIATURA** can be written as an ornament. The interpretation of such an appoggiatura is dependent on the historical period and the context of the music. It is usually played on the beat, and uses a portion of the beat of the note which follows the ornament.

Appoggiatura   Possible interpretations:

A **GRACE NOTE** looks similar to an appoggiatura, but it has a slash through the stem. The grace note is played quickly, before the beat of the main note.

Grace Note

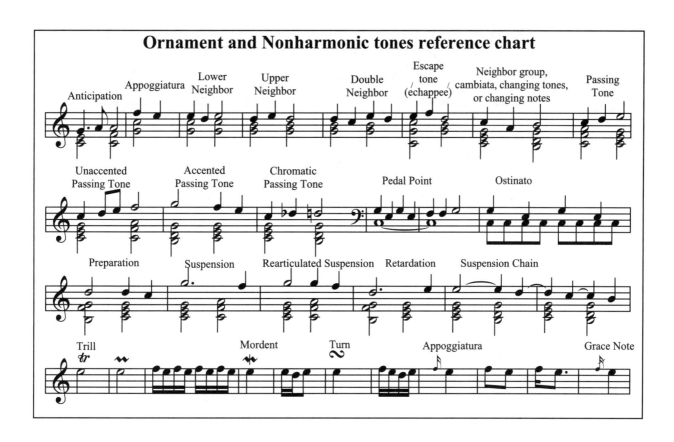

1. Name the nonharmonic tone or ornament that is circled in each example.

a. From *Sonata, Hob. XVI:35,* by Haydn. _____

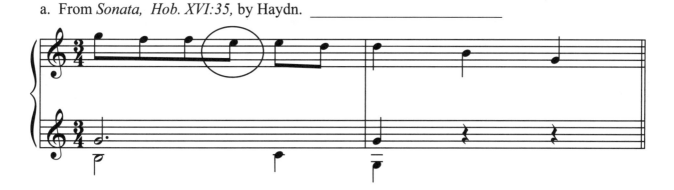

b. From *Sonata, Hob. XVI:50,* by Haydn. _____

c. From *Sonata, Hob. XVI:49,* by Haydn.

d. From *Sonata, K. 309,* by Mozart. _____

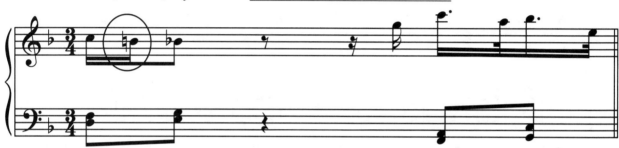

e. From *Sonata, K. 311,* by Mozart. _____

f. From, *Sonata, K. 311,* by Mozart. _____

g. From *Sonata, K. 330,* by Mozart. _____

h. From *Sonata K. 330,* by Mozart. _____

i. From *Sonata K. 331,* by Mozart. _____

j. From *Sonata K. 331,* by Mozart. _____

k. From *Sonata K. 333,* by Mozart. _____

l. From *Sonata XVI:35,* by Haydn. _____

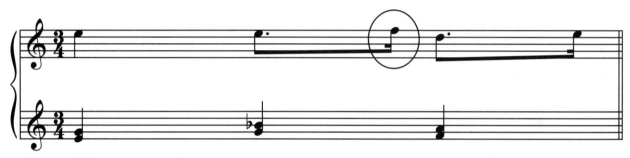

m. From *Sonata XVI:35,* by Haydn. _____

n. From *Short Prelude No. 2* by J.S. Bach. _____

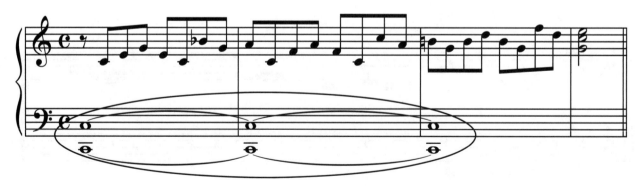

o. From *Sonata, in E♭ Major* by Haydn. _____

p. From *Sonata in E Minor* by C.P.E. Bach. _____

q. From *French Suite No. 5: Sarabande,* by J.S. Bach. _____

r. From *Waltz Op. 42 No. 1,* by Chopin. _____

s. From *Sonata Hob. XVI:37,* by Haydn.

Check the correct performance for each ornament.

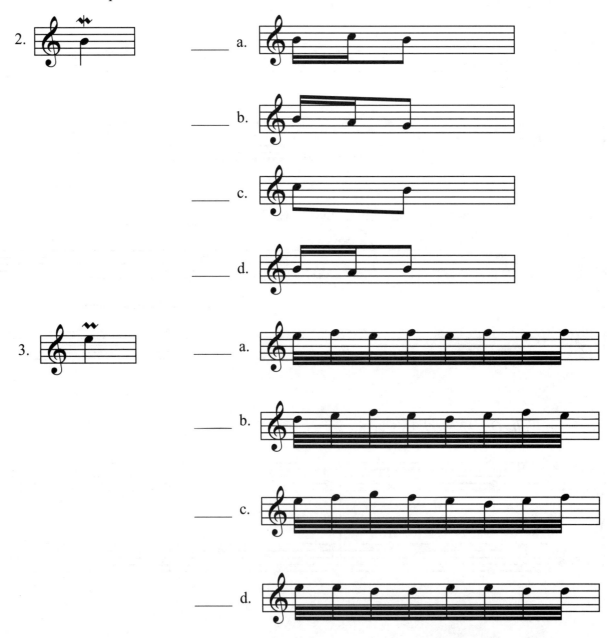

Check the correct answer for each example.

6. What is another name for a neighbor group?

_____ a. Escape Tone or échappée

_____ b. Ornament

_____ c. Passing Tone

_____ d. Cambiata

7. What makes a passing tone an accented passing tone?

_____ a. It occurs on a weak beat

_____ b. It is followed by a cadence

_____ c. It occurs on a strong beat

_____ d. It has a trill

8. Which of these describes an escape tone?

_____ a. Ascends by step, descends by skip

_____ b Repeats the same tone mulitple times

_____ c. Steps down

_____ d. Is a note from the preceding chord

9. What name is used for a persistently repeated note or pattern?

_____ a. Trill

_____ b. Mordent

_____ c. Appoggiatura

_____ d. Ostinato

10. What is another name for ornaments?

_____ a. Frills

_____ b. Embellishments

_____ c. Passing Tones

_____ d. Cambiata

11. The following example shows a mordent, followed by the realization (performance of) the mordent. What is the name for the circled note?

_____ a. Auxiliary Tone

_____ b. Pedal Point

_____ c. Turn

_____ d. Anticipation

12. What name is used for a suspension in which the suspended note is repeated rather than tied?

_____ a. Rearticulated Suspension

_____ b. Reanticipated Suspension

_____ c. Repeated Suspension

_____ d. Recharged Suspension

SIGHT SINGING
ORNAMENTS AND NONHARMONIC TONES

Sing each of the following melodies. Adjust the octave to fit your vocal range.

EAR TRAINING
ORNAMENTS AND NONHARMONIC TONES

Listen to Examples 111-115. Each example will be played three times. Check the ornament or non-harmonic tone that is played.

Example 111: _____ Suspension Chain _____ Ostinato _____ Pedal Point

Example 112: _____ Turn _____ Mordent _____ Trill

Example 113: _____ Neighbor Tone _____ Suspension _____ Anticipation

Example 114: _____ Ostinato _____ Trill _____ Escape Tone (échappée)

Example 115: _____ Cambiata _____ Preparation _____ Accented Passing Tone

Listen to Examples 116 to 120. Each example will be played three times. Complete each melody.

Example 116:

Example 117:

Example 118:

Example 119:

Example 120:

LESSON 13
HARMONIC FUNCTION

FUNCTION refers to the tendency of a chord to progress to certain other chords.

The I chord (tonic) is the only chord with **TONIC FUNCTION**. It is the strongest primary functioning chord. The tonic chord defines the key, and is usually used at both the beginning and the end of the music.

The second most important functioning chords are those with **DOMINANT FUNCTION**. The following chords can function as dominant:

        V   V7   vii°

Chords that have **PRE-DOMINANT FUNCTION** come immediately before, and prepare for dominant chords. These chords often act with a predominant function:

        IV   ii   vi

If the music has temporarily moved to a new key, the chords act as Tonic, Dominant, or Pre-dominant function based on the new key, not based on the key in which the music began.

This example shows the primary triads, and how they function within this chord progression.

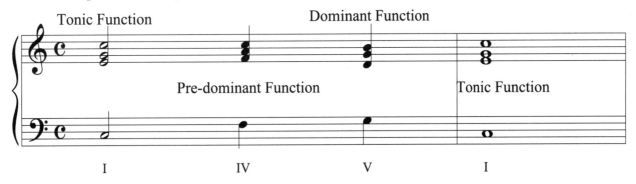

In this example, the key is G Major, but the music has temporarily moved to C Major. The chords and their functions are analyzed as if in C Major.

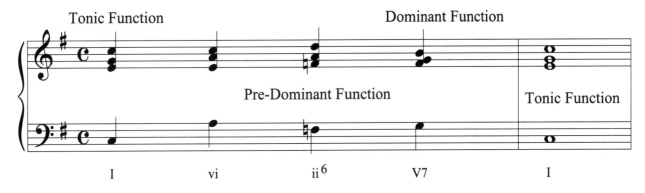

1. For each example, name the function of each circled chord (tonic function, dominant function, or pre-dominant function).

   a. From *Sonata, K. 284,* by Mozart. Key of _____

   b. From *Sonata No. 40* by Scarlatti. Key of _____

   c. From *Grillen* by Schumann. Key of _____

d. From *French Suite No. 3: Menuet II,* by J.S. Bach. Key of: _____ minor. This section is temporarily in the key of _____.

e. From *Sonata, Hob. XVI:42,* by Haydn. Key of: _____

f. From *French Suite No. 1: Menuet,* by J.S. Bach. Key of: ____ minor . This section is temporarily in the key of _____.

g. From *Sonata, K. 283,* by Mozart. Key of _____ Major. This section is temporarily in the key of _____.

Second inversion chords ($^6_4$ chords) often have specific functions.

The **CADENTIAL** $^6_4$ occurs when a I$^6_4$ chord immediately precedes a dominant (V) chord at a cadence.

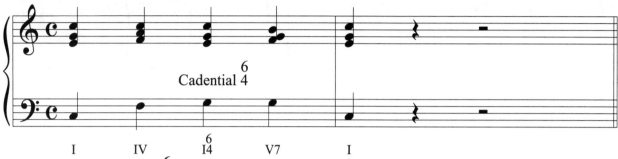

An **ARPEGGIATING** $^6_4$ occurs when the chord tones are broken in the bass, while the chord remains in the upper voices.

A **NEIGHBORING** $^6_4$ or **PEDAL** $^6_4$ is created when the third and fifth of a chord are followed by their upper neighbors, while the bass stays on the chord tone that is the root of the first chord and the fifth of the neighboring chord.

A **PASSING** $^6_4$ occurs when the bass note steps up or down, and creates a $^6_4$ chord between the first and third chords.

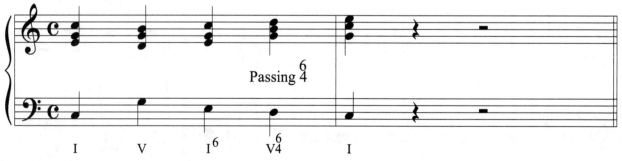

2. Tell whether each of the circled $^6_4$ chords is arpeggiating, cadential, neighboring (pedal) or passing.

a. From *Sonata, KV 309,* by Mozart.

b. From *Moments Musicaux, Op. 94, No. 4,* by Schubert.

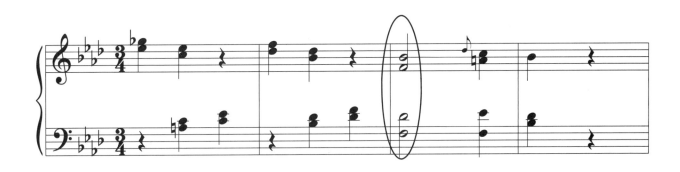

d. From *French Suite No. 3: Menuet II,* by J.S. Bach.

Sometimes, the <u>Circle of Fifths</u> is used to create the harmony. In the first example below, the circle of fifths is present, each chord being major.

In this example, beginning wth the second chord (the e minor chord), the progression goes through a portion of the circle of fifths, but the quality of the chords are adjusted to fit within the key of C Major (for example, the D Major chord is changed to d minor).

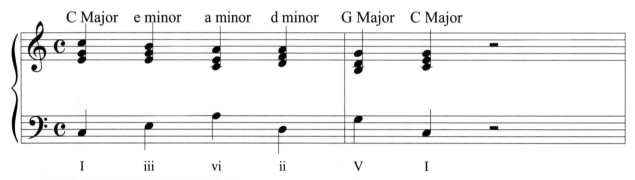

A **DECEPTIVE PROGRESSION** occurs when the listener expects the music to move in a certain harmonic direction, but the music strays from what is expected. This example ends with a deceptive cadence. The expectation would be for the music to end on I, but instead it ends on vi.

NEIGHBORING CHORDS, also known as **PEDAL CHORDS**, occur when the bass remains the same while the other notes move to neighbor notes and back.

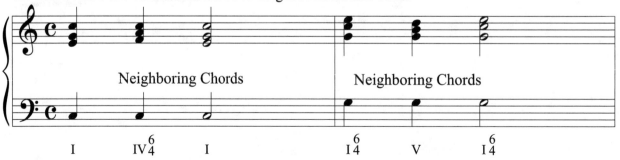

RETROGRESSION occurs when chords move in a manner that is opposite of a typical progression, such as moving from V-IV rather than IV-V, or from ii-vi rather than vi-ii.

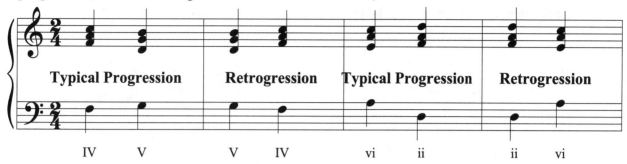

HARMONIC RHYTHM or the **RATE OF HARMONIC CHANGE** is the rhythmic pattern provided by the changes in harmony. In this example, the harmonic rhythm occurs in half notes.

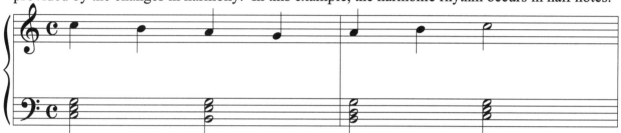

In this example, the harmonic rhythm consists of three beats, one change per measure.

Answer the following question or questions about each example.

3. From *Sonata, K. 280,* by Mozart.

   What is the harmonic rhythm for this example? _____

4. From *Etude, Op. 10, No. 5,* by Chopin.

   Circle the neighboring chords on the music.

5. From *Rhapsody, Op. 119, No. 4,* by Brahms.

   a. Which is the rate of harmonic change, fast or slow? _____

   b. Is the progression at the end of the example normal or deceptive? _____

6. From *Sonata Hob. XVI:23,* by Haydn.

   a. Write the root and quality for the basic chords under each measure. The first chord is given.

   b. Look at the chord names from question 6-a. What is the relationship of these keys?
   _____ _____ _____

A Major

7. From *Nocturne, Op. posth. 72, No. 1,* by Chopin.

   Does this example contain a fast harmonic rhythm or a slow harmonic rhythm? _____

8. From *Sonata, K 281,* by Mozart.

   Which of these is in this example: a deceptive progression, the circle of fifths, or neighboring chords? _____

Check each correct answer.

9. The circled chord in this example is a:

_____ a. Passing $^6_4$

_____ b. Neighboring chord

_____ c. Circle of fifths

_____ d. Cadential $^6_4$

10. What is the function of the circled chord?

_____ a. Tonic Function

_____ b. Dominant Function

_____ c. Pre-dominant Function

_____ d. Neighboring Function

11. What is the name for the circled chord?

_____ a. Neighboring or pedal $^6_4$

_____ b. Passing $^6_4$

_____ c. Cadential $^6_4$

_____ d. Arpeggiating $^6_4$

12. What term describes the circled chord?

_____ a. Retrogression

_____ b. Tonic Function

_____ c. Passing $^6_4$

_____ d. Harmonic Rhythm

13. What is the function of the circled chord?

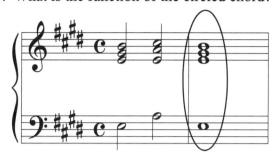

_____ a. Dominant Function

_____ b. Tonic Function

_____ c. Deceptive Progression

_____ d. Pre-dominant Function

14. What term describes this chord progression?

_____ a. Retrogression

_____ b. Deceptive Progression

_____ c. Circle of fifths

_____ d. Tonic Function

15. What best describes the harmonic rhythm for this passage?

_____ a. Fast rate of change

_____ b. Changing on every downbeat

_____ c. Slow rate of change

_____ d. Changing on every beat

16. What term describes this chord progression?

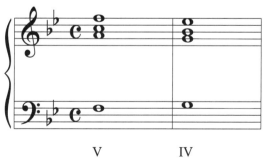

V   IV

_____ a. Neighboring chord

_____ b. Dominant Function

_____ c. Circle of fifths

_____ d. Retrogression

17. What is the function of the circled chord?

     _____ a. Dominant Function

     _____ b. Pre-dominant Function

     _____ c. Post-dominant Function

     _____ d. Tonic Function

18. Which is the strongest functioning chord?

     _____ a. Pre-dominant Function

     _____ b. Tonic Function

     _____ c. Dominant Function

     _____ d. Neighboring Chord

19. What is another name for harmonic rhythm?

     _____ a. Pace of harmonic change

     _____ b. Rhythm of harmonic change

     _____ c. Rate of harmonic change

     _____ d. Timing of harmonic change

20. Which is the only chord with tonic function?

     _____ a. V

     _____ b. V7

     _____ c. I or i

     _____ d. IV or iv

SIGHT SINGING
HARMONIC FUNCTION

Sing each of the following melodies. Adjust the octave to fit your vocal range.

EAR TRAINING
HARMONIC FUNCTION

Listen to Examples 121-125. Each example will be played three times. Check the answer that describes what is played.

Example 121: _____ Fast rate of harmonic change _____ Slow rate of harmonic change

Example 122: _____ Deceptive Progression _____ Cadential $^6_4$ _____ Neighbor chords

Example 123: _____ Circle of Fifths _____ Retrogression _____ Neighboring (pedal) $^6_4$

Example 124: _____ Arpeggiating $^6_4$ _____ Deceptive Progression _____ Circle of Fifths

Example 125: _____ Neighbor chords _____ Circle of Fifths _____ Retrogression

Listen to Examples 126-130. Each example will be played three times. The melody for each example is given. Write the Roman numeral and harmonic function where indicated. The first chord is given.

Example 126:

    IV
  Predominant

Example 127:

Example 128:

middle chord's function: _____

Example 129:

middle chord's function: _____

Example 130:

ii⁶

first chord's function: _____

LESSON 14
TONICIZATION AND MODULATION

Music often changes keys temporarily during the course of the composition. If the key change is relatively short (just a few measures, for example) the temporary key change is called **TONICIZATION**. A longer key change, which lasts for many phrases or for much of a section, is called **MODULATION**.*

This example, from *Song of War* by Schumann, modulates from D Major to F# Major.

The following example, from *25 Progressive Pieces, Op. 100, No. 25* by Burgmuller, contains tonicization.

*Two important 20th Century theorists, Schoenberg and Schenker, taught that music does not truly modulate.

PIVOT CHORD MODULATION occurs when the new key is prepared by a **PIVOT CHORD.** The pivot chord is common to both the original key and the key to which the music modulates. The pivot chord is circled in this example.

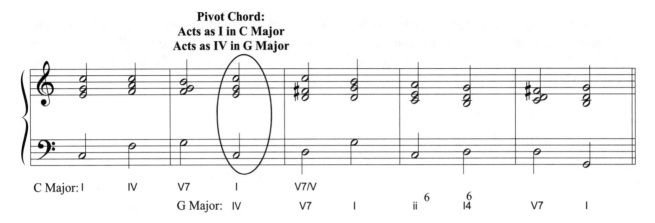

COMMON TONE MODULATION occurs when the last chord of the original key and the first chord of the new key have notes in common, but there is not a pivot chord (a chord that is common to both the original and the new key).

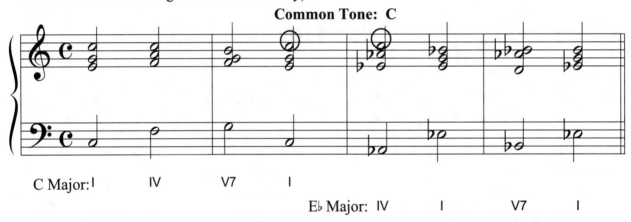

PHRASE MODULATION occurs when the key change takes place from one phrase to the next, without a pivot chord or a common tone.

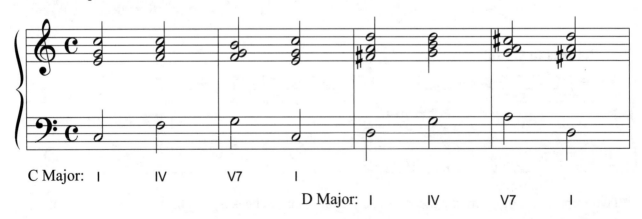

1. Name the key in which each example begins, the key to which it modulates, and the type of modulation (common tone modulation, pivot chord modulation, or phrase modulation).

a. From *Sonata, KV 309,* by Mozart.

Original key: _____ Modulates to: _____ Type: _____

b. From *Intermezzo, Op. 118, No. 2,* by Brahms.

Original key: _____ Modulates to: _____ Type: _____

c. From *Moments Musicaux, Op. 94, No. 6,* by Schubert.

Original key: a♭ minor   Modulates to: _____   Type: _____

2. From *25 Progressive Pieces, Op. 100. No. 9,* by Burgmuller.

   a. In which measures does this example use tonicization? _____

   b. What term describes the relationship of the original key and the key that occurs during the section that uses tonicization? _____

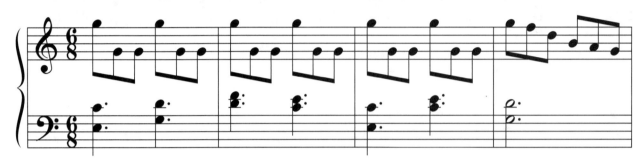

Measure 1

Measure 5

Measure 9

173

Measure 13

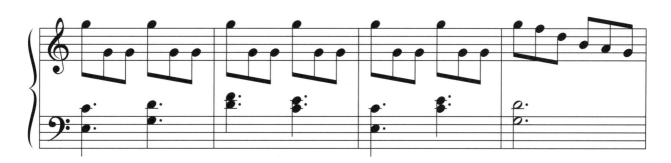

Measure 17

Measure 21

3 Circle the pivot chord in this example.

From *Sonata Hob.-Verz. XVI: 35* by Haydn.

Check the correct answer for each question.

4. What type of modulation is used in this example?

_____ a. Pivot Chord Modulation

_____ b. Common Tone Modulation

_____ c. Phrase Modulation

_____ d. Perfect Modulation

5. What term is used for a change of key that lasts for a considerable length of time?

_____ a. Modification

_____ b. Modulation

_____ c. Tonicization

_____ d. Modulization

6. What name is used for a chord that is common to both the original key and the key to which the music modulates?

_____ a. Primary Chord

_____ b. Pivot Chord

_____ c. Perfect Chord

_____ d. Pedal Chord

7. What type of modulation is used in this example?

_____ a. Pivot Chord Modulation

_____ b. Common Tone Modulation

_____ c. Phrase Modulation

_____ d. Primary Modulation

175

8. Which type of modulation changes key without using a chord or a note that is common to both keys?

_____ a. Modern Modulation

_____ b. Common Tone Modulation

_____ c. Phrase Modulation

_____ d. Pivot Chord Modulation

9. What type of modulation is used in this example?

_____ a. Pivot Chord Modulation

_____ b. Secondary Modulation

_____ c. Phrase Modulation

_____ d. Common Tone Modulation

10. Which type of modulation uses a note, but not a chord, that is the same?

_____ a. Pivot Chord Modulation

_____ b. Common Tone Modulation

_____ c. Phrase Modulation

_____ d. Imperfect Modulation

11. Which is the pivot chord in this example?

_____ a. Measure 1, beat 4

_____ b. Measure 2, beat 1

_____ c. Measure 1, beat 3

_____ d. Measure 2, beat 2

SIGHT SINGING
MODULATION AND TONICIZATION

Sing each of the following examples. Adjust the octave to fit your vocal range.

EAR TRAINING
TONICIZATION AND MODULATION

Listen to Examples 131-138. Each example will be played three times. Check tonication or the type of modulation for each example.

Example 131:
_____ Pivot chord modulation
_____ Common tone modulation
_____ Phrase modulation
_____ Tonicization

Example 132:
_____ Pivot chord modulation
_____ Common tone modulation
_____ Phrase modulation
_____ Tonicization

Example 133:
_____ Pivot chord modulation
_____ Common tone modulation
_____ Phrase modulation
_____ Tonicization

Example 134:
_____ Pivot chord modulation
_____ Common tone modulation
_____ Phrase modulation
_____ Tonicization

Example 135:
_____ Pivot chord modulation
_____ Common tone modulation
_____ Phrase modulation
_____ Tonicization

Example 136:
_____ Pivot chord modulation
_____ Common tone modulation
_____ Phrase modulation
_____ Tonicization

Example 137:
_____ Pivot chord modulation
_____ Common tone modulation
_____ Phrase modulation
_____ Tonicization

Example 138:
_____ Pivot chord modulation
_____ Common tone modulation
_____ Phrase modulation
_____ Tonicization

LESSON 15
ALTERED CHORDS AND SUSPENSIONS

Chord alterations can be labeled using the name of the chord with an additional accidental and number, written to the right of the chord symbol.

A sharp before a number indicates that the chord tone has been raised a half step.

A flat before a number indicates that the chord tone has been lowered a half step.

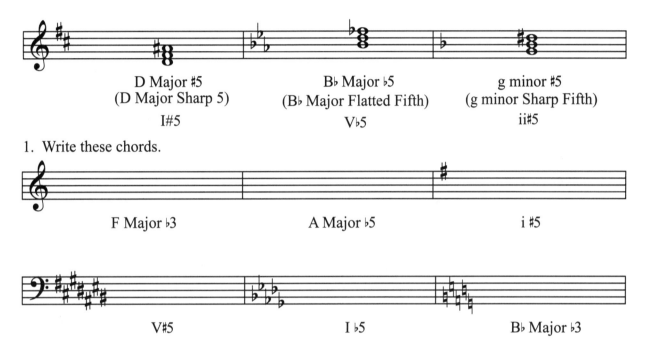

A number with a slash (6) or a plus (4+) indicates that the chord tone is raised a half step.

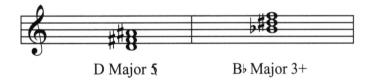

2. Write these chords.

A **PICARDY THIRD** occurs when a composition in a minor key ends with a Major chord. The G♯ on the last chord of this example is the Picardy third.

RESOLUTION is a term used for the chord tones that follow a nonharmonic tone, moving the music from a dissonant sound to a consonant sound.

In a suspension, the relationship of notes above the bass are identified using numbers. The numbers represent the basic interval (simple intervals, not compound intervals, except in the case of the 9th), compared with the bass note of the second chord.

In the first measure, the treble clef A is a 9th above the bass clef G, while the G (the resolution) is an 8th above. The suspension is a 9-8 suspension.

The second measure is a 7-6 suspension, because the treble clef F♯ is a 7th above the bass clef G, and the resolution note E is a 6th above the bass clef G.

The third measure is a 4-3 suspension, because the treble clef C is a 4th above the bass clef G, and the B (the resolution) is a 3rd above the bass clef G.

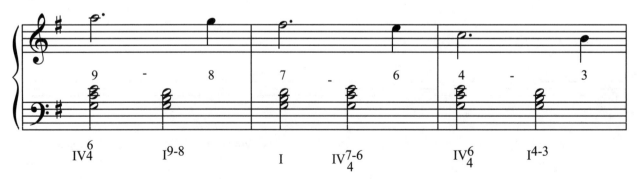

3. Label each chord with its Roman numeral, adding numbers for the suspensions.

Suspensions often occur in inner voices, as in this example, which has two suspended notes.

4. What is the major chord at the end of the example called? _____

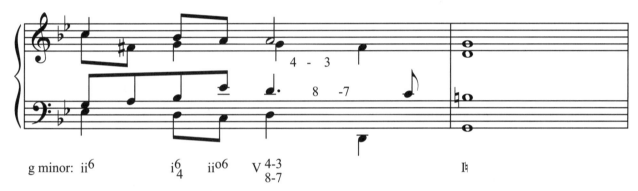

g minor: ii⁶   i⁶₄   ii°⁶   V 4-3 / 8-7   I♮

5. Label the circled suspension in each example with a Roman numeral for the chord and numbers for the suspension. The first one is given.

a. From *Herr Gott, dich loben wir,* by J.S. Bach. Key of: _____

(G Major): IV⁴⁻³   _____

b. From *Das heil'gen Geistes reiche Gnad'* by J.S. Bach. Key of _____

_____

c. From *Herzlich lieb hab'ich dich, O Herr*, by J.S. Bach. Key of _____

Check the correct answer for each example.

6. To determine the type of suspension, which note will be the lowest note of the interval?

   _____ a. The highest note

   _____ b. The bass note

   _____ c. The name of the key

   _____ d. The first chord of the piece

7. When a number has a slash (6̸, for example), what does it indicate?

   _____ a. The note is raised a half step

   _____ b. The note is lowered a half step

   _____ c. The note is raised a whole step

   _____ d. The note is lowered a whole step

8. When a number has a plus after it (4+, for example,) what does it indicate?

   _____ a. The note is raised a half step

   _____ b. The note is lowered a half step

   _____ c. The note is raised a whole step

   _____ d. The note is lowered a whole step

9. Which note creates the resolution for this suspension?

   _____ a. C

   _____ b. A

   _____ c. E

   _____ d. F

SIGHT SINGING
ALTERED CHORDS AND SUSPENSIONS

Sing each of the following melodies. Adjust the octave to fit your vocal range.

EAR TRAINING
ALTERED CHORDS AND SUSPENSIONS

Listen to examples 139-142. Each example will be played three times. A chord will be played, followed by the same chord with an alteration. Check the alteration that is played.

Example 139: _____ ♭5   _____ 5   _____ 3   _____ ♭3

Example 140: _____ ♭5   _____ 5   _____ #3   _____ ♭3

Example 141: _____ ♭5   _____ #5   _____ 3   _____ ♭3

Example 142: _____ ♭5   _____ 5+   _____ 3+   _____ ♭3

Listen to Examples 143-146. Each example will be played three times. Each example contains a suspension. Check the type of suspension that is played.

Example 143: _____ 9-8   _____ 7-6   _____ 4-3

Example 144: _____ 9-8   _____ 7-6   _____ 4-3

Example 145: _____ 9-8   _____ 7-6   _____ 4-3

Example 146: _____ 9-8   _____ 7-6   _____ 4-3

LESSON 16
INTRODUCTION TO FOUR PART HARMONY

Four Part Harmony (or four part writing) is the term typically used for music that is written in choral style. The four parts include soprano, alto, tenor and bass.

Four part choral music is written with the soprano and alto voices in the treble clef, and the tenor and bass voices in the bass clef. The stems for all soprano and tenor notes go up, and stems for all alto and bass notes go down.

Piano style:

Four part style:

In four-part vocal music, each voice should be written within a range that is comfortable for singing. It is best to stay within the following ranges:

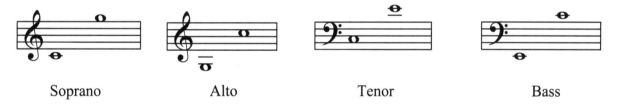

      Soprano   Alto   Tenor   Bass

1. Name the voice or voices for which each note may be used. Write S for Soprano, A for Alto, T for Tenor, and B for Bass.

> Lessons 19-22 are intended only to be a basic introduction to the complex subject of part writing. For further study, see the references on pages 387-388.

2. The following hymn is written in a style that is appropriate for piano. Rewrite the music on the empty staff using four-part choral style.

Kingsley: *Ferguson*

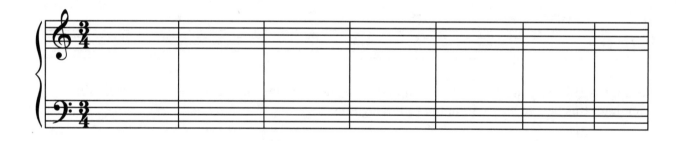

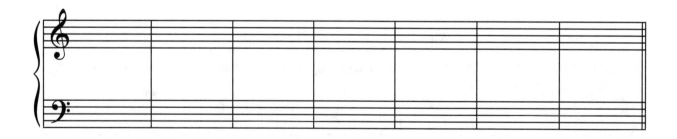

Because there are four different parts, and most chords have only three different notes, one of the notes in each chord will be used twice. This is called **DOUBLING**.

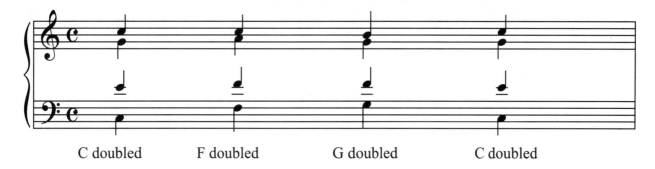

C doubled   F doubled   G doubled   C doubled

3. Label each chord with its Roman Numeral and figured bass. Name the note that is doubled with its letter name and its position in the chord (R, 3, 5, or 7). The first two chords are given. When a nonharmonic tone is present, analyze the chord using the resolution. If no note is doubled, write N.

J.S. Bach: *Dir, dir, Jehova, will ich singen*

Bb Major: __I__ __I⁶__ ____ ____ ____ ____ ____ ____
           __N__ __Bb, R__ ____ ____ ____ ____ ____ ____

When a four part piece is written in **CLOSE POSITION**, the tenor, alto and soprano have no chord tones between them.

Four part harmony style:

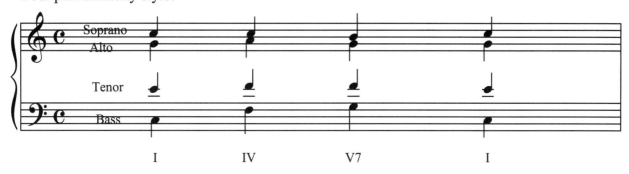

I   IV   V7   I

4. Write each chord in close position. Use the major key for each.

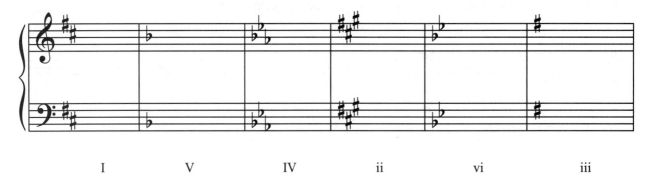

5. Using close position, complete the alto line for this example.

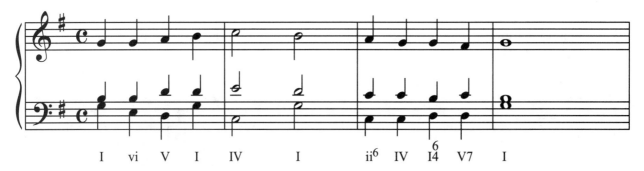

6. Using close position, complete the tenor line for this example.

7. Using close position, complete the soprano line for this example.

Chords that are in **OPEN POSITION** are separated. A note from the chord could be written between some of the voices. It is best to keep the soprano, alto and tenor within an octave of each other. The bass may be far from the tenor, but not more than two octaves away.

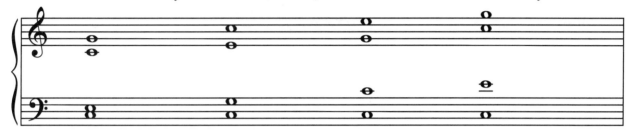

OPEN POSITION

8. Tell whether each of these chords is in open position or close position.

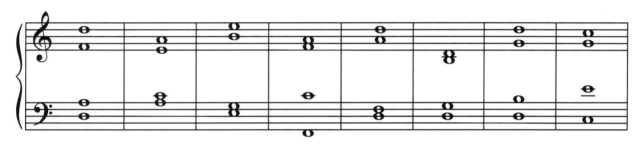

9. Write each chord in open position. Use the major key for each. Double the root for each chord. Do not put too much distance between the upper voices.

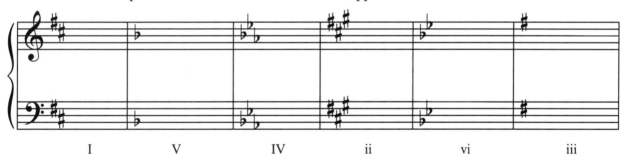

10. Write the Roman numerals and figured bass for the following example from *As with Gladness Men of Old* by Kocher.

190

Check the correct answer for each question.

11. Which note is doubled in this chord?

_____ a. Root
_____ b. Third
_____ c. Fifth
_____ d. Seventh

12. Check the type of position for this chord.

_____ a. Open position
_____ b. Double position
_____ c. Close position
_____ d. Alto position

13. Check the type of position for this chord.

_____ a. Open position
_____ b. Double position
_____ c. Close position
_____ d. Alto position

14. Check the voice for this vocal range.

_____ a. Soprano
_____ b. Alto
_____ c. Tenor
_____ d Bass

15. Check the voice for this vocal range.

_____ a. Soprano
_____ b. Alto
_____ c. Tenor
_____ d. Bass

SIGHT SINGING
INTRODUCTION TO FOUR PART HARMONY

Sing each part, soprano, alto, tenor and bass, for the following example. Adjust the octave of each part to fit your vocal range.

Johann Crüger: *Nun Danket*

EAR TRAINING
INTRODUCTION TO FOUR PART HARMONY

Listen to Example 147. The example will be played four times. Complete the Chorale below by notating the soprano voice.

J.S. Bach: *Aus meines Herzens Grunde*

LESSON 17
DOUBLING

Chords used in Common Practice Style have only three notes, with the exception of seventh chords. Therefore, when writing in four parts, most chords will have one note that is doubled.

Although any note can be doubled, there are basic guidelines that should be followed. Which note to double will depend on several factors:

- The position and scale degree of the chord
- The best voice leading
- The scale degree of the note being doubled

Therefore, there is some flexibility when determining which voice to double.

If a chord is in root position, the root is often the best choice for doubling.

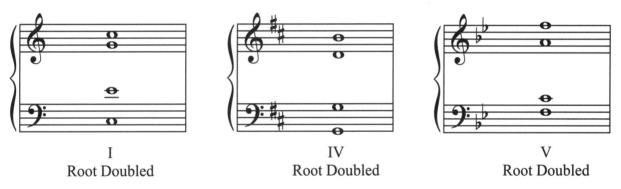

          I   IV   V
Root Doubled   Root Doubled   Root Doubled

1. Write the following chords using four voices. Double the root of each chord. Determine whether to use the major or minor key by the quality of the Roman numeral unless indicated.

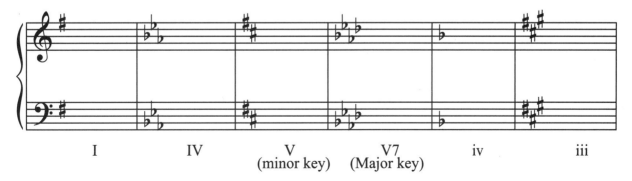

  I   IV   V   V7   iv   iii
                              (minor key) (Major key)

When writing I, I⁶, ii and IV chords, the root is most commonly doubled. The fifth may also be doubled. The third is rarely doubled, but is acceptable.

2. Write the following chords using four voices. Use the indicated doubling for each chord.

The leading tone of the key should not be doubled. The third of the V chord is the leading tone. When writing V chords in any position, the root or fifth should be doubled, but not the third.

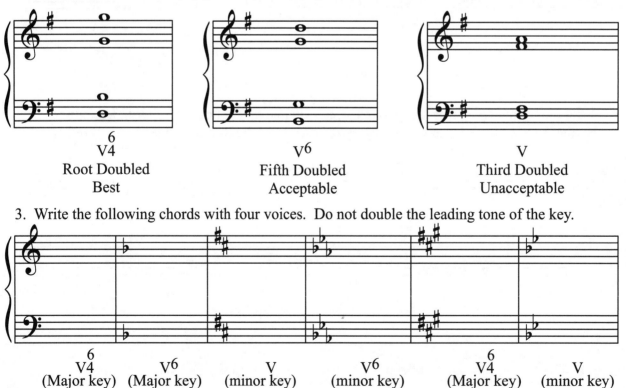

3. Write the following chords with four voices. Do not double the leading tone of the key.

The root of the vii° chord is also the leading tone of the key. The vii° chord also contains the interval of a diminished 5th between the root and fifth of the chord. These two notes act as **TENDENCY TONES** (see p. 216), with the fifth resolving down, and the root resolving up. Therefore, only the third of the vii° chord should be doubled.

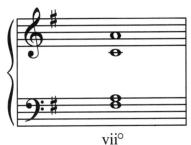

vii°
Third Doubled - Only Acceptable Doubling

4. Write the following chords using four voices. Only double the third of each chord. Use the major key for each example.

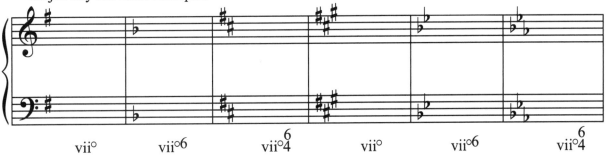

vii°   vii°6   vii°$^6_4$ vii°   vii°6   vii°$^6_4$

The best note to double in the vi chord is the third. The root may also be doubled, but is not as desirable.   The fifth should be avoided. In minor keys, only the third should be doubled in the VI chord.

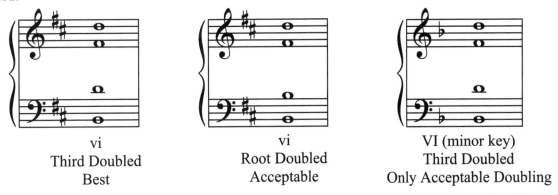

vi   vi   VI (minor key)
Third Doubled   Root Doubled   Third Doubled
Best   Acceptable   Only Acceptable Doubling

5. Write the following chords in four voices, using an appropriate doubling for each chord.

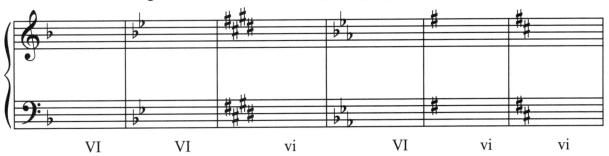

VI   VI   vi   VI   vi   vi

When writing I⁶, IV⁶ or V⁶ triads, the best note to double is the Root, which should be matched in the Soprano voice. Doubling the fifth is also acceptable. The third may be doubled in the I⁶ and IV⁶ chords, but is less desirable. The third should not be doubled in the V⁶ chord.

I⁶
Root Doubled - Best
Matched in Soprano

V⁶
Fifth Doubled
Acceptable

IV⁶
Third Doubled
Avoid

6. Write the following chords in four voices, using an appropriate doubling for each chord.

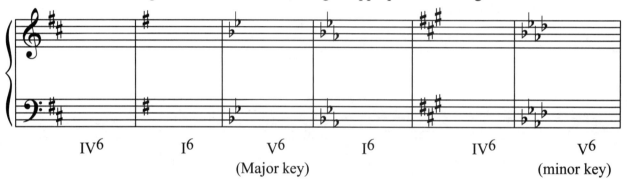

IV⁶   I⁶   V⁶   I⁶   IV⁶   V⁶
(Major key)   (minor key)

When writing ii⁶, iii⁶, iv⁶ or vi⁶ chords, the best note to double is the third. The root may be doubled, but doubling the fifth is less desirable.

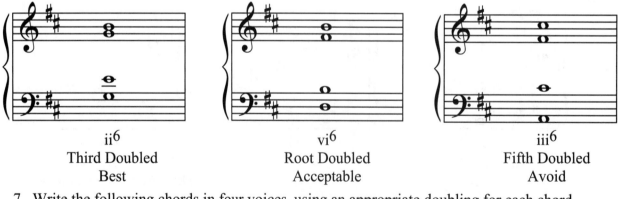

ii⁶
Third Doubled
Best

vi⁶
Root Doubled
Acceptable

iii⁶
Fifth Doubled
Avoid

7. Write the following chords in four voices, using an appropriate doubling for each chord.

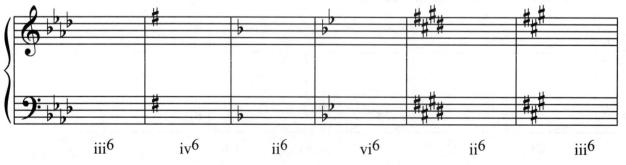

iii⁶   iv⁶   ii⁶   vi⁶   ii⁶   iii⁶

When writing second inversion chords, the fifth should be doubled. The root and third should be avoided, especially if the second inversion chord is a cadential $^6_4$.

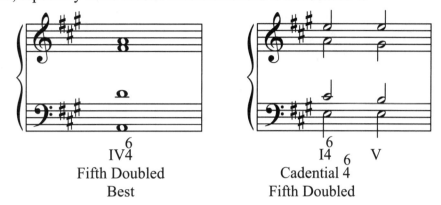

8. Write the following chords in four voices, using an appropriate doubling for each chord.

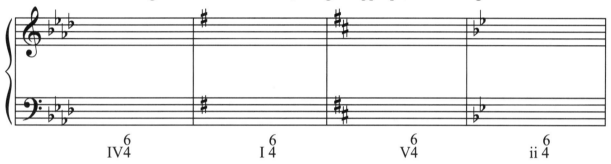

Since dominant seventh chords have four notes, all four may be used, or the fifth may be omitted. The third should not be doubled because it is the leading tone. The seventh should not be doubled.

9. Using the major key for each example, write each of the following seventh chords using four voices, and omitting the 5th.

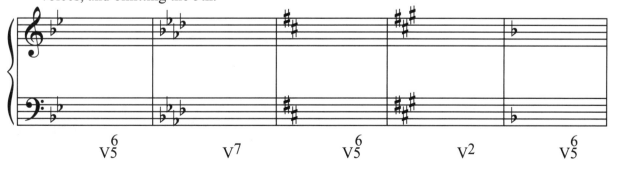

When writing augmented or diminished chords, the third should be doubled. The root may be doubled, except in the vii° chord. If a chord is altered, the altered note should not be doubled unless it is the root.

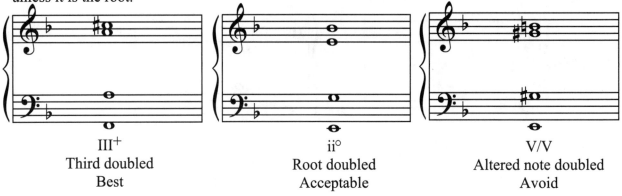

III⁺   ii°   V/V
Third doubled   Root doubled   Altered note doubled
Best   Acceptable   Avoid

10. Write the following chords in four voices, using an appropriate doubling for each chord.

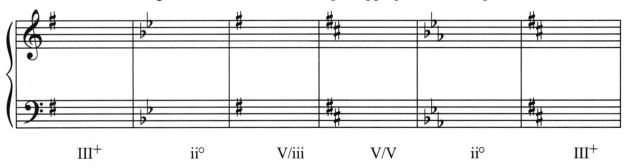

III⁺   ii°   V/iii   V/V   ii°   III⁺

The scale degrees that are most often doubled are the 1st (tonic), 4th (subdominant) and 5th (dominant) tones. Doubled less frequently are 2 (supertonic), 3 (mediant) and 6 (submediant). Doubling the 7th scale degree (leading tone) should be avoided.

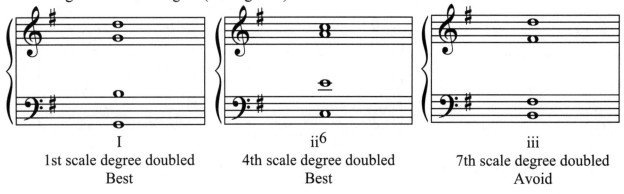

I   ii⁶   iii
1st scale degree doubled   4th scale degree doubled   7th scale degree doubled
Best   Best   Avoid

11. Using the major key for each example, name the scale degree that is doubled in each of the following triads. The first one is given.

1 (tonic)   _____   _____   _____   _____   _____

If a chord only has two notes, they are most likely the root and third. The third is rarely omitted because it is important in giving the chord its quality. When the root and third are the only notes present, the root should be tripled.

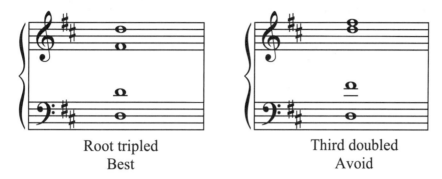

Root tripled
Best

Third doubled
Avoid

12. Using only the root and third, write the following chords with four voices.

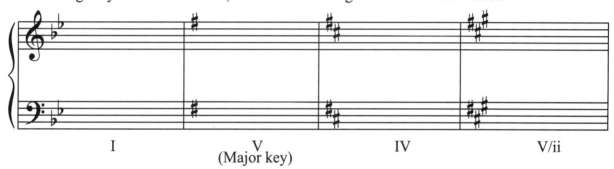

I   V (Major key)   IV   V/ii

Doubling Reference Chart

Chord	Best	Acceptable	Avoid	Unacceptable
Root position	R	See exceptions in this chart		
I I⁶ ii IV	R	5th 3rd		
V	R	5th		3rd
vii°	3rd			R 5th
vi	3rd	R	5th	
VI	3rd			R 5th
I⁶ IV⁶ V⁶	R (match in soprano)	5th	3rd (I⁶ IV⁶)	3rd (V⁶)
ii⁶ iii⁶ iv⁶ vi⁶	3rd	R	5th	
$^6_4$ chords	5th		R 3rd	R 3rd (cadential $^6_4$)
V7 w/o 5th	R			3rd, 7th
Aug, dim.	3rd	R		R (vii°)
altered chords				altered note
Scale degrees	1 4 5	2 3 6		7
R & 3rd only	Triple R			

Check each correct answer.

13. What is the best choice for doubling most root position chords?

  _____ a. Root
  _____ b. Third
  _____ c. Fifth
  _____ d. Seventh

14. Which note or notes may be doubled when writing a V chord?

  _____ a. Root only
  _____ b. Root or third
  _____ c. Root or fifth
  _____ d. Third or fifth

15. Which note or notes should be doubled in a VI chord when using the minor key?

  _____ a. Root
  _____ b. Third
  _____ c. Fifth
  _____ d. Root or Fifth

16. What note should be used in the tenor voice to complete the following chord?

  _____ a. C♯
  _____ b. E
  _____ c. G
  _____ d. B

vii°

17. Which note may be omitted from a dominant seventh chord?

  _____ a. Root
  _____ b. Third
  _____ c. Fifth
  _____ d. Seventh

18. Which note should be doubled when writing an incomplete V7 chord?

　　_____ a. Root
　　_____ b. Root or Fifth
　　_____ c. Third
　　_____ d. Fifth

19. Which note should be doubled in a vii° chord?

　　_____ a. Root
　　_____ b. Root or Fifth
　　_____ c. Fifth
　　_____ d. Third

20. In order of preference, which two notes are the best choices for the soprano in this chord?

　　_____ a. F♯ or C♯
　　_____ b. A or C♯
　　_____ c. C♯ or F♯
　　_____ d. A or F♯

ii6

21. When writing a cadential $^6_4$, which note or notes may be doubled?

　　_____ a. Root or fifth
　　_____ b. Third or Root
　　_____ c. Fifth only
　　_____ d. Root only

22. On which note or notes should doubling be avoided when writing an altered chord?

　　_____ a. Root
　　_____ b. Third
　　_____ c. Fifth
　　_____ d. Altered note

SIGHT SINGING

Sing each part (soprano, alto, tenor, and bass) of the following Chorale. Adjust each part to fit your vocal range.

J.S. Bach: *Christus, der ist mein Leben*

EAR TRAINING

Listen to Example 148. The example will be played four times. Complete the following chorale by notating the bass voice.

J.S. Bach: *O Ewigkeit, du Donnerwort*

LESSON 18
HARMONIC PROGRESSION

HARMONIC PROGRESSION refers to the tendency of a chord to move smoothly from one chord to another. While any chord may be used, and progressions do not have to follow set rules, there are many progressions that are extremely common.

The ultimate goal of most musical compositions is to end on the I chord (tonic). The V chord, or the dominant, is the second most common chord. Many melodies can be harmonized by using only these two chords.

The following example, *Mary Had a Little Lamb,* can be harmonized using only I and V. Notice how the chords match the majority of the notes in the melody.

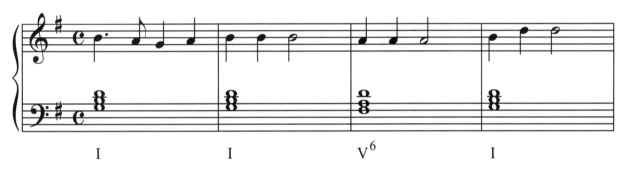

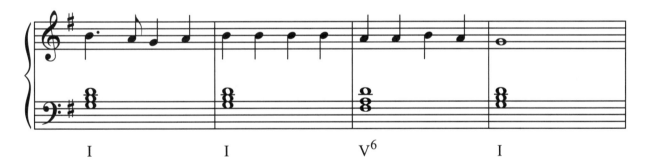

1. Using only the I chord and the V chord, add Roman numerals to each of the following melodies. Place one Roman numeral on each blank line. Choose the chord that matches the melody best.

    a. **Hot Cross Buns**

b. **The Itsy, Bitsy Spider**

The IV chord (subdominant) is the also frequently used chord for harmonizing melodies. Many melodies can be harmonized using only the I, IV, and V chords.

Twinkle, Twinkle, Little Star is shown below. It is harmonized using only the I, IV, and V chords.

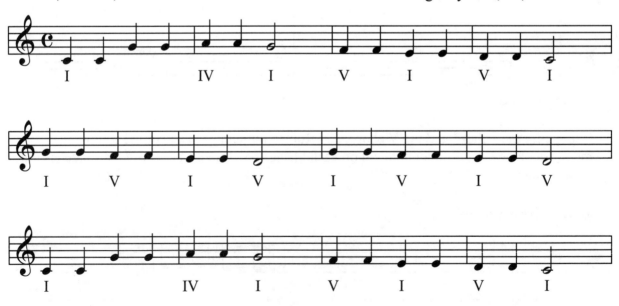

2. Using only I, IV and V chords, add Roman numerals to each of the following melodies. Place one Roman numeral on each blank line. Choose the chord that matches the melody best.

a. **I've Been Working on the Railroad**

b. **Jingle Bells** (Pierpont)

The IV (subdominant), ii (supertonic) and less frequently the vi (submediant) chords are used as preparation for the V (dominant) chord.

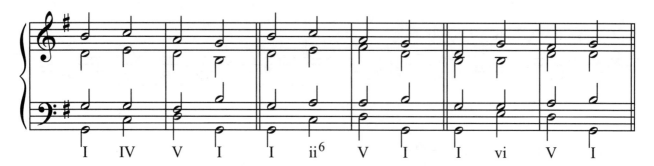

3. Each of the following phrases is from the end of a song. Determine whether the missing chord should be a IV chord, a ii chord, or a vi chord, and write the correct Roman numeral on the blank line.

a. From *The Girl I Left Behind Me*

b. From *While Shepherds Watched*

c. From *Bobby Shafto*

The relationship of the fifth is important in harmonic progression. This applies not only to the V-I progression, but to the other fifth relationships, including ii-V, iii-vi, vi-ii, I-IV, and rarely IV-vii°.

These fifth relationships are often linked together to create a progression that includes a variety of chords.

In Major keys:

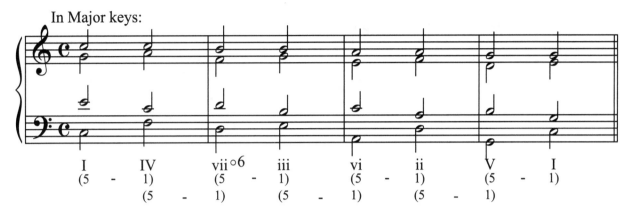

In minor keys:

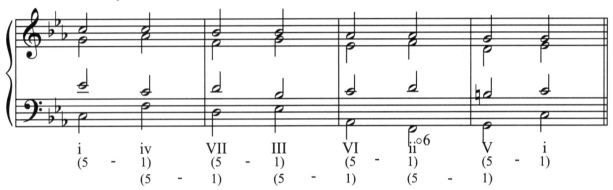

4. Write the Roman numeral that would follow each given Roman numeral when using the fifth relationship. Circle the fifth relationship that is rare.

   a. iii _____ b. V _____ c. ii _____ d. vi _____ e. IV _____ f. vii° _____

5. Complete the Roman numerals for each of the following melodies. Use a fifth relationship for each set of missing chords.

The following chart shows some of the ways in which chords progress.

Common	Sometimes	Rare
I-IV I-V	I-vi	I-ii I-iii
ii-V	ii-vi	ii-I ii-iii ii-IV
iii-vi	iii-IV	iii-ii iii-V
IV-V	IV-I IV-ii	IV-iii IV-vi
V-I	V-vi V-IV	V-iii V-ii
vi-ii vi-V	vi-iii vi-IV	vi-I

6. a. Refer to the chart above. Using only harmonic progressions listed as Common, add Roman numerals to the following melody.

b. Using at least one harmonic progression listed under "Sometimes," add Roman numerals to the following melody.

c. Using at least one harmonic progression listed under "Rare," add Roman numerals to the following melody.

Chords can sometimes be substituted for other chords. This gives variety and color to harmonic progressions. The following melody is shown with two different harmonic progressions. Notice how the second progression is more interesting.

The following chords are often good alternates or substitutes for one another:

   I, vi, iii

   V, V7, vii°

   IV, ii

7. Enhance the harmonic progression for each of the following melodies by adding alternate or substitute chords on each blank line.

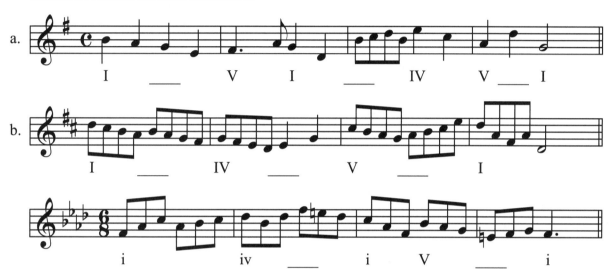

Inversions can also add variety to a harmonic progression, and create smoother progressions. Some of the most common uses of inversions include the following: I^6 - ii^6; ii^6-I_4^6; IV_4^6-V_5^6, and the cadential $_4^6$.

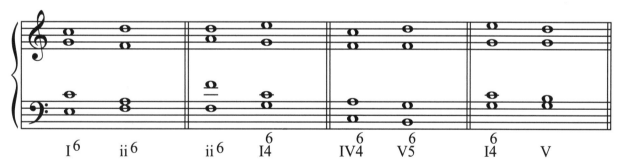

I^6 ii^6 ii^6 I_4^6 IV_4^6 V_5^6 I_4^6 V

8. Using Roman numerals, add chords to the following melody. Use some inversions.

Check the correct answer for each of the following questions.

9. Which of the following examples shows an acceptable alternate chord or substitution?

   _____ a. I and V
   _____ b. IV and V
   _____ c. IV and ii
   _____ d. vii° and I

10. Which two chords are used most frequently?

    _____ a. I and V
    _____ b. IV and I
    _____ c. ii and V
    _____ d. IV and I

11. Which chords are often used as preparation for V?

    _____ a. iii, I and IV
    _____ b. vii°, ii and vi
    _____ c. IV, ii and vi
    _____ d. iii, IV and vii°

12. Which of these shows a fifth relationship?

    _____ a. ii-iii
    _____ b. vi-IV
    _____ c. V-IV
    _____ d. vi-ii

13. Which of these is the best choice for a traditional harmonic progression?

    _____ a. I ii IV vi vii° I
    _____ b. I vi ii V I
    _____ c. I iii ii IV I
    _____ d. I vi vii° ii I

SIGHT SINGING

Sing each part (soprano, alto, tenor, and bass) of the following Chorale.

J.S. Bach: *Du Friedensfurst, Herr Jesu Christ*

EAR TRAINING

Listen to Example 149. The example will be played four times. Complete the following chorale by notating the soprano voice.

J.S. Bach: *Ach wie nichtig, ach wie fluchtig*

LESSON 19
INTRODUCTION TO VOICE LEADING

VOICE LEADING is a term that is used to describe the manner in which each part, or voice, moves within the music. Good voice leading leads to a clean, smooth sound. Poor voice leading causes unusual sounds, and can be very difficult to sing.

The soprano voice usually contains the main melodic line. A good soprano line will be mostly conjunct (stepwise motion), with some leaps to create variety and interest. A disjunct melody can a choppy sound, and may be difficult to sing.

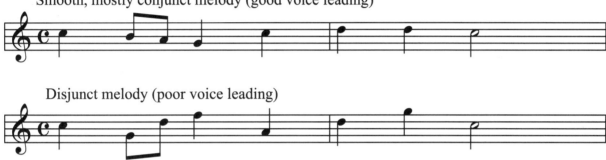

The bass line creates the harmonic support for all voices above it. It is often, but not always, the root of the chord. Bass lines are typically disjunct.

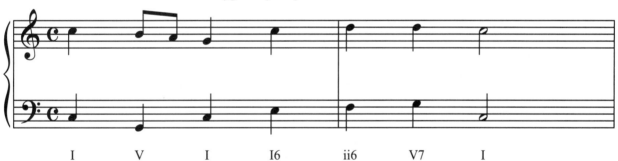

I   V   I   I6   ii6   V7   I

The primary function of the inner voices (alto and tenor) is to complete the chords by filling in the chords that are missing from the soprano and bass.

COMMON TONE is a term used for chord tones that remain the same, even though the chord is changing. The common tones are circled in the example above.

When the voices move in the same directions but the interval between the voices changes, they are moving in **SIMILAR MOTION**. The lines in this example show similar motion between the soprano and bass voices.

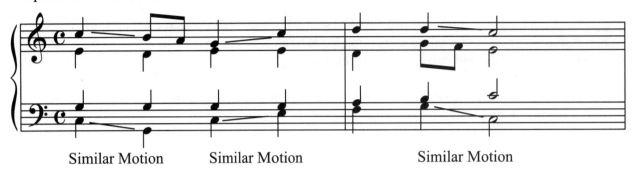

Similar Motion   Similar Motion   Similar Motion

When the voices move in opposite directions, they are moving in **CONTRARY MOTION**. The lines in this example show contrary motion between the tenor and bass voices.

Contrary Motion

When one voice stays the same and the other voice moves, they are moving in **OBLIQUE MOTION**. The lines in this example show oblique motion between the tenor and bass voices.

Oblique Motion

When two voices move in the same direction and the interval between them stays the same, they are moving in **PARALLEL MOTION**. The lines in this example show parallel intervals of 6ths between the soprano and alto voices in the first meausre, and parallel 3rds between the tenor and bass voices in the second measure.

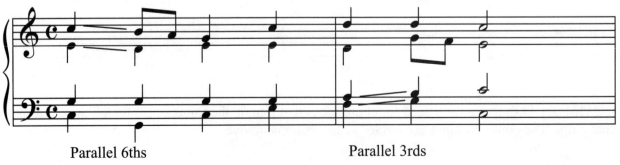

Parallel 6ths   Parallel 3rds

1. Name the type of motion used in each example (similar, contrary, oblique, or parallel).

When two voices exchange position, for example, if the alto voice moves below the tenor voice, it is called **CROSSED VOICES** or **VOICE CROSSING**. This should only be done occasionally.

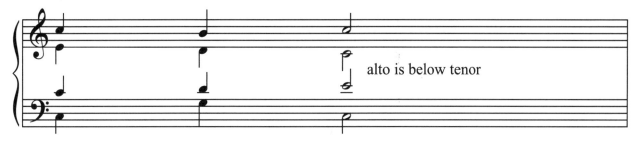

alto is below tenor

Crossed Voices (Voice Crossing)

Fifths or octaves that are approached by similar motion are called **DIRECT FIFTHS** or **HIDDEN FIFTHS**, or **DIRECT OCTAVES** or **HIDDEN OCTAVES**. Direct fifths and octaves are not strictly forbidden in four part writing, but they are not the most desirable voice leading.

Direct Fifth (Hidden Fifth)   Direct Octave (Hidden Octave)

VOICE EXCHANGE occurs when two voices trade parts, such as E-C in the soprano part, with C-E in the alto part.

Voice Exchange

2. Tell whether each measure contains crossed voices, direct fifths, direct octaves, or uses voice exchange.

Chord tones that tend to move stepwise to a note that is a resolution are called **<u>TENDENCY TONES</u>**. These are most commonly found in V7-I or vii°-I progressions, where the 7th scale degree tends towards tonic (7-8), and the fourth scale degree tends toward the third (4-3).

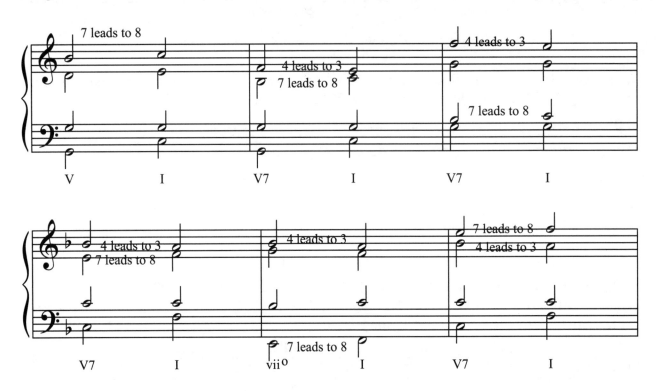

3. Find and circle the tendency tone in each example. Mark the notes with the numbers that indicate their voice leading (7-8 or 4-3).

Check the correct answer for each example.

4. What term is used for voices that move in the same direction regardless of the intervals?

　　_____ a. Parallel motion

　　_____ b. Similar motion

　　_____ c. Oblique motion

　　_____ d. Contrary motion

5. What term is used for voices that move in opposite directions?

　　_____ a. Contrary motion

　　_____ b. Oblique motion

　　_____ c. Parallel motion

　　_____ d. Crossed voices

6. What is the term for the voice leading in this example?

　　_____ a. Similar motion

　　_____ b. Contrary motion

　　_____ c. Oblique motion

　　_____ d. Common tone

7. Direct fifths are approached by:

　　_____ a. Half step

　　_____ b. Whole step

　　_____ c. Contrary motion

　　_____ d. Similar motion

8. The tendency tone 7 wants to move in which direction?

　　_____ a. Down to 6

　　_____ b. Up to 8

　　_____ c. Up to 9

　　_____ d. Down a half step

9. What term describes the voice leading in this example?

_____ a. Similar 6ths

_____ b. Parallel 6ths

_____ c. Oblique 6ths

_____ d. Contrary 6ths

10. What term describes the alto and tenor voices in this example?

_____ a. Voice exchange

_____ b. Direct fifths

_____ c. Crossed voices

_____ d. Parallel 3rds

11. What term describes the soprano and bass voices in this example?

_____ a. Voice exchange

_____ b. Crossed voices

_____ c. Direct octaves

_____ d. Parallel 6ths

12. What term is used for notes that stay the same when the chord changes?

_____ a. Similar tones

_____ b. Contrary tones

_____ c. Same tones

_____ d. Common tones

13. What term is used for the voice leading in this example?

_____ a. Perpendicular 3rds

_____ b. Perfect 3rds

_____ c. Parallel 3rds

_____ d. Particular 3rds

SIGHT SINGING

Sing each part (soprano, alto, tenor, and bass) of the following Chorale. Adjust each octave to fit your vocal range.

J.S. Bach: *Gelobet seist du, Jesu Crhist*

EAR TRAINING

Listen to Example 150. The example will be played four times. Complete the following chorale by notating the bass voice.

J.S. Bach: *Was Gott thut, das ist wohlgethan*

LESSON 20
POOR VOICE LEADING

Certain types of voice leading should be avoided. These include:

CROSS RELATION or **FALSE RELATION**: The interval of an Augmented 4th (tritone) or chromatic movement from the soprano voice to the bass voice should be avoided. (This is acceptable when moving from an inner voice.)

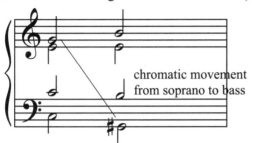
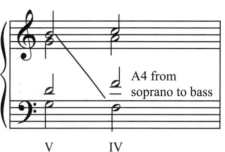

OVERLAPPING VOICES: When two voices move up or down in similar motion, the lower voice is not allowed to move to a higher note than the upper voice just left, and vice versa.

Certain parallel intervals are considered **OBJECTIONABLE PARALLELS.**. These include parallel 5ths, parallel 8ths (octaves), and sometimes parallel 4ths.

PARALLEL PERFECT 5THS

PARALLEL PERFECT OCTAVES

PARALLEL 4THS are acceptable when they are supported by parallel thirds.

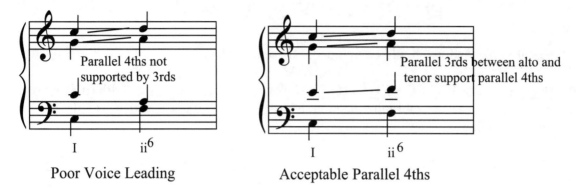

Four part writing should not contain **UNRESOLVED LEADING TONES.** When a 7th is the leading tone of the key, the 7th should resolve by going up a half step, ending on tonic.

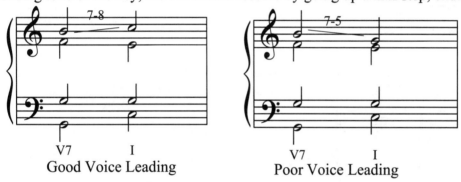

When the 7th is used in a secondary dominant, it should resolve by going down a half step.

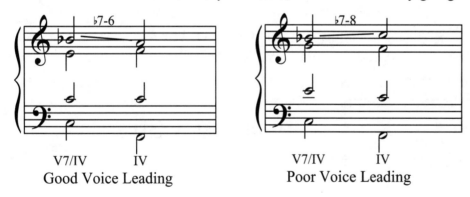

1. Each example includes poor voice leading. Name the problem and the voices in which it occurs. The first one is given.

a.    Parallel 5ths between soprano and alto

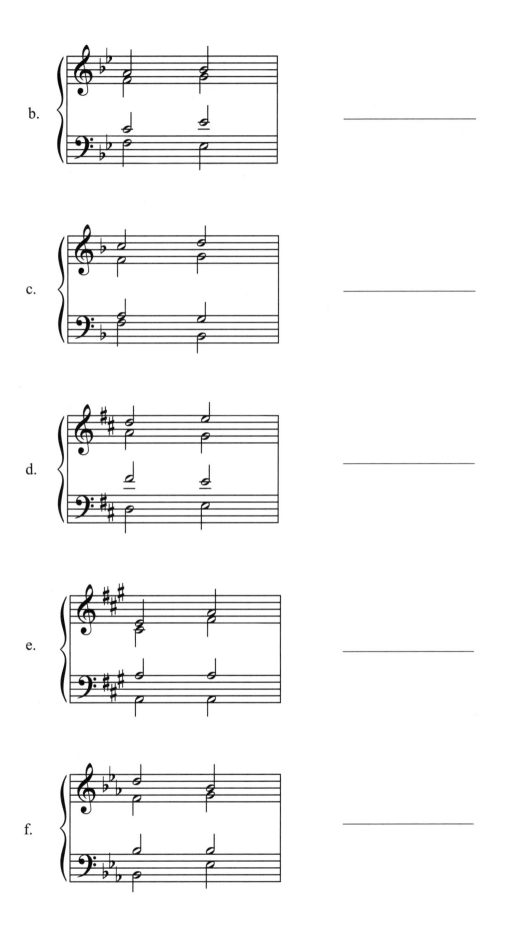

Check each correct answer.

2. What term is used for this voice leading?

    _____ a. Contrary Octaves

    _____ b. Similar Octaves

    _____ c. Parallel Octaves

    _____ d. Oblique Octaves

3. What term indicates the movement of two voices in similar motion, with the lower voice moving to a higher position than the upper voice just left?

    _____ a. Overlapping Voices

    _____ b. Oversinging Voices

    _____ c. Underlapping Voices

    _____ d. Mixed Voices

4. What term is used for voices that create a tritone or chromatic movement when moving from one voice to another?

    _____ a. Unresolved leading tone

    _____ b. Cross Relation

    _____ c. Overlapping Voices

    _____ d. Common Practice Style

5. Which of these parallels should be avoided?

    _____ a. 4ths and 3rds

    _____ b. 6ths and 8ths

    _____ c. 5ths and 3rds

    _____ d. 5ths and 8ths

6. How should 7ths be treated?

    _____ a. Resolved stepwise

    _____ b. Resolved by skips

    _____ c. Resolved by 5ths

    _____ d. Resolved by 8ths

SIGHT SINGING

Sing each part (soprano, alto, tenor, and bass) of the following Chorale. Adjust each octave to fit your vocal range.

J.S. Bach: *O Haupt voll Blut und Wunden*

EAR TRAINING

Listen to Example 151. The example will be played four times. Complete the following chorale by notating the soprano and bass voices.

J.S. Bach: *Hast du denn, Jesu. dein Angesicht*

LESSON 21
REALIZING FIGURED BASS

The term **FIGURED BASS** comes from a practice during the Baroque period in which the composer did not write out the entire keyboard or *continuo* part of an ensemble piece, but instead wrote the bass line with symbols indicating the desired chords. The chords that a bass line represent are determined by the use of figured bass symbols, without the Roman numerals for each chord. Determining the correct chords is called **REALIZING THE FIGURED BASS.**

Root position ($^5_3$) chords have no symbols below them. The chord is determined by using the bass note as the root of the chord, and the quality is determined by the key signature.

No figured bass symbols given

I   iii   vi   IV   ii   V   I

The number "6" represents a first inversion chord. The bass note will act as the third of the chord, and the quality will still be determined by the key signature.

"6" indicates first inversion

I   I⁶   vi   ii⁶   ii   V   I

Second inversion chords are indicated by the numbers $^6_4$. The bass note will be the fifth of the chord. The quality will be determined by the key signature.

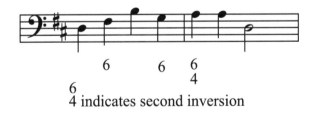
$^6_4$ indicates second inversion

I   I⁶   vi   ii⁶   I$^6_4$ V   I

1. For each of the following examples, realize the following figured bass by writing the Roman numerals for each chord. Use the major key for each example.

Seventh chords and their inversions are as follows:

2. Realize the following figured bass by completing each of the indicated chords.

Chord alterations can be indicated by the figured bass. An accidental by itself indicates that the chord is in root position, and that the third of the chord (the third above the bass) is altered.

3. Realize the following figured bass by completing each chord.

An accidental next to a figure (such as ♯6, 6♯, ♮4 or 4♮) indicates that the note creating the interval is raised a half step. For example, ♯6 indicates a first inversion chord, and the note that is a sixth above the bass will have a sharp.

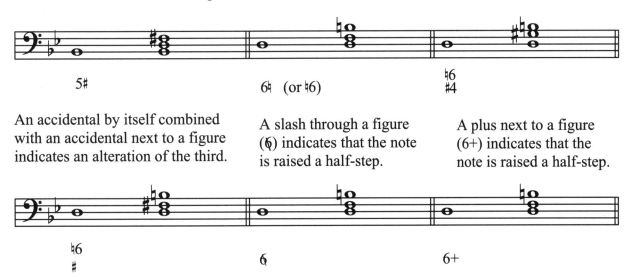

| An accidental by itself combined with an accidental next to a figure indicates an alteration of the third. | A slash through a figure (⑥) indicates that the note is raised a half-step. | A plus next to a figure (6+) indicates that the note is raised a half-step. |

4. Realize the following figured bass by completing each chord.

229

Figured bass can also be used to indicate melodic direction or chord changes, normally to identify suspensions. The figures indicate the intervallic relationship between the bass note and the suspension and its resolution.

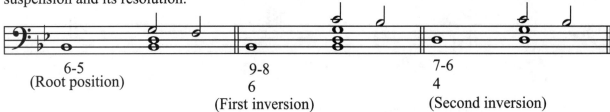

5. Write figured bass (no Roman numerals, numbers only) to show the melodic movement and inversion (if present) for each of the following examples. The first one is given.

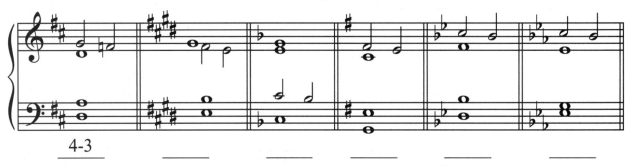

6. Write figured bass under the following example. Do not use Roman numerals. Only put numerical symbols where needed, not on every chord.

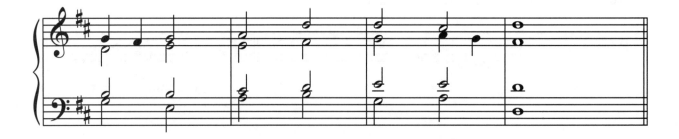

Check the correct answer for each of the following examples.

7. What is the name of the chord that is represented by this figured bass?

(bass clef, 4 sharps, whole note with figured bass $^6_4$)

_____ a. G Major

_____ b. C# minor

_____ c. G# minor

_____ d. E Major

8. Which Roman numeral is represented by this figured bass?

(bass clef, whole note with figured bass 6)

_____ a. I^6

_____ b. vi^6

_____ c. ii^6

_____ d. IV^6

9. Which notes do the numbers 7-6 indicate in this example?

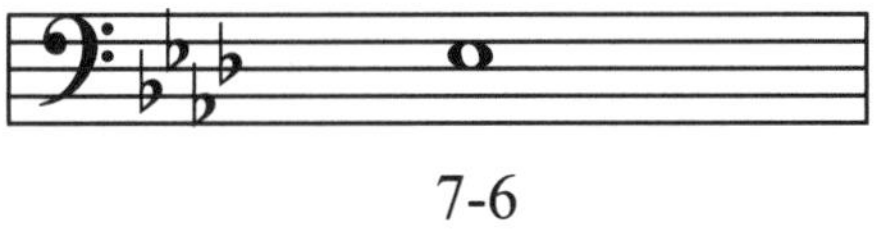

(bass clef, 2 flats, whole note with figured bass 7-6)

_____ a. D♭-C

_____ b. F-E♭

_____ c. C-B♭

_____ d. D♭-E♭

10. Which notes to the numbers 4-3 indicate in example?

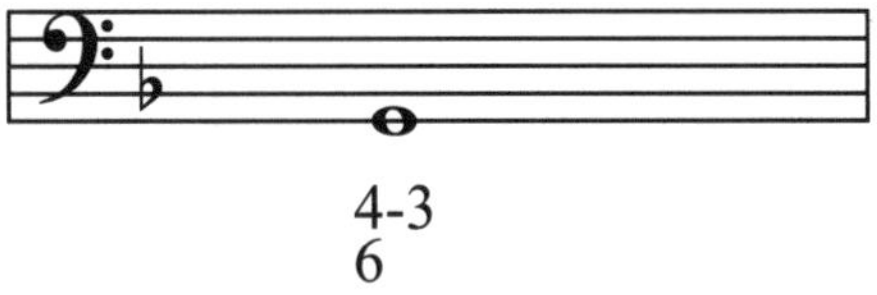

(bass clef, 1 flat, whole note with figured bass $^{4-3}_{6}$)

_____ a. D-C

_____ b. A-G

_____ c. C-B♭

_____ d. B♭-A

11. Which notes are represented by the following figured bass?

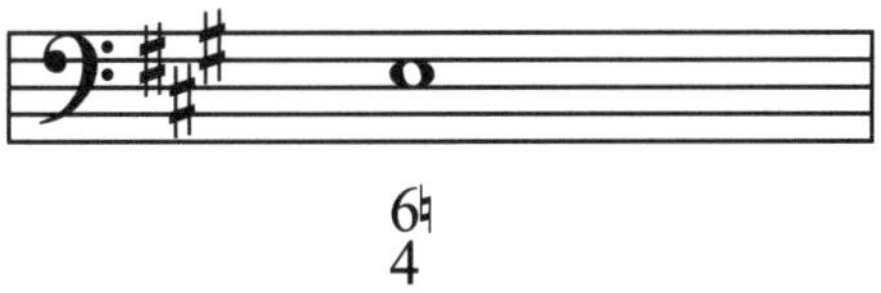

(bass clef, 2 sharps, whole note with figured bass $^{6♮}_{4}$)

_____ a. E-A-C♮

_____ b. E-A-C♭

_____ c. E-G♮-C#

_____ d. E-G#-C♮

12. Which notes are represented by the following figured bass?

    (bass clef, key signature one flat, note F, figure ♭5)

    _____ a. F-A♭-C
    _____ b. F-B♭-D♭
    _____ c. F-A-C♭
    _____ d. F-A♭-C♭

13. Which notes are represented by the following figured bass?

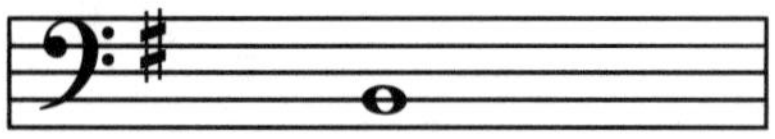

    (bass clef, key signature one sharp, note B, figure 6)

    _____ a. B-E-G♯
    _____ b. B-D-G♯
    _____ c. B-D-F♯
    _____ d. B-D♯-F♯

14. What change is made by the figured bass in this example?

    (bass clef, key signature two flats, note F, figure 4+)

    _____ a. F becomes F♯
    _____ b. D becomes D♭
    _____ c. B♭ becomes B♭♭
    _____ d. B♭ becomes B♮

15. Which chord is represented by the following figured bass?

    (bass clef, key signature two sharps, note E, figure ♯)

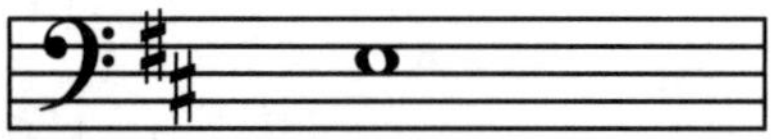

    _____ a. E Augmented
    _____ b. E Major
    _____ c. e diminished
    _____ d. e minor

16. Which chord is created by the following figured bass?

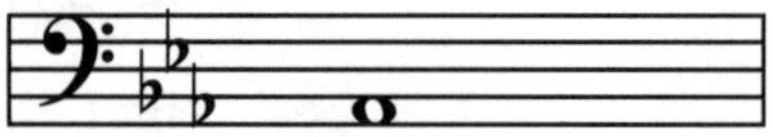

    (bass clef, key signature two flats, note A♭, figure 6♭ 4♭)

    _____ a. D♭ Major
    _____ b. A♭ Major
    _____ c. d♭ minor
    _____ d. f♭ minor

SIGHT SINGING

Sing each part (soprano, alto, tenor, and bass) of the following Chorale. Adjust each octave to fit your vocal range.

J.S. Bach: *Wach auf, mein Herz*

EAR TRAINING

Listen to Example 152. The example will be played four times. Notate the soprano and bass parts, and provide the Roman numerals indicating each chord and its inversion. The first notes and Roman numeral are given.

Gauntlett: *University College*

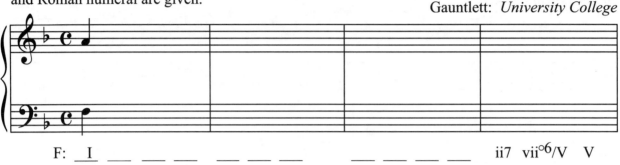

F: I __ __ __   __ __ __   __ __ __ __   ii7 vii°6/V V

__ __ __ __ __   __ __ __   __ __ __ __ __   __ __ __

LISTENING

Listen to Example 153. Questions 17-21 below are based on the music, which is from *Sonata, 1766* by Haydn. The example will be played three times. Circle each correct answer.

17. What is the name for the ornament heard several times in the first phrase?

    a. appoggiatura   b. anticipation
    c. trill   d. passing tone

18. What term best describes the accompaniment at the beginning of the example?

    a. Alberti bass   b. ostinato
    c. arpeggiation   d. cadential $^6_4$

19. What melodic device is used in the melody at the beginning of the example?

    a. arpeggiation
    b. upper auxiliary tones
    c. diminution
    d. cadential extension

20. What type of melodic device occurs in the second half of the example?

    a. repetition   b. augmentation
    c. truncation   d. consequent

21. To which scale degree does the music modulate?

    a. tonic
    b. subdominant
    c. mediant
    d. dominant

LESSON 22
FOUR PART WRITING

Complete each of the examples in this lesson, based on the guidelines taught in Lessons 16 to 21.

1. Add the alto voice to this example.

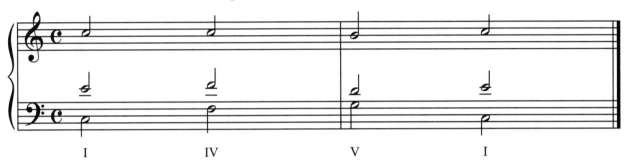

2. Add the alto voice to this example.

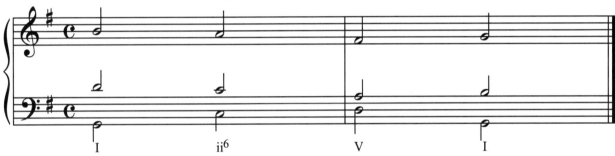

3. Add the tenor voice to this example.

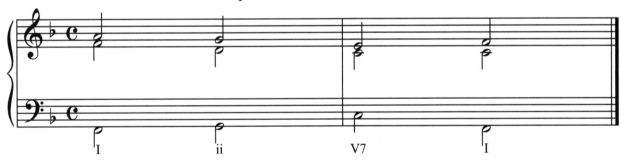

4. Add the tenor voice to this example.

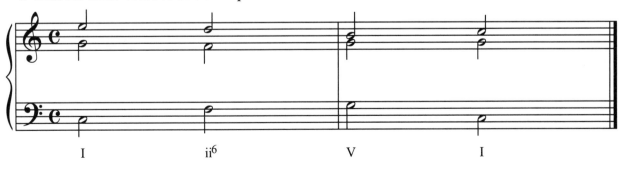

5. Add the soprano voice to this example.

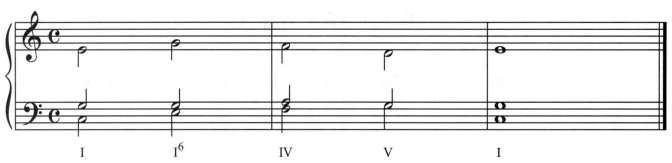

6. Add a bass line to the following example.

7. Add a bass line to the following example.

8. Add a bass line to the following example.

9. Write the bass line and add Roman numerals to the following example.

10. Write the bass line and add Roman numerals to the following example.

11. Realize figured bass for the following example by adding the soprano, alto, and tenor parts.

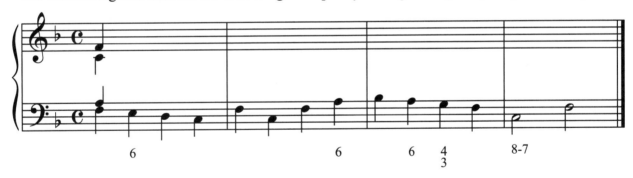

12. Realize figured bass for the following example by adding the soprano, alto, and tenor parts.

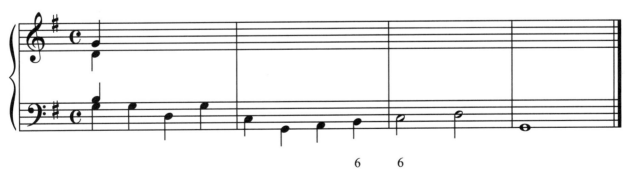

13. Harmonize the following melody using Common Practice style (also called traditional eighteenth-century voice-leading procedures). Add Roman numerals and figured bass under each chord.

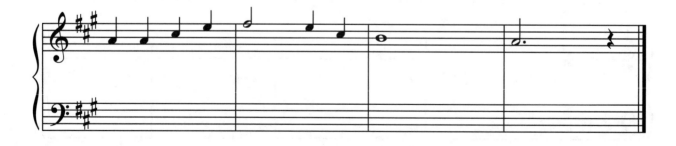

SIGHT SINGING

Sing each part (soprano, alto, tenor, and bass) of the following Chorale. Adjust each part to fit your vocal range.

J.S. Bach: *Von Gott will icn nicht lassen*

EAR TRAINING

Listen to Example 154. Notate the soprano and bass parts, and provide the Roman numerals indicating each chord and its inversion. The first notes and Roman numeral are given. The example will be played four times.

William Croft: *St. Anne*

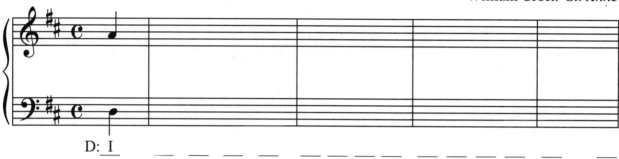

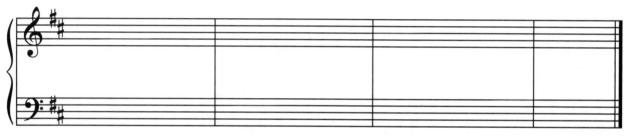

LISTENING

Listen to Example 155, which is from *Sonata K. 279* by Mozart. The example will be played three times. Questions 14-18 are based on the music. Circle each correct answer.

14. What type of melodic movement takes place in the first measure?

    a. alberti bass   c. escape tone (échappée)
    b. arpeggio   d. suspension

15. In what inversion is the first broken chord?

    a. Root position   c. 6/4
    b. 6/3   d. Dominant 7th

16. Immediately following the break with the two single right hand notes, what type of melodic device is used in the next two phrases?

    a. Sequence   c. canon
    b. literal repetition d. pedal point

17. What term describes the accompaniment at the end of the example?

    a. ostinato   c. arpeggiated
    b. pedal point d. Alberti bass

18. What is the function of the final two chords?

    a. Subdominant - Tonic
    b. Dominant - Tonic
    c. Tonic - Dominant
    d. Dominant - Tonic

REVIEW
LESSONS 10-22

1. Match each of the following terms with its definition.

   a. transposition　　　　　_____ motive is repeated a 2nd or 3rd above or below
   b. augmentation　　　　　_____ melody repeated backwards
   c. rhythmic transformation　_____ note values doubled
   d. conjunct　　　　　　　_____ intervals of melody have leaps
   e. octave displacement　　_____ melody is mostly stepwise
   f. contour　　　　　　　　_____ rise and fall of the melody
   g. truncated　　　　　　　_____ notes are added to the middle of a melody
   h. retrograde　　　　　　_____ melody changed to a different key
   i. diminution　　　　　　_____ note values changed
   j. disjunct　　　　　　　_____ part of melody raised or lowered an octave
   k. melodic inversion　　　_____ intervals in melody turned upside down
   l. internal expansion　　　_____ contrasting melody that can stand on its own
   m. extension　　　　　　_____ portion of theme deleted
   n. countermelody　　　　_____ notes are added to the end of the motive or theme
   o. sequence　　　　　　_____ motive is repeated exactly as originally presented
   p. imitation　　　　　　　_____ note values halved
   q. literal repetition　　　_____ only a portion of the motive appears
   r. fragmented　　　　　　_____ motive repeated in a different voice

2. Name each of the following ornaments or non-harmonic tones.

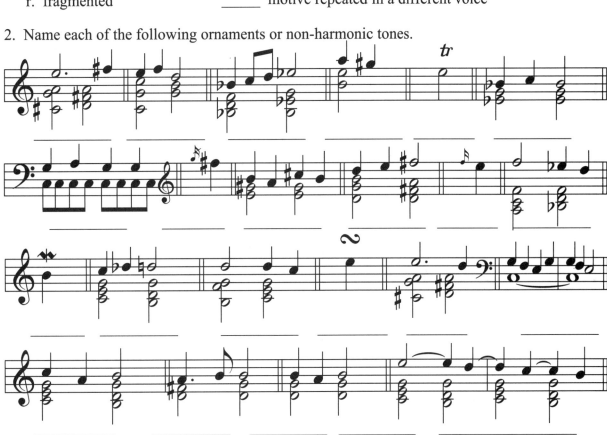

3. Give the name for each of these types of phrase structures.

a. _____ Period with two phrases that begin using the same starting pitch and motive, and have the same harmonic structure.

b. _____ Two consecutive periods with four phrases. The second period closely resembles the first period, with the first and third phrases being similar melodically and harmonically. The first three phrases end with incomplete cadences, and the fourth phrase ends with a complete cadence.

c. _____ Irregular grouping of related pharases, such as three or five phrases

d. _____ Question/answer phrases

e. _____ Period with two phrases that contain different motivic or harmonic material.

d. _____ The overlapping of two phrases.

4. a. Which chord or chords may act with tonic function? _____

   b. Which chord or chords may act with dominant function? _____

   c. Which chord or chords may act with pre-dominant function? _____

5. Name the type of $\frac{6}{4}$ that is used in each of the following examples.

a. _____   b. _____

c. _____   d. _____

6. Give the name for each of the following types of harmonic function.

   a. _____ The bass remains the same while the other notes move stepwise to a new chord.

   b. _____ A Major to E Major to B Major to F# Major to C# Major

   c. _____ The music moves in an unexpected harmonic direction

   d. _____ Harmonic movement that is opposite of typical, such as V-IV

   e. _____ Term that describes the frequency of chord changes

7. Write the term for each of the following definitions.

   a. _____ Short change of key, for only a few measures

   b. _____ Long change of key, for many phrases or a section

   c. _____ Change of key achieved by using a chord that is common to both the original key and the key to which the music changes

   d. _____ Change of key achieved by using chords that have some notes that stay the same and some notes that change

   e. _____ Change of key in which the music jumps to the new key without any connecting elements (no similar notes, no similar chords)

8. Notate the preferred lowest and highest note for each of the following vocal ranges.

   Soprano   Alto   Tenor   Bass

9. Tell whether each of the following chords is in close position or open position.

10. Tell whether each of the following harmonic progressions are common, used sometimes, or are rare. (Use C for common, S for sometimes, and R for rare.)

   _____ a. I-ii   _____ d. vi-I   _____ g. I-vi

   _____ b. iii-vi   _____ e. vi-iii   _____ h. IV-V

   _____ c. vi-IV   _____ f. I-IV   _____ i. ii-V

11. Complete the bass line for the following melody, and write Roman numerals to indicate an appropriate harmony.

   I   I^6 IV

12. Using Roman numerals and figured bass, label the chords in the following example.

13. Realize the figured bass below, using four voices. Write the Roman numeral for each chord.

   6    $^6_4$ 8-7

14. Complete the following progression in four voices, using only quarter notes and half notes.

   I   V$^6_5$ V7/IV   IV$^6_4$ ii   V 6-5   I

LESSON 23
INTERPRETING LEAD SHEETS

A **LEAD SHEET** is a type of notation for a musical composition that includes only the melody, words if applicable, and chord symbols. The performer or performers then improvise the melody with accompaniment, or just an accompaniment, based on those elements. Unlike figured bass, inversions are not indicated by the chord symbols.

In this example of *Mary Had a Little Lamb,* only the melody, words, and chord symbols are given.

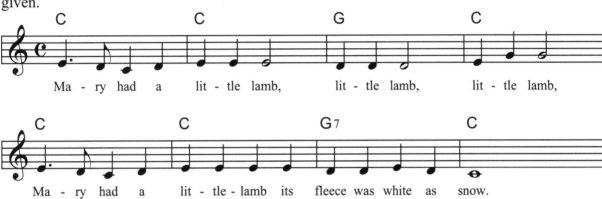

In its simplest form, this lead sheet would be interpreted as in the following example. Proficient musicians will create a more interesting accompaniment, which will include smooth voice leading, inversions, broken chords, other embellishments, and a style that is appropriate to the music.

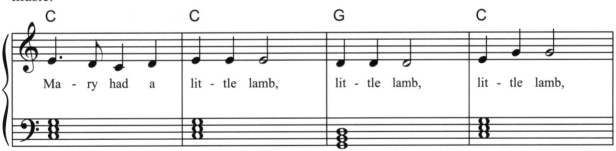

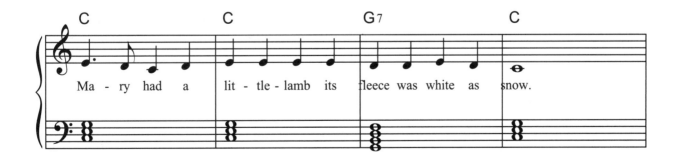

Major chords are indicated on a lead sheet by a capital letter, such as C for C Major chord, or G for G Major chord.

Minor chords are indicated by a capital letter followed by "m," "min.," or rarely "-."

1. In each example below, a melody with chord symbols is given in the treble clef. Write the chord indicated by each chord symbol. Use root position for each chord, or select an inversion that will give a smooth progression.

Augmented chords are labeled with a capital letter and one of the following: aug., +, (♯5), or +5. (Parentheses may or may not be present.)

Diminished chords are labeled with a capital letter and with one of the following: dim., °, m(♭5), or m(-5). (Parentheses may or may not be present.)

2. Write the chord indicated by each chord symbol, in root position.

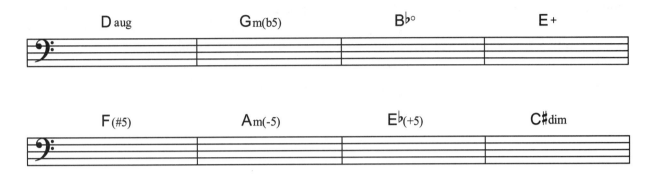

Symbols for the various seventh chords are most commonly written as follows:

Dominant 7th chords: C7
Major 7th chords: CMaj7 (or Cmaj7)
Minor 7th chords: Cmin7
Half-diminished 7th chords: Cmin7♭5
Diminished 7th chords: Cdim7

3. Write the chord indicated by each chord symbol, in root position.

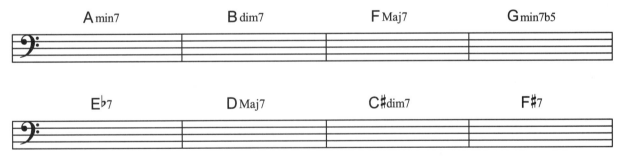

Ninth chords contain a note that is the interval of a ninth above the root of the chord. Most common uses of ninth chords are:

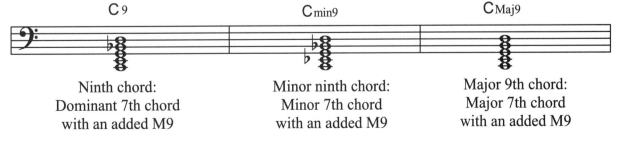

Ninth chord:
Dominant 7th chord
with an added M9

Minor ninth chord:
Minor 7th chord
with an added M9

Major 9th chord:
Major 7th chord
with an added M9

Other notes may be added to chord symbols by the use of numbers and accidentals. Numbers indicate the distance above root of the chord (for example, 4 indicates that the added note is the interval of a fourth above the root). Accidentals, if present, raise or lower the added note.

Some examples of added notes are given below, but many more possibilities exist.

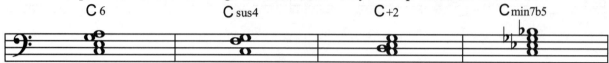

4. Write the chord indicated by each of the following chord symbols, in root position.

5. Write the chord symbol for each of the following chords above the staff, using the style of labeling that is found on lead sheets.

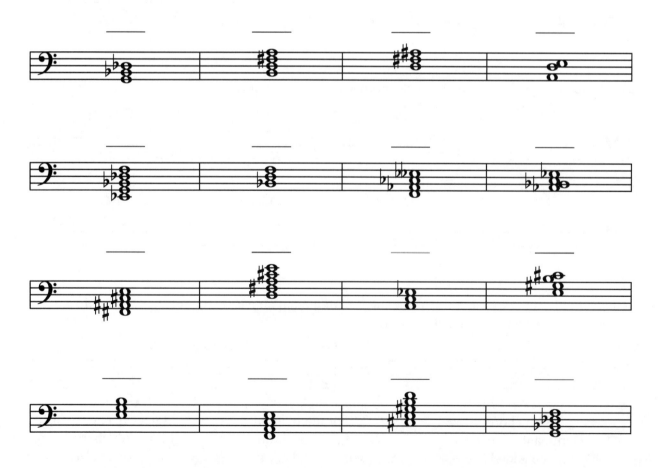

Check the correct answer for each of the following examples.

6. What is the meaning of the number 6 when used in a lead sheet?

   _____ a. First inversion

   _____ b. Add a note that is a sixth above the root

   _____ c. Add a note that is a sixth above the bass

   _____ d. Second inversion

7. What is the symbol for this chord?

   _____ a. fm♭3

   _____ b. fm♭7

   _____ c. fm♮5

   _____ d. fm7

8. Which of these notes make up a B♭ m♭5 chord?

   _____ a. B♭ D♭ F

   _____ b. B♭ D F

   _____ c. B♭ D♭ F

   _____ d. B♭ D♭ F♭

9. Which of these notes make up a Gm9 chord?

   _____ a. G B♭ D F A

   _____ b. G B♭ D♭ F A

   _____ c. G B♭ D F A♭

   _____ d. G B♭ D F♭ A

10. What is the symbol for this chord?

    _____ a. D♯4

    _____ b. D♭4

    _____ c. Dsus4

    _____ d. Dm4

11. Which symbol is correct for a chord with the notes C# E G B?

_____ a. C#M7

_____ b. C#dim7

_____ c. C#min7♭5

_____ d. C#min7

12. What is the symbol for this chord?

_____ a. E

_____ b. EAug

_____ c. EMaj5

_____ d. Emin

13. Which set of two symbols mean the same as Cm?

_____ a. Cmin and CMaj

_____ b. C° and C⁺

_____ c. Cmin and C⁻

_____ d. C and C⁻

14. Which of these symbols means the same as Cdim7?

_____ a. C°

_____ b. C°7

_____ c. Cdim

_____ d. C⁻7

15. Which of these statements are true about lead sheets?

_____ a. Chord symbols are written above the music

_____ b. Performers may use any inversion

_____ c. Many types of chords may be written several ways

_____ d. All of the above

SIGHT SINGING

Sing the following melodies. Adjust the octave to fit your vocal range.

W.A. Mozart: *Clarinet Concerto K. 622*

Grieg: *Morning* from *Peer Gynt Suite*

Grieg: *Anitra's Dance* from *Peer Gynt Suite*

EAR TRAINING

Listen to Example 156. The example will be played four times. Notate the soprano and bass parts, and provide the Roman numerals indicating each chord and its inversion. The first notes and Roman numeral are given.

W. Horsley: *Horsley*

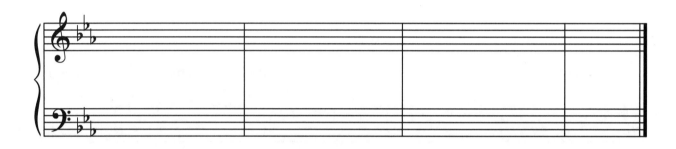

LISTENING

Listen to Example 157, which is from *Sonata, Hob. XVI:41* by Haydn. The example will be played three times. Questions 16-19 are based on the music. Circle each correct answer.

16. What type of rhythmic pattern is used in the melody for the first four measures?

    a. quarter notes
    b. half notes
    c. eighth notes
    d. dotted eighth - sixteenth notes

17. What type of movement takes place when the accompaniment begins to move in the second measure?

    a. skipping downward
    b. stepping downward
    c. skipping upward
    d. stepping upward

18. Which of the following takes place in the lowest voice in the second measure?

    a. ostinato
    b. pedal point
    c. suspension
    d. anticipation

19. What type of cadence ends the example?

    a. Authentic cadence
    b. Plagal cadence
    c. Half cadence
    d. Deceptive cadence

LESSON 24
FORM AND STRUCTURE

The term **FORM** refers to the manner in which the sections of a musical composition are put together, or the basic structure of the music.

BINARY FORM consists of two contrasting sections of similar length, called **A** and **B**, as in this Minuet by J.S. Bach.

Answer these questions about the Minuet by J.S. Bach.

1. Check the attributes that are similar in the A and B sections.   ___ Rhythm
   ___ Melody
   ___ Harmony

2. Check the attributes that are different from each other in the A and B sections.   ___ Rhythm
   ___ Melody
   ___ Harmony

3. In what key does the A section begin? _____ _____

4. In what key does the B section begin? _____ _____

5. What secondary dominant is functioning in measures 20-21? _____ / _____

6. In which measure does the music return to the original key? _____

ROUNDED BINARY FORM consists of an A section, followed by an extended B section after which the A section returns briefly. This Minuet by J.S. Bach is in Rounded Binary Form.

Answer these questions about the above example.

7. Are the A and B sections the same length? _____

8. In what key does the A section begin? _____ _____

9. In what key does the B section begin? _____ _____

10. In what measure does the B section return to the original key? _____

11. In what measure does the A section return, creating the rounded binary form? _____

12. Is the second occurance of the A section longer or shorter than the original A section?

_____

TERNARY FORM consists of three sections with the form **ABA**. The second occurance of the A section may be exactly the same as the first, or it can be slightly different. If it is different, the form is identified as **ABA'**. This March by Shostakovich is in ABA' form.

Answer these questions about the music above.

13. Are the three sections of equal length? _____

14. Is the B section very similar to or very different from the A section? _____

15. In what measure does the A' section begin to vary from the A section? _____

A **SONATA** is a composition for piano or another instrument which has several separate sections called **movements.**

The typical scheme for the movements of a sonata are:

Allegro: Sonata form (also known as Sonata Allegro form)

Adagio: Binary or Ternary form, in a key different but closely related to that of the first movement (such as the dominant or relative minor).

Scherzo or Minuet: Ternary form (Scherzo and Trio or Minuet and Trio), in the same key as the first movement.

Allegro (or Presto): Rondo form or Variations, in the same key as the first movement.

This scheme is not always followed. Often there are fewer than four movements (in which case it is usually the Scherzo/Minuet movement that is missing), or a Sonata may begin with a slow movement rather than a fast movement.

The first movement of a Sonata is usually in **Sonata form** (sometimes called **Sonata Allegro form**). There are three sections:

EXPOSITION		DEVELOPMENT	RECAPITULATION	
Theme 1 (Tonic key)	Theme 2 (Dominant or related key)	Motives based on Themes 1 and 2 are developed in various ways	Theme 1 (Tonic key)	Theme 2 (Tonic key)

Typically, the Exposition is repeated, then the Development and Recapitulation are repeated.

The first movement of Sonata, XVI:27 by Haydn, is given below. The sections and themes (with their keys) are marked.

The second movement of this sonata is a Minuet and Trio in the key of G Major (Tonic).

The third movement is a Rondo in the key of G Major (Tonic). (Music for the second and third movements are not included in this workbook.)

Answer these questions about the Haydn Sonata.

16. In what key does the Development begin? _____ _____

17. What is the function of the key in which the Development begins?   _____ Tonic
　　　　　　　　　　　　　　　　　　　　　　　　　　　　　　　　　　　　　_____ Dominant
　　　　　　　　　　　　　　　　　　　　　　　　　　　　　　　　　　　　　_____ Subdominant

18. In which measure does the music clearly return to tonic?   _____ Measure 71
　　　　　　　　　　　　　　　　　　　　　　　　　　　　　　　　_____ Measure 80
　　　　　　　　　　　　　　　　　　　　　　　　　　　　　　　　_____ Measure 88

THEME AND VARIATIONS are compositions made of multiple independent sections. The theme is usually stated clearly in the first section, followed by variations of the theme. The variations are created by alterations in the rhythm, harmony, or melody, while keeping certain components of the original theme to tie the variations together.

The following music is the theme and the first two variations from *Variations on a Russian Folk Song, Opus 51, No. 1,* by Kabalevsky.

　　Theme

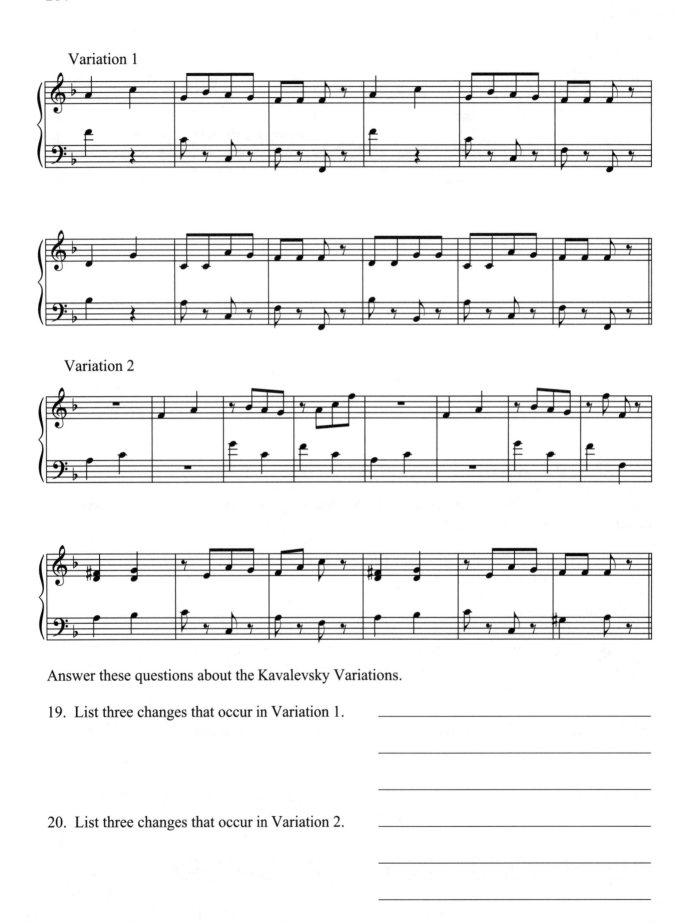

Answer these questions about the Kavalevsky Variations.

19. List three changes that occur in Variation 1. _____

20. List three changes that occur in Variation 2. _____

An **INTRODUCTION** sometimes precedes the opening theme. An introduction may be short, as in the first two measures of this excerpt (which is the first ten measures of an *Arabesque* by Burgmuller), or it may be relatively long. The term introduction can also be applied to an entire movement which introduces a larger composition.

Answer these questions about the example above.

21. Is the introduction in a key that is different from the opening theme? _____

22. Does the harmony change when the opening theme appears? _____

A **CODA** is an ending added at the end of a composition. It is not part of the standard form and does not contain the main themes.

A **CODETTA** is a coda that occurs at the end of the exposition in a sonata, rather than at the end of the movement. The term codetta also means a short coda.

The first movement of this Sonatina by Beethoven contains a coda. The form is ABA Coda, or may also be considered Exposition, Development, Recapitulation, Coda.

Answer these questions about the above example.

23. Does the Coda begin on the I chord? _____

24. Does the Coda contain any of the melodies or themes from earlier in the music? _____

25. Does the Coda end in the original key? _____

Vocal music is often made up of **VERSES** or **STANZAS** and **CHORUSES** or **REFRAINS**. The verses or stanzas have the same melody, but the words are different for each verse. The chorus or refrain contains the same words and music, and is sung after each verse. *We Three Kings of Orient Are* is an example of verses or stanzas with a chorus or refrain. This example shows the first three of five verses, and the chorus.

Answer these questions about the above music.

26. Are the verses and the chorus in the same key? _____

27. Is the rhythm of the chorus similar to the rhythm of the verses? _____

In **STROPHIC** music, each verse of the text is sung to the same melody. *Mary Had a Little Lamb* is an example of strophic music.

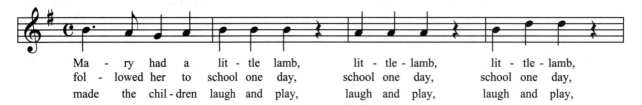

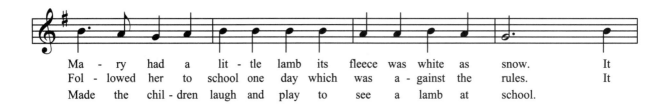

Answer these questions about the above music.

28. What makes this example strophic? _____

29. Does the melody vary from one verse to another? _____

Songs or choral compositions that are **THROUGH-COMPOSED** consist of a different melody for each verse. While through-composed music is typically more complicated than this example, *I've Been Workin' on the Railroad* is a simple example of music that is through-composed.

Verse 1

Answer these questions about *I've Been Workin' on the Railroad*.

30. Which element remains similar throughout? _____ Rhythm
    _____ Melody
    _____ Words

31. Are all three verses the same length? _____

An **ANTIPHON** is call (or verse) and response style, in which a melody is sung or chanted, followed by a response that is repeated after each chant. For example:

Call: Give thanks to God
Response: His love endures forever
Call: For He is good
Response: His love endures forever
Call: Give praise
Response: His love endures forever

ANTIPHONAL music is a more general term that refers to music in which two choirs or two ensembles alternate parts. *Misericordias Domini* by Durante, written for two choirs, is an example of this type of music.

Answer these questions about the following example.

32. In this excerpt from the music, to the two choirs ever overlap? _____

33. When the second choir begins in measure 4, is the music the similar or very different? _____

34. Are all the phrases in the excerpt the same length? _____

Check the correct answer for each example.

35. What is ternary form?
    _____ a. AB
    _____ b. ABA
    _____ c. ABBA
    _____ d. ABCD

36. Which is sonata form?
    _____ a. Exposition, Development, Recapitulation
    _____ b. Development, Recapitulation, Exposition
    _____ c. Recapitulation, Development, Exposition
    _____ d. Exposition, Recapitulation, Development

37. Which is binary form?
    _____ a. ABA
    _____ b. ABA'
    _____ c. ABC
    _____ d. AB

38. Which is rounded binary form?
    _____ a. AB short B
    _____ b. ABA short A
    _____ c. AB short A
    _____ d. AB short C

39. Which term is used to describe a composition with multiple independent sections, with the first section introducing a melody, followed by sections that are different but closely related?
    _____ a. Theme and variations
    _____ b. Sonata form
    _____ c. Strophic
    _____ d. Antiphon

40. What other term can be used for "verse?"

_____ a. Stanza

_____ b. Chorus

_____ c. Refrain

_____ d. Melody

41. What term is used for a vocal style that includes call and response?

_____ a. Strophic

_____ b. Through-composed

_____ c. Antiphon

_____ d. Introduction

42. What term is used for vocal music in which each verse has a different melody?

_____ a. Verse and Chorus

_____ b. Through-composed

_____ c. Antiphon

_____ d. Strophic

43. What term is used for a section at the beginning of the music that does not contain the theme?

_____ a. Coda

_____ b. Codetta

_____ c. Development

_____ d. Introduction

44. What term is used for a section that is added at the end of the music, but does not contain the theme or themes?

_____ a. Recapitulation

_____ b. Coda

_____ c. Development

_____ d. Exposition

45. Which two definitions describe Codetta? (Check two answers.)

_____ a. Coda at the beginning of the music

_____ b. A short coda

_____ c. A long coda

_____ d. A coda at the end of the Exposiiton

46. What term is used for music in which two choirs or two instrumental groups alternate parts?

_____ a. Through-composed

_____ b. Theme and variations

_____ c. Antiphonal

_____ d. Stanza

47. What term is used for vocal music in which the verses all contain the same melody?

_____ a. Strophic

_____ b. Through-composed

_____ c. Aniphonal

_____ d. Chorus

SIGHT SINGING

Sing the following melody. Adjust the octave to fit your vocal range.

Smetena: *The Moldau*

EAR TRAINING

Listen to Example 158. The example will be played four times. Notate the soprano and bass parts, and provide the Roman numerals indicating each chord and its inversion. The first notes and Roman numeral are given.

Beethoven: *Gorton*

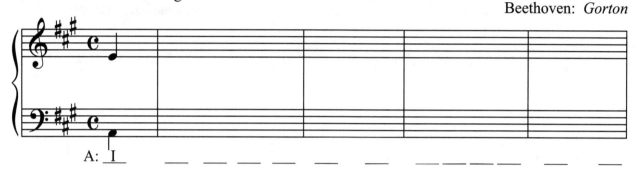

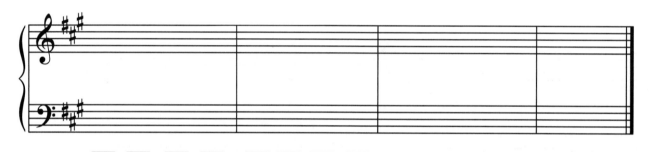

LISTENING

Listen to Example 159, which is from *Song of War* by Schumann. The example will be played three times. Questions 45-48 are based on the music. Circle each correct answer.

48. What harmony is used for the first phrase?

    a. sixths only
    b. octaves only
    c. thirds only
    d. fourths only

49. Which of the following indicates the scale degrees at the beginning of the example?

    a. 1 - 4 - 3 - 1
    b. 1 - 5 - 6 - 1
    c. 1 - 4 - 5 - 1
    d. 1 - 5 - 3 - 1

50. Which of these happens to this music?

    a. It modulates
    b. It gets softer
    c. It has an unsteady meter
    d. It uses minor tonality

51. What is the function of the final chord?

    a. Subdominant
    b. Dominant
    c. Tonic
    d. Cadential $^6_4$

LESSON 25
THE FUGUE

The **Fugue** is a style of composition in which 3 or more voices enter in imitation of one another. Several terms associated with a Fugue are:

Subject: The principle theme of the fugue.

Answer: A restatement of the subject.

Real Answer: An exact transposition of the subject to the dominant.

Tonal Answer: An answer in which the transposition is adjusted so that it can move back to tonic.

Countersubject: A second theme, sometimes defined as a continuation of the subject, which is used repeatedly throughout the fugue.

Exposition: The introduction of all voices at the beginning of the fugue.

Episode: Sections without subjects, that often facilitate key changes.

Stretto: Usually used near the end of a fugue, the entrances of the subjects are close together, causing them to overlap. (The term *stretto* is also used in non-fugal music to mean a concluding sections which is faster than the preceding music.)

Study this Fugue by J. S. Bach. The various terms used in a fugue are marked on the score.

278

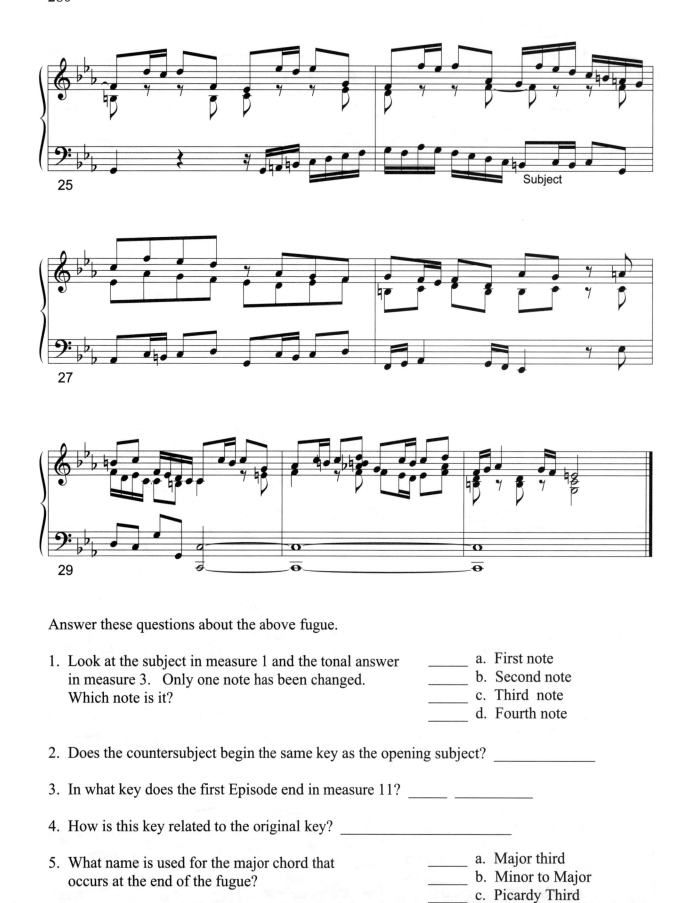

Answer these questions about the above fugue.

1. Look at the subject in measure 1 and the tonal answer in measure 3.   Only one note has been changed. Which note is it?

   _____ a. First note
   _____ b. Second note
   _____ c. Third note
   _____ d. Fourth note

2. Does the countersubject begin the same key as the opening subject? _____

3. In what key does the first Episode end in measure 11? _____ _____

4. How is this key related to the original key? _____

5. What name is used for the major chord that occurs at the end of the fugue?

   _____ a. Major third
   _____ b. Minor to Major
   _____ c. Picardy Third
   _____ d. Augmented Third

Check each correct answer.

6. In which measure does the subject of a fugue first appear?
   - _____ a. Second
   - _____ b. First
   - _____ c. Last
   - _____ d. Fourth

7. What term is used for a section of the fugue in which the full melodies are not present?
   - _____ a. Exposition
   - _____ b. Stretto
   - _____ c. Episode
   - _____ d. Answer

8. What term is used when the subject has the same intervals as the original?
   - _____ a. Real Answer
   - _____ b. Tonal Answer
   - _____ c. Regular Answer
   - _____ d. Minor Answer

9. What term is used for the first section of the fugue, in which all voices appear?
   - _____ a. Episode
   - _____ b. Countersubject
   - _____ c. Exposition
   - _____ d. Answer

10. What term is used for the secondary melody of the fugue?
    - _____ a. Variation
    - _____ b. Development
    - _____ c. Countermelody
    - _____ d. Countersubject

11. What term is used to describe an entrance of the subject that has been adjusted to fit the harmony of the fugue?

_____ a. Tonal Answer
_____ b. Real Answer
_____ c. Right Answer
_____ d. Changed Answer

12. What term is used for the first restatement of the subject?

_____ a. Question
_____ b. Countersubject
_____ c. Melody
_____ d. Answer

13. What term is used to describe the overlapping of subjects in a fugue?

_____ a. Allegro
_____ b. Stretto
_____ c. Sforzando
_____ d. Presto

LISTENING

Listen to Example 160, which is from *Clarinet Concerto, K. 622* by Mozart. The example will be played three times. Check each correct answer about the example.

14. Which term best describes the phrase structure of the example?

_____ a. Antecedent/Consequent
_____ b. Phrase Group
_____ c. Parallel Phrase
_____ d. Double Period

15. How is the cadence embellished at the end of the example?

_____ a. Appoggiatura
_____ b. Mordent
_____ c. Trill
_____ d. Turn

16. What is the basic harmonic progression of the first phrase?

_____ a. I - IV
_____ b. I - V
_____ c. I - vi
_____ d. V - I

17. Which of these occurs in the example?

_____ a. Transposition
_____ b. Countersubject
_____ c. Ostinato
_____ d. Retrogression

SIGHT SINGING

Sing each voice of the following fugue excerpt. Adjust the octave of each part to fit your vocal range.

J.S. Bach: *Fugue, WTC Book II, BWV 870*

EAR TRAINING

Listen to Example 161. The example will be played four times. Notate the missing notes in the highest and lowest voices of the following fugue.

J.S. Bach: *Fugue, BWV 871*

LESSON 26
RHYTHM AND METER

RHYTHM gives music its feeling of motion. The music may have a regular pattern of movement, created by an equal number of beats in each measure, or may have an irregular pattern of movement, caused by mixing various numbers of beats in each measure.

BARLINES divide music into **MEASURES**. In most music, the measures maintain the same number of beats throughout. A **TIME SIGNATURE** (sometimes called a **METER SIGNATURE**), found at the beginning of the music, reveals the number of beats in each measure, and the **DURATION** of the note (or type of note) that receives one beat.

2 = two beats per measure
4 = quarter note (♩) receives one beat

BEATS are the individual pulses within a measure. Some time signatures indicate **SIMPLE BEATS**. In these time signatures, one beat is given to each note that is indicated by the bottom number of the time signature. Other time signatures may be divided into **COMPOUND BEATS**. **RHYTHM** is created by combining notes of various durations.

Four equal SIMPLE BEATS

Six simple beats, or two **COMPOUND BEATS**
RHYTHM created by combining
notes of different durations

A **DOT** following a note is worth half the value of the previous note.

$\frac{4}{4}$ ♩. = ♩ + ♪   or 1 1/2 beats when a quarter note receives one beat

𝅗𝅥. = 𝅗𝅥 + ♩   or three beats when a quarter note receives one beat

A **DOUBLE DOT** is worth 3/4 the value of the previous note. (The second dot is worth half the value of the first dot.)

♩.. = ♩ + ♪ + 𝅘𝅥𝅯   or 1 3/4 beats when a quarter note receives one beat

𝅗𝅥.. = 𝅗𝅥 + ♩ + ♪   or 3 1/2 beats when a quarter note receives one beat

The following chart shows note values and the number of beats they receive in the most common time signatures. (Time signatures listed below are examples. Others are possible.)

Note Value	Note	Rest	Note Value that Receives One Simple Beat		
			Quarter Note $\left(\begin{smallmatrix}2&3&4&5&7\\4&4&4&4&4\end{smallmatrix}\right)$	**Eighth Note** $\left(\begin{smallmatrix}3&6&9\\8&8&8\end{smallmatrix}\right)$	**Half Note** $\left(\begin{smallmatrix}2&4&6\\2&2&2\end{smallmatrix}\right)$
64th note	♪		1/16 beat	1/8 simple beat	1/32 beat
32nd note	♪		1/8 beat	1/4 simple beat 1/12 compound beat	1/16 beat
16th note	♪		1/4 beat	1/2 simple beat 1/6 compound beat	1/8 beat
Eighth note	♪		1/2 beat	1 simple beat 1/3 compound beat	1/4 beat
Quarter note	♩		1 beat	2 simple beats	1/2 beat
Dotted quarter note	♩.		1 1/2 beats	3 simple beats 1 compound beat	3/4 beat
Half note	♩	—	2 beats	4 simple beats	1 beat
Dotted half note	♩.		3 beats	6 simple beats 2 compound beats	1 1/2 beats
Whole note	o	—	4 beats	not usually used	2 beats
Double whole note	‖o‖		8 beats	not usually used	4 beats

The symbol **C** is often used instead of $\frac{4}{4}$, and **₵** may be used in place of $\frac{2}{2}$.

Often, musicians use counting to work out a rhythmic pattern. Each new measure begins with the beat number 1, and each measure is given the number of "counts" indicated by the top number of the time signature. There are many ways to count rhythms, and many other ways to determine the correct way to play a rhythmic pattern.

Here are a few examples of counting, using some of the most common rhythmic patterns:

The last note of one measure and the first note of the following measure may be added together by the use of a **TIE**. The note that occurs on the first beat of the second measure (the end of the tie) is held, it is not played.

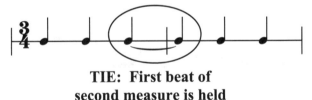

TIE: First beat of second measure is held

TUPLETS are divisions of notes that vary from the normal pattern, such as three eighth notes in the time of two eighth notes. The most common tuplets are **DUPLETS** and **TRIPLETS**.

TRIPLETS occur when three notes are performed in the time of two notes of the same value, such as three eighth notes in the same time as two eighth notes, or three quarter notes within the same time as two quarter notes.

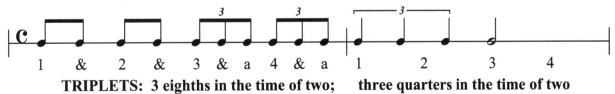

TRIPLETS: 3 eighths in the time of two;   three quarters in the time of two

DUPLETS occur when two notes of the same value occur in the time of three, such as two eighth notes in the time of three eighth notes, or two quarter notes in the time of three quarter notes.

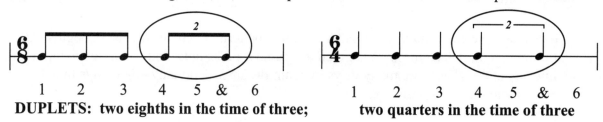

An **ANACRUSIS**, more commonly known as an **UPBEAT** or **PICKUP**, occurs when an incomplete measure is found at the beginning of the music. When music has an anacrusis, the final measure of the music has the number of beats that are missing from the upbeat measure.

When counting a rhythmic pattern that includes an anacrusis, the final numbers of the measure are used for the incomplete measure at the beginning, and the first numbers are used in the last measure.

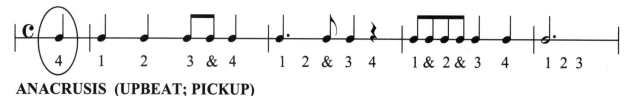

ANACRUSIS (UPBEAT; PICKUP)

1. Write counts under the notes for each of the following rhythms.

2. Which of the above examples has an anacrusis? _____
3. Which of the above examples have ties? (There are two.) _____
4. Which of the above examples has a duplet? _____
5. Which of the above examples has a triplet? _____

METER is a term that is used in reference to division of music into regular patterns or the basic **PULSE** of the music, based on the number of beats are in each measure. For example, a time signature with three beats per measure will have a strong pulse every three beats, while a time signature with two beats per measure will have a strong pulse every two beats, of which the first beat of each measure being the strongest.

DUPLE METER means that the composition has two basic pulses per measure.

TRIPLE METER means that the composition has three basic pulses per measure.

QUADRUPLE METER means that the composition has four basic pulses per measure.

Time signatures that have the number of basic beats as the top number are called **SIMPLE** meters.

If the time signature has a 2 on the top, the meter is **SIMPLE DUPLE**. The first beat of each measure is strongest. There are two pulses per measure.

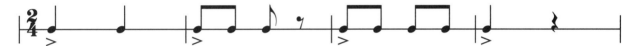

If the time signature has a 3 on the top, the meter is **SIMPLE TRIPLE**. The first beat of each measure is strongest. There are three pulses per measure.

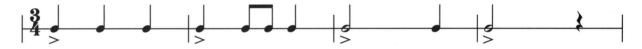

If the time signature has a 4 on the top, the meter is **SIMPLE QUADRUPLE**. The first beat of each measure is strongest, and the third beat is slightly emphasized. There are four pulses per measure.

Note: The accents above are only intended to demonstrate where strong and weak beats occur within the given meter. They are not meant to imply that every strong beat receives an accent.

COMPOUND METERS occur when the music has two, three, or four basic beats, but those beats are subdivided into smaller units or counts. Time signatures that have a 6, 9 or 12 on top are compound.

If the time signature has a 6 on the top, the meter is **COMPOUND DUPLE**. The first beat of each measure is strongest, and the fourth beat is slightly emphasized. There are **two pulses** per measure, each containing three smaller beats.

If the time signature has a 9 on the top, the meter is **COMPOUND TRIPLE**. The first beat of each measure is strongest, and the fourth and seventh beats are slightly emphasized. There are **three pulses** per measure, each containing three smaller beats.

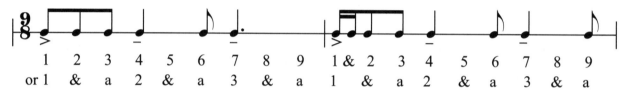

If the time signature has a 12 on the top, the meter is **COMPOUND QUADRUPLE**. The first beat of each measure is strongest, and the fourth, seventh, and tenth beats are slightly emphasized. There are **four pulses** per measure, each containing three smaller beats.

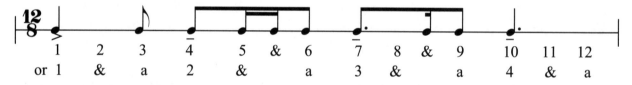

When a time signature has a 5 or 7 on top, the meter is **IRREGULAR** or **ASSYMETRICAL**. In time signatures that have a 5 on top, the beats of each measure are typically divided into two groups of either 3 + 2 or 2 + 3 .

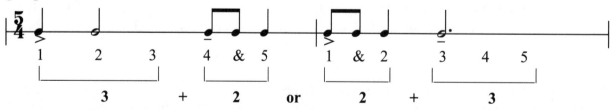

If the time signature has a 7 on top, the beats are typically divided into two groups of either 4 + 3 or 3 + 4.

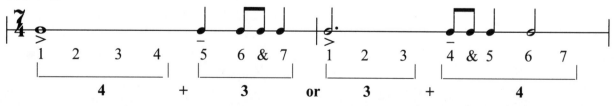

If the time signature changes throughout the course of a composition, the music has **CHANGING METER** or **MULTIMETER**.

6. Complete the time signature and the name of the meter for each of the following rhythmic phrases.

Other Rhythmic Terms

A note that has an **ACCENT** is emphasized in some way. A **DYNAMIC ACCENT** (𝅘𝅥) indicates that the note should be played louder than the others.

Rhythm can also create accents.

A **METRIC** (or **METRICAL) ACCENT** is the natural emphasis on the first beat of each measure. The metric accents are circled in the following example.

METRIC ACCENTS

An **AGOGIC ACCENT** is a rhythmic accent that is created by a note being longer than the others, on a beat that would normally be a weak beat. The agogic accent is circled in the following example.

AGOGIC ACCENT

AUGMENTATION takes place when the pitches of a melody are repeated, but the rhythmic value of each note is doubled.

AUGMENTATION

DIMINUTION takes place when the pitches of a melody are repeated, but the rhythmic value of each note is cut in half.

DIMINUTION

SYNCOPATION is the deliberate disturbance or alteration of the regular pulse or meter in a rhythmic pattern. Syncopation can be accomplished by the use of accented notes on normally weak beats, through agogic accents, dynamic accents, or the use of rests.

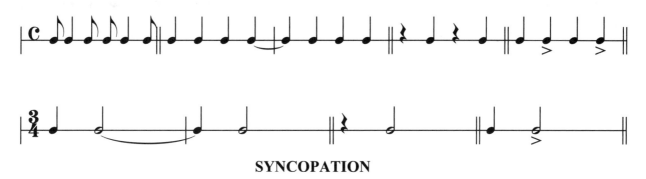

SYNCOPATION

HEMIOLA occurs when the pulse of the rhythm switches from 2 to 3 or from 3 to 2, such as from two beats per measure to three beats per measure.

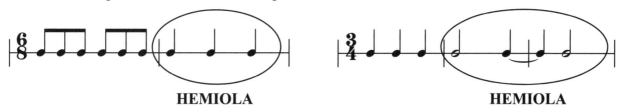

HEMIOLA   **HEMIOLA**

CROSS RHYTHM, also sometimes called **POLYRHYTHM**, is the simultaneous use of conflicting rhythmic patterns, such as two notes against three notes. Cross rhythm may be accomplished by the use of tuplets, or by combining two different time signatures.

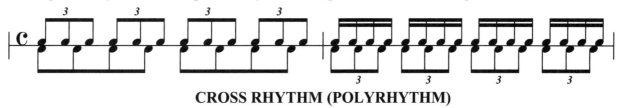

CROSS RHYTHM (POLYRHYTHM)

POLYRHYTHM can also mean the simultaneous use of rhythmic patterns that are very different from one another.

POLYRHYTHM

SWING RHYTHM is a long-short rhythmic pattern, with the feel of a triplet. Sometimes the swing rhythm will be written as it is to be played, and other times a "straight" rhythm will be written, with the following directions given:

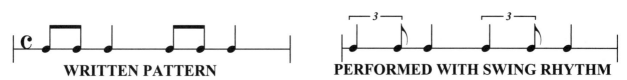

WRITTEN PATTERN   **PERFORMED WITH SWING RHYTHM**

7. Circle the hemiola in the following rhythmic pattern.

8. Write the following rhythmic pattern in the empty measures using augmentation.

9. Circle the swing rhythm in the following rhythmic pattern.

10. Circle the syncopation in the following rhythmic pattern.

11. Write the following rhythmic pattern in the empty measure using diminution.

12. The following example contains a metrical accent, a dynamic accent, and an agogic accent. Circle and name each. (Write the type of accent below the circle.)

Check each correct answer.

13. What does a double dot after a note indicate?

    _____ a. Add half the value of the note

    _____ b. Remove half the value of the note

    _____ c. Play staccato

    _____ d. Add one and a half times the value of the note

14. How many beats will this duplet receive in $\frac{6}{8}$ time when giving an eighth note one beat?

    _____ a. One beat

    _____ b. Three beats

    _____ c. Four beats

    _____ d. Two beats

15. Which of these time signatures indicates duple meter?

    _____ a. $\frac{3}{4}$

    _____ b. $\frac{9}{8}$

    _____ c. $\frac{5}{4}$

    _____ d. $\frac{6}{8}$

16. Which two terms are used for $\frac{5}{4}$? (Check two answers.)

    _____ a. Asymmetrical meter

    _____ b. Compound meter

    _____ c. Irregular meter

    _____ d. Quadruple meter

17. What other term may be used for polyrhythm?

    _____ a. Swing rhythm

    _____ b. Syncopation

    _____ c. Hemiola

    _____ d. Cross rhythm

18. What term is used for an accent that occurs on the first beat (or the downbeat) of each measure?

　　_____ a. Metric accent

　　_____ b. Dynamic accent

　　_____ c. Musical accent

　　_____ d. Agogic accent

19. What other terms may be used for anacrusis? (Check two answers.)

　　_____ a. Pre-beat

　　_____ b. Upbeat

　　_____ c. Pickup

　　_____ d. Last beat

20. What term is used for an accent that is created by a long note on a normally weak beat?

　　_____ a. Dynamic accent

　　_____ b. Metric accent

　　_____ c. Musical accent

　　_____ d. Agogic accent

21. What term is used for this rhythmic pattern?

　　_____ a. Swing rhythm

　　_____ b. Cross rhythm

　　_____ c. Polyrhythm

　　_____ d. Hemiola

22. What two terms are used for compositions that have many different meters? (Check two answers.)

　　_____ a. Duple meter

　　_____ b. Multimeter

　　_____ c. Simple meter

　　_____ d. Changing meter

SIGHT READING RHYTHMIC PATTERNS

Clap or tap each of the following examples.

Tap each of the following examples. Tap the top line with your right hand and the bottom line with your left hand.

EAR TRAINING

Listen to Examples 162-165. Each example will be played four times. Complete each rhythmic pattern. One complete measure will be tapped using the basic beats before the beginning of each example.

Example 162:

Example 163:

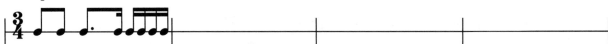

Example 164:

Example 165:

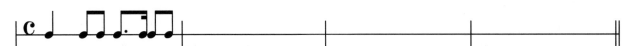

LISTENING

Listen to Example 166, which is from *The Moldau* by Smetena. The example will be played four times. Answer the following questions about the music.

23. What is the meter signature?

    a. $\frac{2}{4}$
    b. $\frac{3}{4}$
    c. $\frac{6}{8}$
    d. $\frac{9}{8}$

24. Which best describes the first two phrases?

    a. Parallel phrases
    b. Contrasting phrases
    c. Double period
    d. Cadential phrases

25. Which of these melodic patterns leads into the key change in the fifth phrase?

    a. Arpeggio
    b. Literal Repetition
    c. Scale
    d. Pedal point

26. What term best describes the lowest voice at the end of the example?

    a. Passing tone
    b. Embellishment
    c. Ostinato
    d. Dissonance

LESSON 27
TEXTURE

TEXTURE is the manner in which the various voices or parts of music are put together. Music consists of vertical elements (harmony), and horizontal elements (melody). How these two components are woven together create the texture.

MONOPHONIC TEXTURE or **MONOPHONY** consists of a single melodic line, with no harmony or accompaniment. This melody is an example

HOMOPHONIC TEXTURE or **HOMOPHONY** occurs when there is one voice which dominates the music, while the other voice or voices serve as an accompaniment. Homophonic texture may either be **chordal** in nature, or may have a **separate melody with accompaniment.**

CHORDAL HOMOPHONY, also known as **HOMORHYTHMIC TEXTURE** or sometimes **CHORDAL TEXTURE**, occurs when the texture consists of a series of solid chords. The top notes of the chords form the melody. This example, from *Deck the Halls,* demonstrates chordal homophony in a four-part vocal setting.

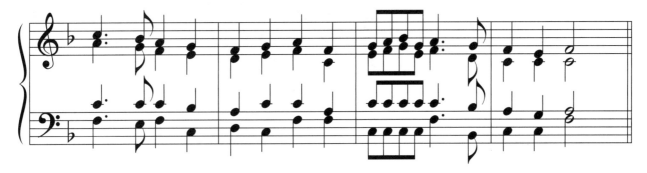

This example, from *Kinderscenen, Op. 15, No. 6,* by Schumann, demonstrates chordal homophony in an instrumental setting.

More commonly, homophonic texture consists of a clear melody with an acccompaniment. This example, from *Sonata, Op. 10, No. 1* by Beethoven, is an example of this use of homophonic texture. The accompaniment styles for music that is homophonic varies. This excerpt from the sonata demonstrates **CHORDAL ACCOMPANIMENT**.

CHORDAL ACCOMPANIMENT

ALBERTI BASS is a style of broken chord with the pattern 1-5-3-5, named for Domenico Alberti (1710-40?), who used it frequently. Alberti bass is shown in the following Sonata (K. 284) by Mozart.

ALBERTI BASS

OSTINATO is a persistently repeated phrase, usually throughout a section of a composition or even throughout the entire composition, in the same voice, and at the same pitch (such as a repeated single note in the bass clef). This excerpt, from *Study for the Left Hand* (For Children, Book 1) by Bartok is an example of the use of ostinato.

OSTINATO

WALKING BASS is created by a steady rhythmic pattern of single notes, such as all quarter notes. It is common in jazz, but is also found in other musical genres. Some possible walking bass patterns include the following (although many more possibilities exist):

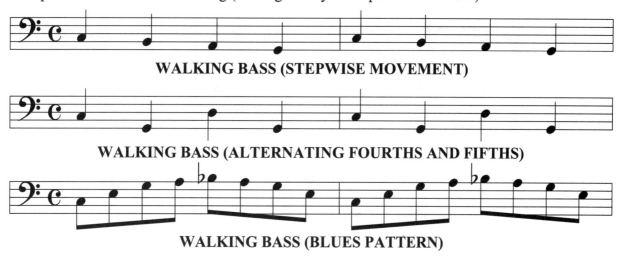

This example, from *March, Op. 65, No. 10* by Prokofiev, uses walking bass.

Homophonic music sometimes includes use of a **COUNTERMELODY.** This is a melody that is subordinate to and distinct from the main melody. This example, from *A Little Song* by Kabalevsky, contains a countermelody.

POLYPHONIC TEXTURE or **POLYPHONY** combines several different melodies or parts, each of which may stand on its own as a melody. The harmonies are the result of the interweaving of the various lines.

The terms **COUNTERPOINT** and **CONTRAPUNTAL** (literally "note against note") are often used as synonyms for the term Polyphony. Counterpoint tends to be used in reference to early music (prior to the 16th century), while Polyphony tends to be used in reference to later works (the 16th to 18th centuries). Theory scholars vary in their interpretation of these terms.

This example, from *Sinfonia No. 3* by J.S. Bach, is an example of polyphonic texture or countrapuntal music. Notice how each individual voice creates a melody.

POLYPHONIC TEXTURE (COUNTERPOINT; CONTRAPUNTAL)

IMITATIVE POLYPHONY (also know as **IMITATIVE COUNTERPOINT**) is based on use of the same thematic material (melodies, themes or motives) throughout the composition. The term **IMITATION** is often used as a general term for vaious melodic terms, including repetition, sequence, and more.

IMITATION, in its strictest definition, is the restatement of a theme, motive, or melody immediately following its introduction, in another voice. This excerpt, from *Invention No. 4* by J.S. Bach, is an example of the strict definition of imitation.

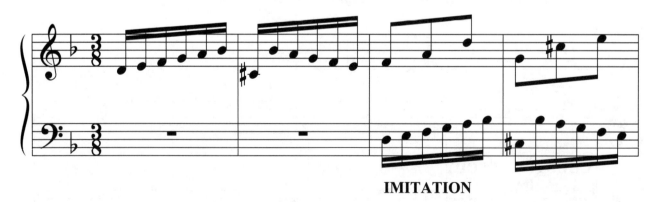

IMITATION

CANON or **CANONIC** music is a type of imitative polyphony in which an extended melody is strictly imitated in another part, often for the entire duration of the music. Popular "rounds," such as *Row, Row, Row Your Boat,* are examples of canonic style. The following example, from *Sonata, K. 576* by Mozart, is a canon.

FUGAL IMITATION is another type of imitative polyphony in which the entire theme is imitated. Fugues contain various subjects (themes) and countersubjects (secondary themes), which form the basis for the entire composition. This example, from a fugue by J.S. Bach, is an example of fugal imitation. See Lesson 25 for more information on fugues.

FUGAL IMITATION

HETEROPHONY or music that is **HETEROPHONIC** consists of two or more performers that are singing or playing the same melody, but with slight differences between the two performers, by the useof ornaments or other variations. This is often used in folk and pop music and music of non-Western cultures. Using the melody from *Twinkle, Twinkle, Little Star*, this example shows heterophony.

HETEROPHONY
(Parts 1 and 2 are sung simultaneously)

NON-IMITATIVE POLYPHONY is contrapuntal or polyphonic music in which the melodies of the various voices do not copy or imitate each other, but are different from one another. The following is an example of non-imitative polyphony.

1. Write the name of the type of texture that each definition describes (homophonic, polyphonic, or monophonic).

   a. Melody with accompaniment _____

   b. Mulitple independent voices _____

   c. Single melody without accompaniment _____

2. Match each excerpt with the term that describes it.

3. Match each definition with its name.

a. Type of polyphony that uses subjects and countersubjects that are imitated throughout the composition

_____ imitative polyphony

b. Type of polyphony that uses melodies that are different from one another in each of the voices

_____ non-imitative polyphony

c. Type of polyphony in which the same melody is performed by two or more performers at the same time, but with variations

_____ canon

d. Type of polyphony in which the entire melody is repeated in the various voices without any changes

_____ fugal imitation

e. Type of polyphony in which the melodies are repeated either in full or in part among the various voices

_____ heterophony

Check the correct term for each example.

4. (Chopin: *Nocturne, Op. posth. 72, No. 1*)

_____ a. homophonic texture

_____ b. homorhythmic texture

_____ c. chordal texture

_____ d. polyphonic texture

5. (J.S. Bach: *French Suite No. 1: Minuet*)

_____ a. walking bass

_____ b. imitation

_____ c. heterophony

_____ d. polyphonic texture

6. (Brahms: *Rhapsody, Op. 119, No. 4*)

_____ a. contrapuntal

_____ b. Alberti bass

_____ c. chordal homophony

_____ d. canon

7. (Scarlatti: *Sonata No. 40*)

_____ a. homophonic texture

_____ b. walking bass

_____ c. ostinato

_____ d. imitation

8. (J.S. Bach: *Invention No. 8*)

_____ a. monophonic texture

_____ b. imitative polyphony

_____ c. heterophony

_____ d. chordal accompaniment

9. (J.S. Bach: *March in D*)

_____ a. walking bass

_____ b. Alberti bass

_____ c. canon

_____ d. chordal homophony

10. (Kabalevsky: *Sonatina, Op. 13, No. 1*)

_____ a. imitative polyphony

_____ b. ostinato

_____ c. heterophony

_____ d. countermelody

11. (Bartok: *Dance from For Children, Book 2*)

_____ a. ostinato

_____ b. polyphonic texture

_____ c. imitation

_____ d. countermelody

12.

_____ a. imitation

_____ b. countermelody

_____ c. heterophony

_____ d. chordal accompaniment

13. (Kabalevsky: *A Little Dance, Op. 39, No. 9*)

_____ a. walking bass

_____ b. monophonic texture

_____ c. chordal accompaniment

_____ d. non-imitative polyphony

14. (Beethoven: *Sonatina in G*)

_____ a. polyphonic texture

_____ b. non-imitative polyphony

_____ c. Alberti bass

_____ d. contrapuntal

15. (Kabalevsky: *Playing, Op. 39, No. 5*)

_____ a. countermelody

_____ b. monophonic texture

_____ c. homophonic texture

_____ d. heterophony

16.

_____ a. chordal accompaniment

_____ b. ostinato

_____ c. monophonic texture

_____ d. canon

17. (J.S. Bach: *Sinfonia No. 2*)

_____ a. contrapuntal

_____ b. homophonic texture

_____ c. Alberti bass

_____ d. heterophony

18. (Kabalevsky: *Improvisation, Op. 39, No. 21*)

_____ a. chordal homophony

_____ b. non-imitative polyphony

_____ c. imitation

_____ d. monophonic texture

SIGHT SINGING

Sing each part (soprano, alto, tenor, and bass) of the following Chorale. Adjust each octave to fit your vocal range.

J.S. Bach: *Liebster Jesu, wir sind hier*

EAR TRAINING

Listen to Example 167. The example will be played four times. Notate the soprano and bass parts, and provide the Roman numerals indicating each chord and its inversion. The first notes and Roman numeral are given.

Luther: *Ein Feste Burg*

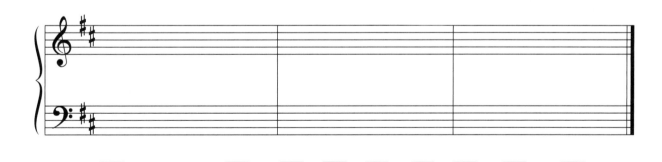

LISTENING

Listen to Example 168, which is from *Sonata, Op. 2, No. 3* by Beethoven. The example will be played four times. The score is printed correctly below, but in the version you will hear there are errors. Check the correct answer for each question.

19. Measure 2 contains an error or errors in

    a. treble staff pitch
    b. bass staff pitch
    c. treble staff rhythm
    d. bass staff rhythm

20. In measure 5, there is an error in pitch on beat

    a. 1
    b. 2
    c. 3
    d. 4

21. In measure 8, there is an error in the

    a. pitch in the treble staff
    b. pitch in the bass staff
    c. rhythm in the treble staff
    d. rhythm in the bass staff

22. Measure 9 contains a pitch error on beat

    a. 1
    b. 2
    c. 3
    d. 4

LESSON 28
PERFORMANCE TERMS

Musical directions for items other than pitch and rhythm are indicated by performance terms or symbols.

ARTICULATION is a term used to indicate the manner in which a performer executes a note or succession of notes. For example, notes may be connected, separated, or attacked vigorously.

Accent: emphasize the note; play the note louder than the others.

Arco: An instruction for string players to bow the strings (as opposed to plucking them).

Legato: Connect the notes, or play smoothly. Legato can be indicated by a slur over the notes, or by the term *legato*.

Marcato: Marked or stressed, emphasizing each note.

Pizzicato: An instruction for string players to pluck the strings (as opposed to bowing them).

Slur: A curved line, used to indicate legato articulation, for one breath in singing, or for one stroke of the bow. (See Example A above.)

 Staccato: Detached, crisp, not connected.

 Tenuto: Hold or sustain the note for its full value.

1. Write the term for each of the following types of articulation.

   a. _____ Bow the strings.

   b. _____ Connect the notes, play smoothly.

   c. _____ Emphasize the note.

   d. _____ Detach the note, play crisply.

   e. _____ Hold the note for its full value.

   f. _____ A curved line indicating to connect the notes.

   g. _____ Pluck the strings.

   h. _____ Marked, emphasizing each note.

DYNAMICS indicate volume or loudness and softness.

    ⟨——— *crescendo (cresc.)*: gradually louder; increasing in volume

    ———⟩ *diminuendo (dimin., dim.)*: gradually softer; decreasing in volume

decrescendo (decresc.): gradually softer, decreasing in volume

pp   *pianissimo*: very soft

p   *piano*: soft

mp   *mezzo piano*: medium soft

mf   *mezzo forte*: medium loud

f   *forte*: loud

ff   *fortissimo*: very loud

Terrace dynamics: Dynamic changes that occur by sections, rather than gradually, such as *p mp mf f*   Terraced dynamics were used primarily in the Baroque Period (appx. 1600-1750), when keyboard instruments were not able to create gradual dynamic changes.

2. Write the dynamic mark for each of the following definitions.

   a. _____ very loud

   b. _____ soft

   c. _____ gradually louder

   d. _____ very soft

   e. _____ loud

   f. _____ medium loud

   g. _____ gradually softer

   h. _____ dynamic changes by section rather than gradually

   i. _____ medium soft

TEMPOS indicate the speed of a composition, and changes in speed during the course of the composition.

Adagio: Slow

Allegro: Fast or quick, cheerful, joyful. (Originally, the term *Allegro* was an expression mark, meaning cheerful, but it has evolved to mean fast or quick.)

Allegretto: Slightly slower than Allegro

Andante: Walking tempo

Andantino: Slightly faster than Andante, although some composers use it to mean slightly slower than Andante.

Grave: Slow, solemn

Largo: Very slow and dignified, broad

Lento: Slow, between Adagio and Largo

Moderato: Moderate tempo, between Andante and Allegro

Presto: Faster than Allegro; very fast.

Vivace: Quick, lively, vivacious.

accelerando: Gradually faster

ritardando (ritard., rit.): Gradually slower

ritenuto: Immediately slower

rubato: Literally "robbed time." Flexible tempo, using slight accelerandos and ritardandos that are determined by the expressiveness of the music.

Fixed tempos from slowest to fastest:

Grave, Largo, Lento, Adagio, Andante, Andantino, Moderato, Allegretto, Allegro, Vivace, Presto

3. Write the tempo for each of the following definitions.

   a. _____ Gradually faster

   b. _____ Flexible tempo, "robbed time"

   c. _____ Walking tempo

   d. _____ Faster than Allegro, very fast

   e. _____ Slow, between Adagio and Largo

   f. _____ Solemn, slow

   g. _____ Slow

   h. _____ Quick, lively, vivacious

   i. _____ Slightly faster than Andante

   j. _____ Immediately slower

   k. _____ Cheerful, joyful, fast

   l. _____ Very slow, broad, dignified

   m. _____ Gradually slower

   n. _____ Moderate tempo

   o. _____ Slightly slower than Allegro

4. Tell whether each of the following terms or symbols indicate articulation, dynamics, or tempo.

   a. marcato _____

   b. diminuendo _____

   c. Arco _____

   d. pizzicato _____

   e. Andante _____

   f. accelerando _____

   g. fortissimo _____

   h. legato _____

Chck each correct answer.

5. Which term or symbol means gradually louder?

   _____ a. >
   _____ b. <
   _____ c. *decrescendo*
   _____ d. *mezzo forte*

6. What is the meaning of *ritenuto*?

   _____ a. gradually slower
   _____ b. gradually faster
   _____ c. immediately slower
   _____ d. immediately faster

7. What term is used to indicate the manner in which a note is executed?

   _____ a. dynamics
   _____ b. arco
   _____ c. allegretto
   _____ d. articulation

8. Which of these tempos is slowest?
   - _____ a. largo
   - _____ b. vivace
   - _____ c. andante
   - _____ d. moderato

9. What name is used for a curved line above or below notes?
   - _____ a. staccato
   - _____ b. rubato
   - _____ c. slur
   - _____ d. pizzicato

10. What term indicates to hold the note for its full value?
    - _____ a. accent
    - _____ b. staccato
    - _____ c. pianissimo
    - _____ d. tenuto

11. Which of these dynamic marks is loudest?
    - _____ a. *p*
    - _____ b. *mp*
    - _____ c. *mf*
    - _____ d. *f*

12. Which of these examples shows the tempos from slowest to fastest?
    - _____ a. vivace, presto, andante
    - _____ b. lento, largo, grave
    - _____ c. moderato, allegro, andantino
    - _____ d. lento, moderato, allegro

13. What term indicates a flexible tempo?
    - _____ a. rubato
    - _____ b. adagio
    - _____ c. legato
    - _____ d. crescendo

SIGHT SINGING

Sing each of the following melodies. Observe all performance terms. Adjust the octave to fit your vocal range.

EAR TRAINING

Listen to Example 169. The example will be played four times. Notate the soprano and bass parts, and provide the Roman numerals indicating each chord and its inversion. The first notes and Roman numeral are given.

A. Sullivan: *St. Gertrude*

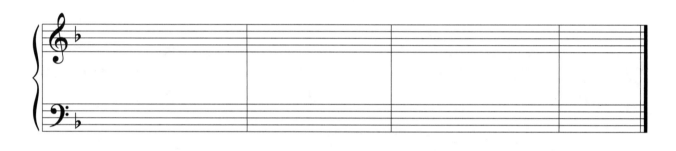

F: I __ __ __   __ __ __ __ __ __

LISTENING

Listen to Example 170, which is from *Symphony No.100* by Haydn. The example will be played four times. Answer the following questions about the music.

14. What is the first interval?

    a. 3rd
    b. 4th
    c. 5th
    d. 6th

15. On which scale degree does the opening motive begin?

    a. Tonic
    b. Subdominant
    c. Dominant
    d. Submediant

16. Compared with the beginning, on which scale degree does the example end?

    a. I
    b. IV
    c. V
    d. vi

17. Which of these terms best describes the tempo?

    a. Allegro
    b. Presto
    c. Vivace
    d. Adagio

LESSON 29
INSTRUMENTAL TERMS

Musical instruments are divided into four basic types:

   Strings
   Woodwinds
   Brass
   Percussion

INSTRUMENTATION is the term that is used for the selection of instruments for a musical composition. Instrumentation may include only one instrument, or any combination of instruments that the composer chooses. Some of the most common instruemtations include full orchestra, marching band, and string quartet, for example. The possibilities are vast.

STRING INSTRUMENTS are those in which the sound is produced by a stretched string which is plucked, bowed, or struck. While "string instruments" can include a wide range of non-orchestral instruments such as those from the guitar family, the term "Strings" typically refers to the stringed instruments used in the orchestra:

   Violin (highest in sound)
   Viola (upper middle range)
   Cello (or Violincello, lower middle to lower range)
   String Bass (low range)

WIND INSTRUMENTS are those in which the sound is produced by blowing into the instrument. Wind instruments are divided into two categories: **WOODWINDS** and **BRASS**.

The **WOODWIND** family includes instruments with varying types of sound production. They include but are not limited to the following:

   Flute and piccolo (sound produced by blowing across the top of the mouthpiece)
   Oboe, English horn, Bassoon, and Double Bassoon (sound produced by blowing between
      two reeds or a "double reed")
   Clarinet, Bass Clarinet, Saxophone (sound produced by blowing between a single reed
      and the mouthpiece)

The sound for **BRASS** instruments is created by the vibration of the performer's lips against the mouthpiece. Brass instruments include, but are not limited to, the following:

   Trumpet
   Horn (also known as French Horn)
   Trombone
   Baritone
   Tuba

PERCUSSION INSTRUMENTS make up the **RHYTHM SECTION** of a band or orchestra. The instruments in this category can be subdivided into various groups:

DRUMS: Side drum, bass drum, tenor drum, tom-tom, bongos, tympani, and more.

MALLET INSTRUMENTS: Xylophone, Vibraphone, Glockenspiel, Marimba, and more.

MISCELLANEOUS INSTRUMENTS: Castanets, wood blocks, triangle, tambourine, cowbell, and more. (Note: use of the term "miscellaneous" to describe this group does not mean that the instruments are not important.)

1. Write the type for each of the following (strings, woodwinds, brass, or percussion).

   a. Trumpet _____

   b. Viola _____

   c. Bassoon _____

   d. Flute _____

   e. Tympani _____

   f. Trombone _____

   g. Cello _____

   h. Saxophone _____

   i. Tuba _____

   j. Clarinet _____

   k. Oboe _____

CONTINUO is a term that is mainly associated with the Baroque Period of music. The term is an abbreviation for *basso continuo*. The continuo part provided a bass line with figured bass (see Lesson 21), and the harmony for that line is interpreted by the performer.

Continuo Part

Performer's Possible Interpretation

CONTINUO may also refer to the keyboard part in an orchestral work. In the Baroque Period, the harpsichord was often included in orchestral music. Sometimes, piano, harpsichord, and clavichord are grouped with the percussion instruments. Other times, they are considered continuo instruments.

OTHER INSTRUMENTAL TERMS

OBBLIGATO means obligatory, required, or necessary. Originally, in the 18th century or earlier, the term referred to a section or part that must be played. In the 19th century, the term came to mean the opposite, and referred to a part that could be omitted.

SOLO or **SOLI** means "alone." It may be applied to music in several ways:

1) A single performer, either alone (such as a piano solo), or as a single instrumentalist with an accompanist (such as a violin solo with piano accompaniment)
2) A passage in orchestral music for a single performer, such as an oboe solo that stands out
3) In a concerto, the solo instrument that is accompanied by the orchestra
4) In Baroque music, orchestral passages that are to be played only by a few of the instrumentalists rather than by the full orchestra

TIMBRE is the unique quality, sound, or tone color of each specific instrument.

TUTTI indicates the entire orchestra. It usually appears in orchestral works after a solo or small ensemble section.

2. Define each of the following terms associated with instrumental music.

   a. Timbre _____

   b. Solo or soli: _____

   c. Obbligato: _____

   d. Tutti: _____

Check each correct answer.

3. Which section of the orchestra contains the rhythm section?
   _____ a. Strings
   _____ b. Woodwinds
   _____ c. Brass
   _____ d. Percussion

4. How many instrumentalists perform when the tutti is indicated?
   _____ a. The entire orchestra
   _____ b. One person
   _____ c. A small group
   _____ d. Nobody

5. Which of these instruments belong in the woodwind section?
   _____ a. bass drum
   _____ b. clarinet
   _____ c. viola
   _____ d. trombone

6. To which section do the violin, viola, cello and string bass belong?
   _____ a. Brass
   _____ b. Woodwind
   _____ c. Percussion
   _____ d. Strings

7. Which instrument performs the continuo part?
   _____ a. Keyboard
   _____ b. Trumpet
   _____ c. Xylophone
   _____ d. Flute

8. What term is used for a section of the music that highlights a single performer?
   _____ a. Timbre
   _____ b. Tutti
   _____ c. Solo
   _____ d. Obbligato

9. What term can mean either a section of the music that must be played, or a section of the music that can be omitted?
   _____ a. Obbligato
   _____ b. Tutti
   _____ c. Solo
   _____ d. Instrumentation

10. What term indicates the tone color of an instrument?
    _____ a. Timbre
    _____ b. Tutti
    _____ c. Solo
    _____ d. Obbligato

Recommended listening: Benjamin Britten's *Young Person's Guide to the Orchestra*, with narration.

SIGHT SINGING

Sing each part (soprano, alto, tenor, and bass) of the following Chorale. Adjust the octave to fit your vocal range.

J.S. Bach: *Wer in dem Schutz des Hochsten*

EAR TRAINING

Listen to Example 171 on CD 3. The example will be played four times. Notate the soprano and bass parts, and provide the Roman numerals indicating each chord and its inversion. The first notes and Roman numeral are given.

Stebbins: *Evening Prayer*

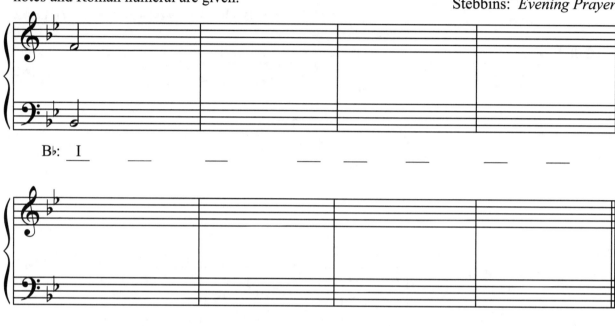

LISTENING

Listen to Example 172, which is from a piece by Bartok. The example will be played four times. Circle the correct answer for each question..

11. For which instrumental group is this example?

    a. Brass
    b. Strings
    c. Percussion
    d. Woodwinds

12. The first twelve notes of the music consist of only which interval?

    a. 2nds
    b. 3rds
    c. 4ths
    d. 5ths

13. Which of the following best describes the various textures as they occur in the music?

    a. polyphony/chordal homophony/monophony/octaves
    b. Alberti bass/polyphony/homophony/counterpoint
    c. homophony/solo/polyphony/fugue
    d. monophony/octaves/chordal homophony/polyphony

14. The opening rhythm is represented by:

LESSON 30
GENRE

The term **GENRE** refers to the kind, sort, or category of a musical composition. The term has a variety of uses, defining not only the type of music such as Classical, pop, rock or jazz, but also to define categories a larger genre, such as the Classical Sonata, symphony, or song. Popular music includes, but is not limited to, the following genre: New Age, Hip Hop, Classic Rock, Heavy Metal, Pop, or Techno.

Within Classical music, the following genre may be found:

CONCERTO: A composition for a soloist with an orchestra. The most common are piano concertos and violin concertos, although there are concertos for most other orchestral instruments.

SONATA: The Italian word literally means "played." A sonata is an instrumental composition, normally for a solo instrument or solo instrument with accompaniment. Sonata form was developed during the Classical Period, and consists of multiple sections called *movements*.
The typical scheme for sonata movements is Allegro - Adagio - Scherzo (or Minuet) - Allegro. The third movement (the Scherzo or Minuet) is often omitted. For more information on Sonata form, see Lesson 24.

SYMPHONY: A sonata for orchestra. (The term symphony is often used as a generic term for other orchestral music, or for the orchestra itself.)

STRING QUARTET: Chamber music for four strings, usually two violins, one viola and one cello.

PRELUDE: A composition that is intended to be played as an introduction to a ceremony, play, service, etc.

INTERLUDE: A composition that is "inserted." Interludes might be written for performance between other pieces, acts of a play, portions of a service, verses of a hymn, etc.

POSTLUDE: A composition that is intended to be played at the end of a ceremony, play, service, etc.

The terms Prelude, Interlude, and Postlude are often used as titles of compositions even though those compositions are not intended specifically for the defined purposes.

SONG: A musical composition with words (lyrics) for solo voice, with or without accompaniment.

OPERA: A dramatic presentation in which all parts are sung and acted, for orchestra and vocalists.

Check the correct answer for each question.

1. Which term refers to a composition that is intended to be performed before a play or ceremony?
   _____ a. Prelude
   _____ b. Postlude
   _____ c. Interlude
   _____ d. Sonata

2. What instrumental configuration is used for a concerto?
   _____ a. Solo and orchestra
   _____ b. Solo and accompanist
   _____ c. Vocal solo
   _____ d. Unaccompanied violin

3. What is the difference between a song and other orchestral compositions?
   _____ a. Songs have accompaniment
   _____ b. Songs are unaccompanied
   _____ c. Songs are hummed
   _____ d. Songs have words or lyrics

4. Which term refers to a sonata for orchestra?
   _____ a. Concerto
   _____ b. Opera
   _____ c. Symphony
   _____ d. String quartet

5. What term is used for the sections of a sonata?
   _____ a. pieces
   _____ b. portions
   _____ c. movements
   _____ d. codas

6. What is the purpose of a Postlude?
   _____ a. Played at the beginning of a ceremony
   _____ b. Played at the end of a ceremony
   _____ c. Played in the middle of a ceremony
   _____ d. Played throughout a ceremony

7. Which is the typical configuration for a string quartet?
   _____ a. Two violins, viola, cello
   _____ b. One violin, two violas, cello
   _____ c. One violin, one viola, two cellos
   _____ d. One each of violin, viola, cello and bass

8. Which term refers to music that is inserted between acts of a play?
   _____ a. Postlude
   _____ b. Concerto
   _____ c. Interlude
   _____ d Opera

9. Which configuration is used for opera?
   _____ a. Piano and orchestra
   _____ b. Violin and piano
   _____ c. Full orchestra
   _____ d. Vocalists and orchestra

10. Which term is used for various types of music?
    _____ a. Concerto
    _____ b. Opera
    _____ c. Prelude
    _____ d. Genre

SIGHT SINGING

Sing each part (soprano, alto, tenor, and bass) of the following Chorale. Adjust the octave to fit your vocal range.

J.S. Bach: *Komm, Gott Schopfer, heiliger Geist*

EAR TRAINING

Listen to Example 173. The example will be played four times. Notate the soprano and bass parts, and provide the Roman numerals indicating each chord and its inversion. The first notes and Roman numeral are given.

C.H.A. Malan: *Welton*

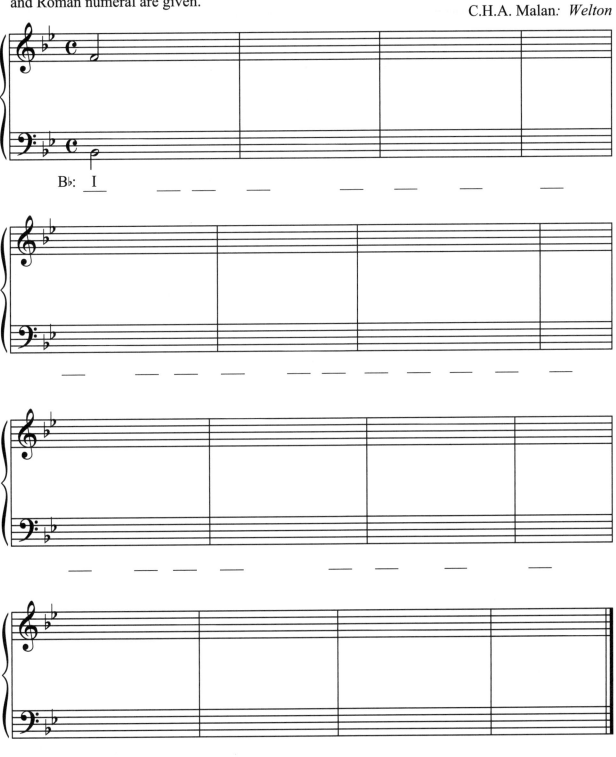

LISTENING

Listen to Example 174, which is from *Swan Lake* by Tchaikovsky. The example will be played four times. Answer these questions about the music.

11. With which of these motivic patterns does the example begin?

    a. Descending scale followed by ascending arpeggio
    b. Descending fourths followed by ascending scale
    c. Descending fifths followed by ascending arpeggio
    d. Descending chromatic scale followed by ascending triplets

12. What is the meter?

    a. Compound triple
    b. Compound quadruple
    c. Simple triple
    d. Simple quadruple

13. With which type of cadence does the example end?

    a. Plagal
    b. Deceptive
    c. Half
    d. Authentic

14. Which of these terms best describes the bass after the introduction?

    a. Ostinato
    b. Walking bass
    c. Pedal point
    d. Alberti bass

LESSON 31
VOCAL TERMS

The following terms are used in vocal music:

LYRICS are the words to a song.

REGISTER is a term used for the various portions of a vocalist's range, such as the "head register" or "chest register."

TESSITURA is the general "lie" of a vocal part, or the part of the range that is most frequently used in the part, whether high or low in its average pitch. It differs from range (the entire area of notes covered by a vocal part, from the lowest note in the piece to the highest), in that it does not take into account the few isolated notes of very high or very low pitch in the part. The following melody has a wide range of two octaves, and a tessitura of one octave.

SYLLABIC: One note for each syllable of text.

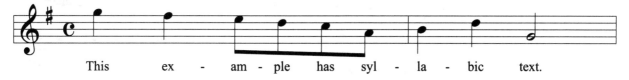

MELISMATIC: Several notes for one word of text.

An **ARIA** is an elaborate vocal composition, usually contained within a larger work such as a cantata or oratorio (works for solo vocalists and choir, usually with orchestra), or in an opera. The following excerpt is from the aria *Il Nocchier Nella Tempesta,* from the opera *Salustia,* by Pergolesi.

An **ART SONG** is a song for piano and vocalist. Art songs are not usually as long or as elaborate as arias. The following excerpt is from the art song *Der Doppelganger,* by Schubert.

Check each correct answer.

1. What term indicates one syllable per note?

    _____ a. Aria

    _____ b. Syllabic

    _____ c. Tessitura

    _____ d. Lyrics

2. Which term indicates the general pitch region of the music, as opposed to the entire range of a song?

    _____ a. Tessitura

    _____ b. Register

    _____ c. Syllabic

    _____ d. Art Song

3. Which term indicates the different portions of a vocalist's range, such as the head voice chest voice?

    _____ a. Lyrics

    _____ b. Syllabic

    _____ c. Register

    _____ d. Tessitura

4. What term is used for the words of a song?

_____ a. Chorus

_____ b. Lyrics

_____ c. Comments

_____ d. Poems

5. Which type of song is elaborate, and usually from an opera, cantata, or oratorio?

_____ a. Art Song

_____ b. Aria

_____ c. Lyrics

_____ d. Melismatic

6. Which term indicates several notes per syllable?

_____ a. Melismatic

_____ b. Lyrics

_____ c. Register

_____ d. Syllabic

7. What type of song is usually written for piano and voice?

_____ a. Aria

_____ b. Opera

_____ c. Art Song

_____ d. Syllabic

SIGHT SINGING

Sing each of the following melodies. Adjust the octave to fit your vocal range.

EAR TRAINING

Listen to Example 175. The example will be played four times. Notate the soprano and bass parts, and provide the Roman numerals indicating each chord and its inversion. The first notes and Roman numeral are given.

W.B. Bradbury: *Abends*

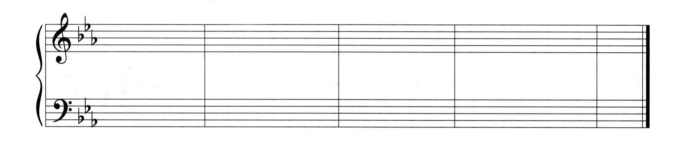

LISTENING

Listen to Example 176, which is from *Symphony No. 5, Opus 67* by Beethoven. The example will be played four times. Circle the correct answer for each of these questions about the music.

8. Which of the following does NOT occur in the excerpt?

   a. Literal repetition
   b. Appoggiatura
   c. Sequence
   d. Changing meter

9. Which of the following represents the scale degrees of the opening melody?

   a. 1 - 3 - 5 - 4 - 3 - 2 - 1 - 2 - 1
   b. 1 - 3 - 4 - 3 - 3 - 2 - 1 - 2 - 1
   c. 1 - 2 - 5 - 4 - 3 - 2 - 1 - 3 - 1
   d. 1 - 4 - 5 - 4 - 3 - 2 - 1 - 2 - 1

10. What type of cadence ends the example?

    a. Plagal
    b. Half
    c. Perfect authentic
    d. Imperfect authentic

11. Which term describes the end of the example?

    a. Coda
    b. Codetta
    c. Recapitulation
    d. Cadential extension

LESSON 32
JAZZ AND POP TERMS

The following terms are associated with jazz, blues, and popular music:

TWELVE-BAR BLUES is a the following harmonic pattern (using one chord per measure):

I I I I IV IV I I V IV I I

Jazz, pop, and rock music have their foundations in twelve-bar blues. The **BLUES SCALE** is often used in conjunction with twelve-bar blues harmony.

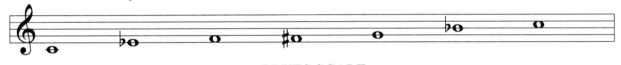

BLUES SCALE

TWELVE-BAR BLUES

In the example on page 341, the music ended on a I chord. If the music is to continue, the performer often uses a **TURNAROUND**. The turnaround is a series of chords that lead from the end of the first section to the beginning of the next section of the music.

This example is the last four measures of the previous example, followed by a repeat of the music. A turnaround of I - ii6 - V and chromatic movement are used to lead into the new section.

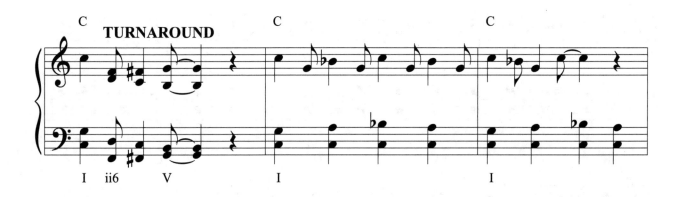

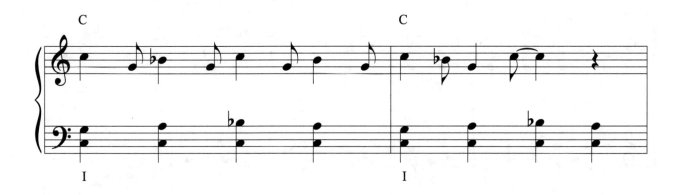

The term **CHORUS** is also used in jazz. In this context, it refers to the entire melody (or "tune") played one time through. Jazz performances often consist of the same melody played by various soloists, who **IMPROVISE** (not following the notes as written, but creating the music as the performer plays), using the melody and harmony as a basis.

SONG FORM for jazz and pop is **A A B A.** In jazz, the B section is referred to as the **BRIDGE**, and consists of material that is contasting in both melody and harmony.

Check each correct answer.

1. What term is used for the form AABA?
   - _____ a. Vocal form
   - _____ b. Melody form
   - _____ c. Harmony form
   - _____ d. Song form

2. What term is used for the B section in Song Form?
   - _____ a. Bridge
   - _____ b. Cadence
   - _____ c. Turnaround
   - _____ d. Chorus

3. What term is used for the entire melody from beginning to end?
   - _____ a. Chorus
   - _____ b. Bridge
   - _____ c. Section
   - _____ d. Selection

4. Which of these progressions is twelve-bar blues?
   - _____ a. I I IV IV I I V V IV IV I I
   - _____ b. I I I I IV IV I I V IV I I
   - _____ c. I I V I IV IV V I IV I V I
   - _____ d. I I IV V I I IV V I V IV I

5. What term is used for a chord progression at the end of a section that leads into the next phrase?
   - _____ a. Bridge
   - _____ b. Chorus
   - _____ c. Turnaround
   - _____ d. Song form

6. What term is used for creating music as the performer plays?
   - _____ a. Turnaround
   - _____ b. Improvising
   - _____ c. Bridge
   - _____ d. Twelve-bar blues

SIGHT SINGING

Sing the following melody. Adjust the octave to fit your vocal range.

EAR TRAINING

Listen to Example 177. The example will be played four times. Notate the soprano and bass parts, and provide the Roman numerals indicating each chord and its inversion. The first notes and Roman numeral are given.

William James Kirkpatrick

A♭: I

LISTENING

Listen to Example 178, which is from *Symphony No. 4* by Brahms. The example will be played four times. Answer these questions about the music.

7. What type of tonality does the example use?

   a. Major
   b. Minor
   c. Pentatonic
   d. Whole tone

8. Which term best describes the melodic structure?

   a. Modulation
   b. Conjunct
   c. Disjunct
   d. Tonicization

9. What is the opening interval?

   a. 3rd
   b. 2nd
   c. 4th
   d. 5th

10. What type of $^6_4$ chord occurs at the end of the example?

    a. Passing
    b. Neighboring (pedal)
    c. Arpeggiating
    d. Cadential

REVIEW
LESSONS 23-32

1. Using the chord symbols given above the treble clef, write chords in the bass clef for the following example.

2. Using traditional harmony, write chord symbols above the following melody.

3. Match each of the following terms with its definition.

_____ Through-composed   a. ABA

_____ Stanza   b. Several verses sung to the same melody

_____ Ternary form   c. A B shortened A

_____ Strophic   d. AB

_____ Antiphonal   e. The same basic melody and harmonic structure
_____ Introduction   followed by several sections that are based on the
                                   original, but varied

_____ Binary form   f. An extended ending at the end of an exposition

_____ Coda   g. Exposition, Development, Recapitulation

_____ Sonata form   h. Verse: the same melody with different words

_____ Chorus   i. Two choirs or ensembles that alternate parts

_____ Rounded binary form   j. An extended ending that is not part of the standard form

_____ Theme and variations   k. Different melody for each verse

_____ Codetta   l. Same music and words sung between verses

                                m. Music that precedes the opening theme

4. Each of these terms relates to the fugue. Match each with its definition.

   _____ Answer   a. Continuation of the subject, used repeatedly
   _____ Episode   b. Sections without subjects
   _____ Tonal answer   c. Principle theme of the fugue
   _____ Subject   d. Exact transposition of the subject
   _____ Stretto   e. Introduction of all voices at the beginning of the fugue
   _____ Real answer   f. Restatement of the subject
   _____ Exposition   g. Answer with intervallic adjustments
   _____ Countersubject h. Overlapping of subjects

5. Using one number for each eighth note, write counts under the notes for the following rhythmic pattern. The first measure is given.

6. The following questions are based on the rhythmic pattern in question 4.

   a. What three terms may be used for the incomplete measure at the beginning of the example?

      _____, _____, _____

   b. What term is used for the rhythmic pattern on beat 2 of measure 1? _____

   c. What term is used for the rhythmic pattern in measure 2? _____

   d. What term is used for the rhythmic pattern used on beats 1-2 in measure 3? _____

   e. Name the type of accent used on each of the following notes:

      Measure 4, beat 2: _____

      Measure 6, beat 1: _____

      Measure 7, beat 4: _____

7. Write the name for each of the following rhythmic devices.

a. _____ or _____

b. _____

c. _____

8. Write the full name of the meter for each of the following time signatures.

a. 4/4 _____

b. 12/8 _____

c. 2/4 _____

d. 7/4 _____ or _____

e. 3/2 _____

f. 4/4 5/4 3/4 _____ or _____

g. 9/8 _____

h. 6/4 _____

9. Match each of the following terms with its definition.

_____ canon
_____ chordal accompaniment
_____ ostinato
_____ chordal homophony
       (homorhythmic texture)
_____ imitative polyphony
       (imitative counterpoint)
_____ polyphonic texture
_____ homophonic texture
_____ counterpoint
_____ Alberti bass
_____ heterophony
_____ non-imitative polyphony
_____ walking bass
_____ fugal imitation
_____ countermelody
_____ monophonic texture

a. accompaniment that uses solid or blocked chords
b. accompaniment pattern of 1-5-3-5
c. combination of several independent melodies
d. one chord with each melody note
e. strict repetition of entire melody in another voice
f. polyphony in which voices do not copy one other
g. a melody with no accompaniment
h. theme imitated with subjects and countersubjects
i. steady rhythmic accompaniment of single notes
j. "note against note"
k. one melody performed by two musicians at the same time who each perform it differently
l. melody that is subordinate to and distinct from theme
m. polyphonic voices based on same thematic material
n. melody with accompaniment
o. persistently repeated pattern

10. Define each of the following terms.

   a. *p* _____
   b. tenuto _____
   c. Arco _____
   d. slur _____
   e. marcato _____
   f. articulation _____
   g. mezzo forte _____
   h. staccato _____
   i. allegro _____
   j. presto _____
   k. rubato _____
   l. tempo _____
   m. legato _____
   n. diminuendo _____
   o. *mp* _____
   p. pizzicato _____
   q. grave _____
   r. andantino _____
   s. accelerando _____
   t. ritenuto _____
   u. crescendo _____
   v. *pp* _____
   w. dynamics _____
   x. lento _____
   y. moderato _____
   z. largo _____

11. Name the instrumental group for each of these instruments.

    a. Violin _____

    b. Horn _____

    c. Baritone _____

    d. tom-tom _____

    e. Xyolphone _____

    f. Piccolo _____

12. Which instrument is used for continuo? _____

13. Match each of the following terms with its definition.

    _____ solo (soli)   a. All performers play

    _____ timbre   b. Only one performer plays

    _____ tutti   c. A part that may be omitted or that must be played, depending on the historical period of the music

    _____ obbligato

    d. The unique quality, sound or tone color of an instrument

14. Match each genre with its definition.

    _____ Interlude   a. Performed at the end of a ceremony

    _____ Song   b. A sonata for orchestra

    _____ Concerto   c. Performed at the beginning of a ceremony

    _____ Sonata   d. Dramatic presentation that is sung and acted

    _____ Prelude   e. Soloist with orchestra

    _____ String quartet   f. Musical composition with lyrics

    _____ Postlude   g. Two violins, viola and cello

    _____ Opera   h. Performed between acts of a play

    _____ Symphony   i. Composition for solo instrument with multiple movements

15. What is the difference between a vocalist's register and his or her tessitura? _____
_____

16. What is the difference between an aria and an art song? _____
_____

17. What is the difference between syllabic and melismatic? _____
_____

18. Write the Roman numerals for the twelve-bar blues pattern. _____

19. Complete the blues scale on the staff below. The first two notes are given.

20. Match each of the following terms with its definition in relation to jazz music.

    _____ bridge

    _____ turnaround

    _____ chorus

    _____ song form

    _____ improvisation

    a. AABA

    b. Music that is created by the performer during the performance

    c. Chords that lead from the end of one section to the beginning of another section

    d. Section of the music that is contrasting in both melody and harmony

    e. The entire melody or tune

ANSWER KEY

LESSON 1: MAJOR AND MINOR KEY SIGNATURES (Pages 1-12)

Page 4

1. E Major, A♭ Major, A Major, B♭ Major, D Major

   F Major, C♯ Major, C Major, G♭ Major, F♯ Major

   G Major, E♭ Major, D♭ Major, C♭ Major, B Major

Page 5

2.

Page 6

3. c♯ minor, e minor, d minor, c minor, b minor, b♭ minor

Page 7

f♯ minor, g minor, a minor, g♯ minor, f minor, e♭ minor

4.

Page 7, No. 4, cont.

Page 8

5. a. G Major
   b. c♯ minor
   c. g minor

Page 9

d. f minor
e. B♭ Major
f. B♭ Major

Page 10

g. E Major
h. A♭ Major
i. F Major

Page 12

6.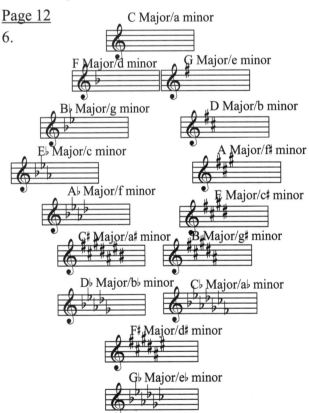

Pages 4-12

354

Page 13	Page 14
7. b	14. d
8. d	15. a
9. d	16. b and c
10. a	17. d
11. b	18. d
12. c	19. d
13. b	20. b

Page 15

Example 1: minor
Example 2: Major
Example 3: Major
Example 4: minor
Example 5: Major
Example 6: minor
Example 7: Major
Example 8: minor
Example 9: Major
Example 10: minor

LESSON 2: SCALES (Pages 16-28)

Page 19

Page 20

Pages 13-21

Page 22

2. a. F# Major
   b. G Major
   c. Ab Major

Page 23

   d. Chromatic
   e. F# Major
   f. Eb Major

Page 24

   g. G Major
   h. Bb Major
   i. Chromatic

Page 25

3. c
4. a
5. d
6. b
7. d

Page 26

8. b
9. c
10. d
11. a
12. b

Page 28

Example 11: melodic minor
Example 12: whole tone
Example 13: chromatic
Example 14: natural minor
Example 15: harmonic minor

Example 16

Example 17

Example 18
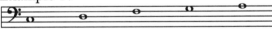

Example 19
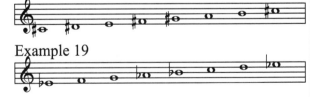

Example 20
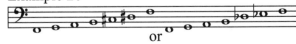

LESSON 3: INTERVALS (Pages 29-38)

Page 31

1. m7, A11, P5, M3, P4, m7, M10, M7

   m10, P12, m2, A6, d13, A8, P4, P8

   d5, m9, m3, M10, P8, d5, d12, A6

2.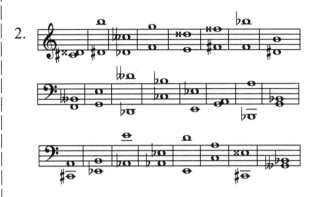

Page 32

3. a. m3, m2, m2, P4, m3, M2, M2

   b. M10, m7, M6, m2, m6

   c. m3, M6, P5, m3, m2, M3

Page 33

4. b
5. a
6. c
7. c
8. d

Page 34

9. a
10. a and c
11. b
12. b and c
13. d

Page 35

14.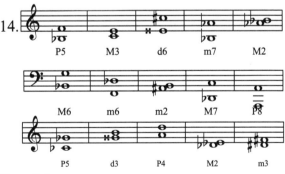

Page 36

15. a   16. c   17. d   18. c   19. a

356

Page 38

Example 21: M3
Example 22: P4
Example 23: m6
Example 24: M2
Example 25: P5

Example 26:

Example 27:

Example 28:

Example 29:

Example 30:

LESSON 4: MODES (Pages 39-50)

Page 41

1. (Given)

2. a. E♭, A♭, B♭
   b. B♭, E♭, A♭
   c. E♭
   d. E♭ to D: 7th note
   e. Locrian

3. a. F♯, G♯, A♯, C♯, D♯, E♯
   b. F♯. C♯, G♯, D♯, A♯, E♯
   c. F♯ Major
   d. F♯ to F♯: first note
   e. Ionian

4. a. C♯, D♯, F♯, G♯
   b. F♯, C♯, G♯, D♯
   c. E Major
   d. E to B: 5th note
   e. Mixolydian

Page 42

5. a. Lydian
   b. Aeolian
   c. Phrygian
   d. Locrian
   e. Mixolydian
   f. Dorian
   g. Ionian
   h. Phrygian

Page 44

6. (Given)

7. a. M3
   b. B♭
   c. B♭, E♭

8. a. M6
   b. E♭
   c. B♭, E♭, A♭

9. a. P5
   b. A
   c. F♯, C♯, G♯

10. a. M7
    b. D
    c. F♯, C♯

Page 45

11. a.
    b.
    c.
    d.
    e.
    f.

Pages 38-45

Page 45, cont.

g.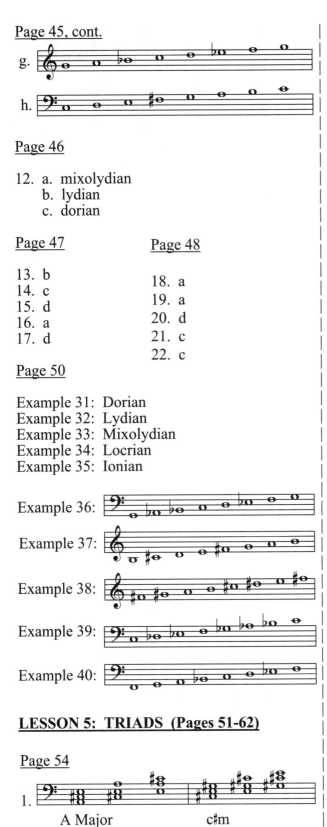

h.

Page 46

12. a. mixolydian
    b. lydian
    c. dorian

Page 47

13. b
14. c
15. d
16. a
17. d

Page 48

18. a
19. a
20. d
21. c
22. c

Page 50

Example 31: Dorian
Example 32: Lydian
Example 33: Mixolydian
Example 34: Locrian
Example 35: Ionian

Example 36:
Example 37:
Example 38:
Example 39:
Example 40:

LESSON 5: TRIADS (Pages 51-62)

Page 54

1. A Major   c#m

   Gb Major   e diminished

Page 54, No. 1, cont.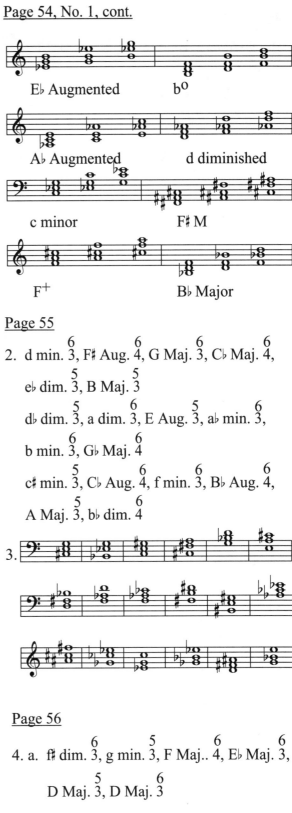

Eb Augmented   b°

Ab Augmented   d diminished

c minor   F# M

F+   Bb Major

Page 55

2. d min. 3, F# Aug. $\substack{6\\4}$, G Maj. $\substack{6\\3}$, Cb Maj. $\substack{6\\4}$,
   eb dim. 3, B Maj. $\substack{5\\3}$
   db dim. $\substack{5\\3}$, a dim. $\substack{6\\3}$, E Aug. $\substack{5\\3}$, ab min. $\substack{6\\3}$,
   b min. 3, Gb Maj. $\substack{6\\4}$
   c# min. $\substack{5\\3}$, Cb Aug. $\substack{6\\4}$, f min. $\substack{6\\3}$, Bb Aug. $\substack{6\\4}$,
   A Maj. $\substack{5\\3}$, bb dim. $\substack{6\\4}$

3.

Page 56

4. a. f# dim. $\substack{6\\3}$, g min. $\substack{5\\3}$, F Maj.. $\substack{6\\4}$, Eb Maj. $\substack{6\\3}$,
   D Maj. $\substack{5\\3}$, D Maj. $\substack{6\\3}$

358

Page 57

4. b. B♭ Maj. $^6_3$, B♭ Maj. $^5_3$, c min. $^6_4$, B♭ Maj. $^6_4$

c. E Maj. $^5_3$, B Maj. $^5_3$, A Maj. $^5_3$, f♯ min. $^5_3$,
d♯ dim. $^6_3$, g♯ min. $^6_3$

d. A♭ Maj. $^5_3$, E♭ Maj. $^6_3$, b♭ min. $^6_3$, A♭ Maj. $^6_3$

Page 58

e. g min. $^5_3$, B♭ Maj. $^5_3$, g♯ dim. $^5_3$, d min. $^5_3$

f. e♭ min. $^5_3$, a♭ min.. $^6_4$, B♭ Maj. $^5_3$, e♭ min. $^5_3$

g. A Maj. $^5_3$, A Maj. $^6_3$, d♯ dim. $^6_3$, d min. $^6_3$,
A Maj. $^6_4$, f♯ min. $^5_3$

Page 59   Page 60

5. a   10. c
6. b   11. a
7. c   12. c
8. a   13. c
9. c   14. d

Page 62

Example 41: Augmented
Example 42: minor
Example 43: diminished
Example 44: Major
Example 45: Augmented
Example 46: $^6_3$
Example 47: $^5_3$
Example 48: $^6_3$
Example 49: $^6_4$
Example 50: $^5_3$

Ex. 51   Ex. 52   Ex. 53   Ex. 54

LESSON 6: PRIMARY AND SECONDARY TRIADS (Pages 63-76)

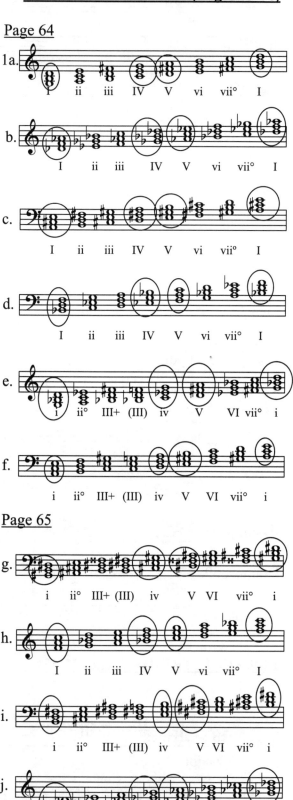

Pages 57-65

Page 65, cont.

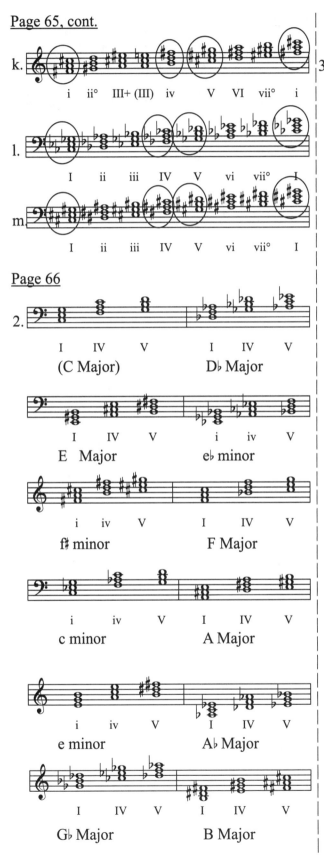

Page 66

Page 67

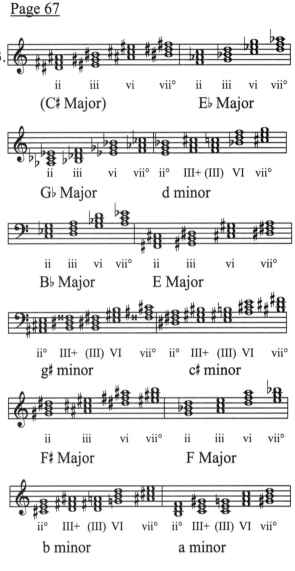

Page 68

4. f, g, a, e, d, c, b

5. Tonic, Supertonic, Mediant, Subdominant, Dominant, Submediant, Leading Tone

Page 70

6. a. Key of B♭ Major: I^6, I, ii^6_4, I^6_4

   b. Key of E Major: I, V, IV, ii, vii^{o6}, iii^6

   c. Key of A♭ Major: I, V^6, ii^6, I^6

360

Page 71

d. Key of d minor: iv, VI, i

e. Key of G Major: I, IV^6, V^6, I, vi^6

f. Key of D Major: I, vi, IV, IV^6, ii^6

Page 72

g. Key of b minor: i$^6_4$, V^6, iv^6

7. IV$^6_4$, vi$^6_3$, I$^6_3$, V$^5_3$, ii$^6_4$, vii°$^5_3$
   I$^6_4$, vii°$^6_3$, ii$^6_3$, IV$^5_3$, vi$^6_3$, vi$^5_4$

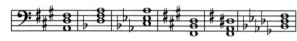

Page 73

9. a
10. d
11. c
12. a
13. a

Page 74

14. b
15. b
16. d
17. a
18. c

Page 76

Example 55: I   IV   V7   I

Example 56: I   IV$^6_4$ V$^6_5$ I

Example 57: I   vi   ii   V7   I

Example 58: i   iv$^6_4$ ii°   V$^6_5$ i

Example 59: I   iii   IV   vii°   I

Example 60: I   vi^6 IV   ii   V   I

Example 61:

Example 62:

Page 76, cont.

Example 63:

Example 64:

Example 65:

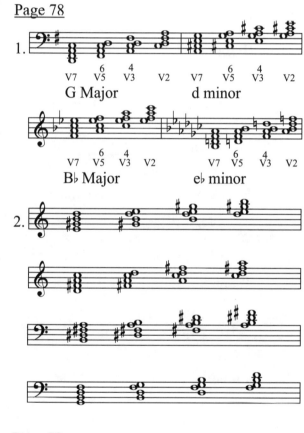

LESSON 7: SEVENTH CHORDS
(Pages 77-88)

Page 78

1.

V7 V$^6_5$ V$^4_3$ V2   V7 V$^6_5$ V$^4_3$ V2

G Major   d minor

V7 V$^6_5$ V$^4_3$ V2   V7 V$^6_5$ V$^4_3$ V2

B♭ Major   e♭ minor

2.

Page 79

3.

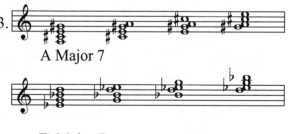

A Major 7

E♭ Major 7

Page 79, No. 3, cont.

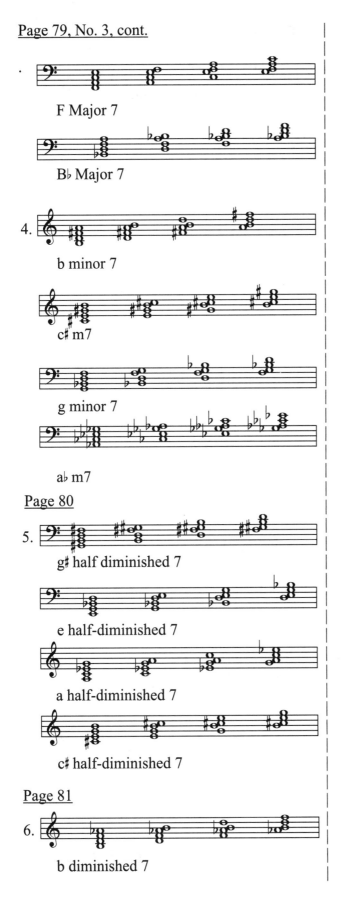

F Major 7

B♭ Major 7

4. b minor 7

c♯ m7

g minor 7

a♭ m7

Page 80

5. g♯ half diminished 7

e half-diminished 7

a half-diminished 7

c♯ half-diminished 7

Page 81

6. b diminished 7

Page 81, No. 6, cont.

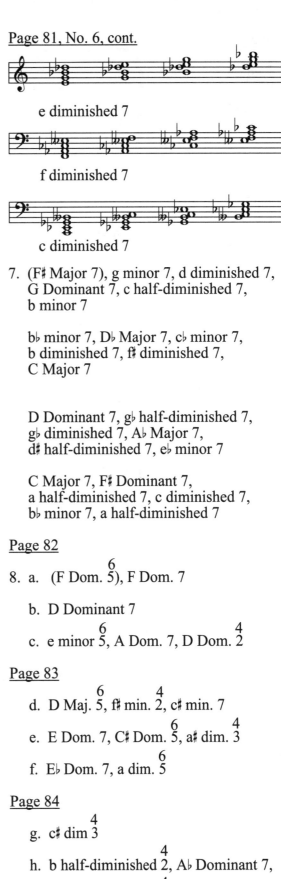

e diminished 7

f diminished 7

c diminished 7

7. (F♯ Major 7), g minor 7, d diminished 7, G Dominant 7, c half-diminished 7, b minor 7

b♭ minor 7, D♭ Major 7, c♭ minor 7, b diminished 7, f♯ diminished 7, C Major 7

D Dominant 7, g♭ half-diminished 7, g♭ diminished 7, A♭ Major 7, d♯ half-diminished 7, e♭ minor 7

C Major 7, F♯ Dominant 7, a half-diminished 7, c diminished 7, b♭ minor 7, a half-diminished 7

Page 82

8. a. (F Dom. $\overset{6}{5}$), F Dom. 7

b. D Dominant 7

c. e minor $\overset{6}{5}$, A Dom. 7, D Dom. $\overset{4}{2}$

Page 83

d. D Maj. $\overset{6}{5}$, f♯ min. $\overset{4}{2}$, c♯ min. 7

e. E Dom. 7, C♯ Dom. $\overset{6}{5}$, a♯ dim. $\overset{4}{3}$

f. E♭ Dom. 7, a dim. $\overset{6}{5}$

Page 84

g. c♯ dim $\overset{4}{3}$

h. b half-diminished $\overset{4}{2}$, A♭ Dominant 7, d half-diminished $\overset{4}{2}$, b minor 7

Pages 79-84

Page 85

9. b
10. c
11. d
12. b
13. d

Page 86

14. a
15. c
16. d
17. a
18. d

Page 88

Example 66: diminished 7th
Example 67: Major 7th
Example 68: half-diminished 7th
Example 69: minor 7th
Example 70: Dominant 7th

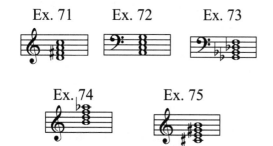

Ex. 71   Ex. 72   Ex. 73

Ex. 74   Ex. 75

LESSON 8: SECONDARY CHORDS
(Pages 90-98)

Page 90

Page 91

Page 92

3. a. Key of F Major: V/vi, vi

   b. Key of A Major: vii^{o6}/IV, IV^6; V^2/V, V^6

Page 93

   c. Key of C Major: V^2/V, V^6; V^2/IV, IV^6

   d. Key of G Major: V$^4_3$/V, V

   e. Key of G Major: V7/IV, IV$^6_4$

Page 94

   f. Key of E♭ Major: vii^{o7}/vi, vi

   g. Key of F Major: V7/IV, IV$^6_4$

   h. Key of G Major: vii^o/V, V; vii^o/IV, IV

Page 95

4. a
5. c
6. b
7. c
8. a

Page 96

9. c
10. c
11. d
12. c
13. a

Page 98

Example 76: V7/V, V
Example 77: V7/IV, IV
Example 78: V7/ii, ii
Example 79: vii^o/iii, iii
Example 80: V/vi, vi

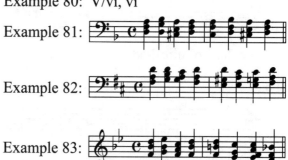

Example 81:

Example 82:

Example 83:

Page 98, cont.

Example 84:

Example 85:

LESSON 9: CADENCES (Pages 99-110)

Page 100

Page 101

2. V^6-I, authentic; iv-i^6, plagal;

   V^6-vi6, deceptive; I-V^6, half

   IV-I^6, plagal; iv^6-V, phrygian half;
   V-i^6_4, authentic; i-V^6_5, half

   V^4_3-i^6, authentic; I-V^6_5, half;
   V^6_4-i^6, authentic; IV^6_4-I, plagal

   iv^6-i^6_4, plagal; ii^6-V7, half;

   V2-I^6, authentic; iv^6-V, phrygian half

Page 102

3. perfect, imperfect, imperfect, perfect, imperfect

Page 103

4. V-I, perfect authentic; i-v, half; IV-I, plagal; V-vi, deceptive

   iv-V, half; V-i^6_4, imperfect authentic; V-i, perfect authentic, iv-i, plagal

   V-I, imperfect authentic; iv^6-V, phrygian half; I-V, half; V-VI, deceptive

Page 104

5. a. Key of e minor: V7-vi, deceptive
   b. Key of A Major; I^6_4-V, half

Page 105

   c. Key of B♭ Major: IV-I, plagal
   d. Key of E♭ Major: V-i, perfect authentic
   e. Key of E♭ Major: V7-I, imperfect authentic

Page 106

   f. Key of D Major: V7-vi, deceptive
   g. Key of B♭ Major: V7-I, perfect authentic
   h. Key of G Major: V7-I, perfect authentic

364

Page 107
6. b
7. c
8. a and d
9. b
10. c

Page 108
11. b
12. a and b
13. d
14. d
15. b

Page 110

Example 86: Plagal
Example 87: Half
Example 88: Phrygian Half
Example 89: Deceptive
Example 90: Perfect Authentic

Example 91:
Example 92:
Example 93:
Example 94:
Example 95:

REVIEW: LESSONS 1-9 (Pages 111-114)

Page 111

1.

2. d harmonic minor

G♭ Major

e melodic minor

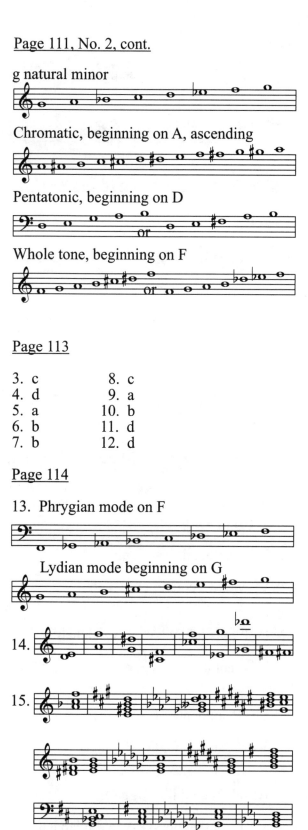

Page 111, No. 2, cont.

g natural minor

Chromatic, beginning on A, ascending

Pentatonic, beginning on D

Whole tone, beginning on F

Page 113

3. c   8. c
4. d   9. a
5. a   10. b
6. b   11. d
7. b   12. d

Page 114

13. Phrygian mode on F

Lydian mode beginning on G

14.

15.

Pages 107-114

Page 114, cont.

iv^6-V, phrygian half; V-VI, deceptive;

V-I, perfect authentic; IV-I, plagal;

V-I$^6_4$, imperfect authentic

LESSON 10: MELODIC DEVICES
(Pages 115-126)

Page 119   Page 120

1. c   6. d
2. d   7. b
3. a   8. b
4. b   9. a
5. c   10. b

Page 121   Page 122

11. b   14. b
12. d   15. a
13. c   16. d

Page 123

22. d, b, c, a

Page 124

23. c
24. a
25. d
26. b

Page 126

Example 96: Rhythmic Transformation
Example 97: Truncation
Example 98: Augmentation
Example 99: Imitation
Example 100: Sequence

Example 101:

Example 102:

Example 103:

Example 104:

Example 105:

LESSON 11: PHRASE STRUCTURE
(Pages 127-138)

Page 131-135   Page 136

1. b   6. a
2. a   7. c
3. d   8. b
4. c   9. c
5. c   10. c
                     11. c

Page 138

Example 106: Contrasting Period
Example 107: Parallel Period
Example 108: Antecedent/Consequent
Example 109: Double Period
Example 110: Phrase Group

LESSON 12: ORNAMENTS AND NON-HARMONIC TONES (Pages 139-152)

Page 143

1. a. anticipation
   b. lower neighbor (neighbor note)

Page 144

   c. upper neighbor (neighbor note)
   d. chromatic passing tone
   e. accented passing tone
   f. appoggiatura

Page 145

   g. ostinato (pedal point)
   h. appoggiatura
   i. lower neighbor (neighbor note)
   j. upper neighbor (neighbor note)

Page 146

   k. double neighbor
   l. escape tone
   m. rearticulated suspension
   n. pedal point

Page 147

   o. trill
   p. turn
   q. mordent
   r. grace note

Page 148

   s. appoggiatura

2. d
3. a

Page 149	Page 150
4. b	7. c
5. c	8. a
6. d	9. d
	10. b
	11. a
	12. a

Page 152

Example 111: Pedal Point
Example 112: Mordent
Example 113: Suspension
Example 114: Ostinato
Example 115: Accented Passing Tone

Example 116:

Example 117:

Example 118:

Example 119:

Example 120:

LESSON 13: HARMONIC FUNCTION (Pages 153-166)

Page 154

1. a. Key of D Major; tonic, pre-dominant, dominant
   b. Key of G Major; tonic, dominant
   c. Key of D♭ Major; dominant, tonic

Page 155

   d. Key of D Major, temporarily in e minor; dominant, dominant, tonic
   e. Key of D Major; dominant, tonic
   f. Key of F Major, temporarily in key of a minor; pre-dominant, dominant, tonic
   g. Key of G Major, temporarily in key of D Major; tonic, pre-dominant, dominant

Page 157

2. a. passing
   b. neighboring
   c. cadential
   d. arpeggiating

Page 160

3. One chord per measure (every 3 beats)

4.

5. a. fast
   b. deceptive

6. a. (A Major), d minor, G Major, C Major
   b. circle of fifths (V-I)

Page 161

7. slow
8. deceptive progression

Page 162	Page 163	Page 164
9. d	13. b	17. a
10. c	14. c	18. b
11. a	15. c	19. c
12. c	16. d	20. c

Page 166

Example 121: Slow rate of harmonic change
Example 122: Deceptive Progression
Example 123: Retrogression
Example 124: Circle of fifths
Example 125: Neighbor chords

Example 126: (IV - Predominant),
   V7 - dominant, I - tonic
Example 127: I$^6_4$ - Cadential $^6_4$,
   V7 - dominant, I - tonic
Example 128: I, I$^6_4$, I - arpeggiating $^6_4$
Example 129: I, IV$^6_4$, I - neighboring $^6_4$
Example 130: I$^6_4$, V7, I - Cadential $^6_4$

LESSON 14: TONICIZATION AND MODULATION (Pages 167-178)

Pages 169-174

1. a. Original key: C Major
      Modulates to: G Major
      Type: Pivot Chord
   b. Original key: A Major
      Modulates to: f♯ minor
      Type: Common tone
   c. Modulates to: E♭ Major
      Type: common tone
2. a. Measures 9-16
   b. Parallel major and minor
3. In measure 4 (second line, first measure):

Page 175	Page 176
4. b	8. c
5. b	9. c
6. b	10. b
7. a	11. c

Page 178

Example 131: Phrase modulation
Example 132: Tonicization
Example 133: Common tone modulation
Example 134: Pivot chord modulation
Example 135: Tonicization
Example 136: Phrase modulation
Example 137: Pivot chord modulation
Example 138: Common tone modulation

LESSON 15: ALTERED CHORDS AND SUSPENSIONS (Pages 179-184)

Page 179

1.

Page 179, cont.

2.

Page 181

3. $V^6_5 - I$ 4-3 $V^6_5 - I$ 9-8 $I - IV^{7-6}_4$

   $V^6_5 - I$ 4-3

4. Picardy third

5. a. Key of a minor: (IV 4-3); I 9-8

   b. Key of d minor: i 4-3

Page 183

   c. Key of C Major: vi 4-3

6. b
7. a
8. a
9. d

Page 184

Example 139: ♯5
Example 140: ♭5
Example 141: ♮5
Example 142: ♭3
Example 143: 9-8
Example 144: 7-6
Example 145: 4-3
Example 146: 7-6

LESSON 16: INTRODUCTION TO FOUR PART HARMONY (Pages 185-192)

Page 185

1. S, A;   S, A, T;   S;   A;   B;

   A, T, B;   A, T;   B

Page 186, No. 2.

Page 187

3. Upbeat and measure 1: (I, N; I6, B♭,);
   vii°6, C, 3; I, B♭, R
   Measure 2: IV, E♭, R; IV6, G, 3
   Measure 3: I, F, 5; vi, G, R; IV, E♭, R
   Measure 4: V, F, R

Page 188

4. (Other voicings are possible)

I   V   IV   ii   vi   iii

5.

I vi V I IV   I   ii6 IV I$^6_4$ V7   I

6.

I I IV I IV   I   IV ii I$^6_4$ V   I

Page 188, cont.

Page 189

8. open, close, open, close, open, close, open, close

9. (Other voicings are possible)

10. I V^6 I I V^6 V$^{8-7}$I IV V$^4_2$ I4^6 IV^6 I4^6 V$^{8-7}$I

Page 190

11. a
12. a
13. c
14. c
15. a

Page 192

Example 147

Page 192, Example 147, cont.

LESSON 17: DOUBLING (Pages 193-200)

Page 193

1. (Other voicings are possible)

Page 194

2. (Other voicings are possible)

3. (Other voicings are possible)

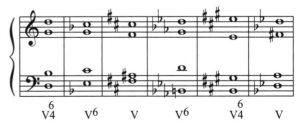

Page 195

4. (Other voicings are possible)

vii°   vii°6   vii°$^6_4$ vii°   vii°6   vii°$^6_4$

5. (Other voicings are possible)

VI   VI   vi   VI   vi   vi

Page 196

6. (Other voicings are possible)

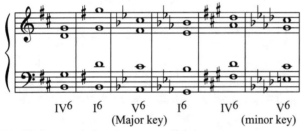

IV6   I6   V6   I6   IV6   V6
(Major key)   (minor key)

7. (Other voicings are possible)

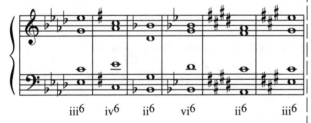

iii6   iv6   ii6   vi6   ii6   iii6

Page 197

8. (Other voicings are possible)

IV$^6_4$ I$^6_4$ V$^6_4$ ii$^6_4$

Page 197, cont.

9. (Other voicings are possible)

V$^6_5$ V7   V$^6_5$ V2   V$^6_5$

Page 198

10. (Other voicings are possible)

III+   ii°   V/iii   V/V   ii°   III+

11. (1, tonic), 5th (dominant), 2nd (supertonic), 1 (tonic), 1 (tonic), 5th (dominant)

Page 199

12. (Other voicings are possible)

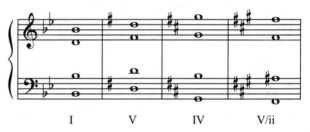

I   V   IV   V/ii

Page 200

13. a
14. c
15. b
16. b
17. c

Page 201

18. a
19. d
20. d
21. c
22. d

Page 202

Example 148

LESSON 18: HARMONIC PROGRESSION
Pages 203-212

Page 203

1. a. I V I   I V I   I V   I V I

Page 204

   b. I I V I
       I I V I
       I I V I
       I I V I

Page 205

2. a. I I IV I
      I I V V
      V I IV I
      IV I I V I

   b. I I I I
      IV I V V
      I I I I
      IV I V I

Page 206

3. a. IV or ii
   b. IV
   c. ii

Page 207

4. a. vi   b. I   c. V   d. ii   e. vii°   f. iii

Page 207, cont.

5. a. ii   V
   b. ii   V
   c. iii   vi

Page 208

6. (Other progressions are possible)
   a. I   IV   V   I
   b. I   vi   IV   I   ii   V   I
   c. I   iii   vi   IV   V   I

Page 209

7. (Other progressions are possible)
   a. vi   vi   V7
   b. vi   ii   V7
   c. vii°   V7

8. (Other progressions are possible)
   I   vi^6 IV$^6_4$ ii   V^6 V$^6_5$ I   V7   I

Page 210

9. c
10. a
11. c
12. d
13. b

Page 212, Example 149

LESSON 19: INTRODUCTION TO VOICE LEADING (Pages 213-220)

Page 215

1. oblique, parallel, similar, oblique, parallel, contrary

2. direct octaves, voice exchange, direct fifths, crossed voices & direct octaves

Page 216

Page 217	Page 218
4. b	9. b
5. a	10. c
6. c	11. a
7. d	12. d
8. b	13. c

Page 220, Example 150

Page 220, Example 150, cont.

LESSON 20: POOR VOICE LEADING (Pages 221-226)

Page 222

1. a. (Parallel 5ths between soprano and alto)

Page 223

   b. Cross relation of A4 from soprano to bass
   c. Parallel 5ths between soprano and alto
   d. Parallel octaves between soprano and bass
   e. Overlapping voices between soprano and alto
   f. 7th resolves down instead of up a half-step in soprano

Page 224

2. c
3. a
4. b
5. d
6. a

Page 226, Example 151

Page 226, Example 151, cont.

LESSON 21: REALIZING FIGURED BASS (Pages 227-234)

Page 227

1. a. I I^6 vi V6 I IV I$^6_4$ V I

   b. I vii^{o6} I^6 IV I$^6_4$ V I

Page 228

2.

Page 229

3.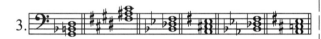

4.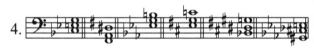

Page 230

5. (4-3) 9-8 8-7 7-6   7-6   6-5
                        4   6

Page 231

7. b
8. d
9. a
10. c
11. a

Page 232

12. c
13. b
14. d
15. b
16. c

Page 234

Example 152:

I I IV I V$^6_5$ I V   I I^6 I V ii7 vii^{o6}/V V

I V vi IV V V7 I   V6/vi vi V I   I V I

Example 153

17. c   20. d
18. b   21. a
19. a

LESSON 22: FOUR PART WRITING

Page 235

Pages 226-235

374

Page 235, cont.

Pages 235-238

Page 240

Example 154

Example 155

14. b   17. d
15. b   18. a
16. a

REVIEW: LESSONS 10-23 (Pages 241-244)

Page 241

1. o, h, b, j, d, f, l, a, c, e, k, n, g, m, q, i, r, p

2. retardation, escape tone, unaccented passing tones, appoggiatura, trill, upper neighbor

   ostinato, grace note, double neighbor, passing tone, appoggiatura, accented passing tone

   mordent, chromatic passing tone, rearticulated suspension, turn, suspension, pedal point

   neighbor group (cambiata, changing tones, or changing notes), anticipation, lower neighbor, suspension chain

Page 242

3. a. parallel period
   b. double period
   c. phrase group (phrase chain)
   d. antecedent/consequent
   e. contrasting period
   f. elision

Page 242, cont.

4. a. I
   b. V, V7, vii°
   c. IV, ii, vi

5. a. neighboring $^6_4$
   b. cadential $^6_4$
   c. passing $^6_4$
   d. arpeggiating $^6_4$

Page 243

6. a. neighboring chords
   b. circle of fifths
   c. deceptive progression
   d. retrogression
   e. harmonic rhythm (rate of harmonic change)

7. a. tonicization
   b. modulation
   c. pivot chord modulation
   d. common tone modulation
   e. phrase modulation

8.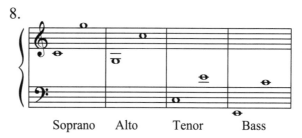

    Soprano   Alto   Tenor   Bass

9. close, close, open, open

Page 244

10. a. R   d. R   g. S
    b. C   e. S   h. C
    c. S   f. C   i. C

11. (Other answers are possible)

Page 244, cont.

12. I I I I V7 I$^6_4$ V V7 I V7/IV IV$^6_4$ ii^6 I$^6_4$ V$^{8-7}$ I

13. (Other answers are possible)

14. (Other answers are possible)

LESSON 23: INTERPRETING LEAD SHEETS (Pages 245-252)

Page 246

1. (Other answers are possible)

Page 247

2.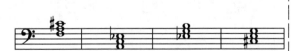

Page 247, cont.

3.

Page 248

4.

5. G dim (G°, G m♭5, Gmin♭5, G-♭5), Bmin7, D Aug (D+5), A sus4

   E♭9, B♭, Fdim7, A♭+2

   F♯7, DMaj9, Adim (Am♭5, Am-5), Esus4

   Em (Emin, E-), FMaj7, C♯min9, G min7♭5

Page 249   Page 250

6. b   11. c
7. d   12. b
8. d   13. c
9. a   14. b
10. c   15. d

Page 252

Example 156

Example 157

16. d   18. b
17. d   19. c

LESSON 24: FORM AND STRUCTURE
Pages 254-276

Page 254

1. Rhythm
2. Melody, Harmony
3. G Major
4. G Major
5. V/V (or V7 of V)
6. 24

Page 256

7. no
8. G Major
9. e minor
10. 25
11. 33
12. shorter

Page 257

13. Yes
14. very different
15. 20 or 21

Page 263

16. d minor
17. Dominant
18. 88

Page 264

19. (Other answers are possible.) Melody is in right hand; steady left-hand accompaniment; motives end with eighth notes instead of half notes
20. (Other answers are possible.) Melody is changed; motives move between hands; introduction of chords

Page 265

21. no
22. no

Page 266

23. no
24. no
25. yes

Page 267

26. no
27. yes

Page 268

28. There are three verses, all sung to the same melody
29. no

Page 269

30. Rhythm
31. no

Page 270

32. no
33. similar
34. yes

Page 272	Page 273	Page 274
35. b	40. a	45. b and d
36. a	41. c	46. c
37. d	42. b	47. a
38. c	43. d	
39. a	44. b	

Page 276

Example 158

Example 159

48. b   50. a
49. d   51. b

LESSON 25: THE FUGUE (Pages 277-284)

Page 280

1. d
2. yes
3. E♭ Major
4. relative major
5. Picardy Third

Page 281

6. b
7. c
8. a
9. c
10. d

Page 282

11. a
12. d
13. b

Example 160

14. a
15. c
16. b
17. c

Page 284

Example 161

LESSON 26: RHYTHM AND METER (Pages 285-298)

Page 288

1. (Sub-beats may be written differently)

2. d
3. c and d
4. b
5. a

Page 291

6. a. $\frac{9}{8}$ compound triple meter

   b. $\frac{6}{8}\frac{9}{8}\frac{12}{8}$ changing meter or multimeter

   c. $\frac{3}{4}$ simple triple meter

   d. $\frac{2}{4}$ simple duple meter

   e. $\frac{4}{2}$ simple quadruple meter

   f. $\frac{5}{4}$ irregular or assymetrical meter

Page 294

Page 294, cont.

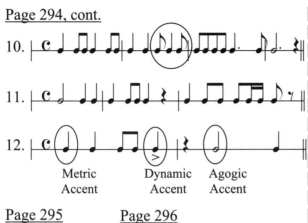

Metric Accent   Dynamic Accent   Agogic Accent

Page 295   Page 296

13. d   18. a
14. b   19. b and c
15. d   20. d
16. a and c   21. a
17. d   22. b and d

Page 298

Example 162:
Example 163:
Example 164:
Example 165:

Example 166

23. a   25. c
24. a   26. c

LESSON 27: TEXTURE (Pages 299-312)

Page 304

1. a. homophonic texture
   b. polyphonic texture
   c. monophonic texture

Page 305

2. c, e, a, d, b, f

Page 306

3. e, b, d, a, c

Page 306, cont.

4. a
5. d

Page 307   Page 307   Page 308

6. c   10. d   14. c
7. d   11. a   15. b
8. b   12. c   16. d
9. a   13. c   17. a

Page 310

18. b

Page 311: Example 167

I   I vi V6 V/V V   I6 V$_3^4$ I IV V$_3^4$

vi   iii vi V6 ii$_5^6$ V/V V   ii IV I vi ii

V/V   vi iii IV I vi ii V7 I

Page 312: Example 168

19. a   21. d
20. d   22. c

LESSON 28: PERFORMANCE TERMS
(Pages 313-320)

Page 314

1. a. arco
   b. legato
   c. accent
   d. staccato
   e. tenuto
   f. slur
   g. pizzicato
   h. marcato

Page 315

2. a. *ff*
   b. *p*
   c. *crescendo, cresc.,* <
   d. *pp*
   e. *f*
   f. *mf*
   g. *decrescendo, dimuendo,* >
   h. terraced dynamics
   i. *mp*

Page 316

3. a. *accelerando*
   b. *rubato*
   c. Andante
   d. Presto
   e. Lento
   f. Grave
   g. Adagio
   h. Vivace
   i. Andantino
   j. *ritenuto*
   k. Allegro
   l. Largo
   m. *ritardando (ritard., rit.)*
   n. Moderato
   o. Allegretto

Page 317

4. a. articulation
   b. dynamics
   c. articulation
   d. articulation
   e. tempo
   f. tempo
   g. dynamics
   h. articulation

Page 317, cont.

5. b
6. c
7. d

Page 318

8. a   11. d
9. c   12. d
10. d   13. a

Page 320

Example 169

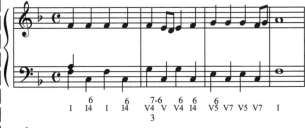

Example 170
14. b   16. c
15. c   17. d

LESSON 29: INSTRUMENTAL TERMS
(Pages 321-326)

Page 322

1. a. brass
   b. strings
   c. woodwinds
   d. woodwinds
   e. percussion
   f. brass
   g. strings
   h. woodwinds
   i. brass
   j. woodwinds
   k. woodwinds

Page 323

2. a. The unique quality, sound, or tone color of each specific instrument
   b. Alone: a single performer, a passage in an orchestral work for a single performer, a solo instrument in a concerto, or orchestral passages played by only a few of the instrumentalists
   c. A part that can be omitted, or in music of the 18th century, a part that must be played
   d. The entire orchestra

3. d
4. a

Page 324

5. b
6. d
7. a
8. c
9. a
10. a

Page 326

Example 171

Example 172

11. b   13. d
12. a   14. a

LESSON 30: GENRE (Pages 327-332)

Page 328   Page 329

1. a   6. b
2. a   7. a
3. d   8. c
4. c   9. d
5. c   10. d

Page 331

Example 173

Page 332

Example 174

11. a
12. c
13. c
14. b

LESSON 31: VOCAL TERMS
(Pages 333-338)

Page 337   Page 338

1. b   4. b
2. a   5. b
3. c   6. a
                7. c

Page 340

Example 175

Example 176

8. d   10. b
9. a   11. d

LESSON 32: JAZZ TERMS
(Pages 341-346)

Page 344

1. d   4. b
2. a   5. c
3. a   6. b

Page 346

Example 177

Page 346, Example 177, cont.

Example 178

7. b   9. a
8. c   10. d

REVIEW: LESSONS 23-32 (Pages 347-352

Page 347

1. (Other inversions are possible)

2. (Other answers are possible)

3. k, h, a, b, i, m, d, j, g, l, c, e, f

Page 348

4. f, b, g, c, h, d, e, a

5.

6. a. anacrusis, upbeat, pickup
   b. duplet (tuplet)
   c. hemiola
   d. syncopation
   e. measure 4, beat 2: agogic
      measure 6, beat 1: metric
      measure 7, beat 4: dynamic

Page 349

7. a. crossrhythm or polyrhythm
   b. polyrhythm
   c. swing rhythm

8. a. simple quadruple
   b. compound quadruple
   c. simple duple
   d. irregular or assymetrical
   e. simple triple
   f. changing meter or multimeter
   g. compound triple
   h. compound duple

9. e, a, o, d, m, c, n, j, b, k, f, i, h, l, g

10. a. soft
    b. hold the note for its full value
    c. bow the strings
    d. curved line that indicates legato
    e. marked or stressed
    f. terms or symbols that indicate how to execute the notes
    g. medium loud
    h. detached
    i. cheerful, joyful, fast, quick
    j. faster than allegro
    k. robbed time, flexible tempo
    l. signs or terms that indicate speed
    m. connected, smooth
    n. gradually softer
    o. medium soft
    p. pluck the strings
    q. slow, somber
    r. slightly faster than andante
    s. gradually faster
    t. immediately slower
    u. gradually louder
    v. very soft
    w. terms/symbols that indicate volume
    x. slow
    y. medium or moderate tempo
    z. very slow and dignified, broad

Page 351

11. a. strings
    b. brass
    c. brass
    d. percussion
    e. percussion
    f. woodwinds

Page 351, cont.

12. keyboard

13. b, d, a, c

14. h, f, e, i, c, g, a, d, b

Page 352

15. register is all notes a vocalist can sing, tessitura is the general lie of the voice or the most comfortable region of the voice

16. Aria is an elaborate vocal composition, usually contained in a larger work such as a cantata or oratorio. An Art Song is a song for piano and vocalist, usually not as long or as elaborate as Arias.

17. Syllabic music has one note for each word. Melismatic music has many notes for one word.

18. I I I I IV IV I I V IV I I

19.

20. d, c, e, a, b

References

Aldwell, Edward and Carl Schachter. *Harmony and Voice Leading, Third Edition.* United States: Thompson/Schirmer, 2003.

Apel, Willi, ed. *Harvard Dictionary of Music, Second Edition.* Massachusetts: The Belknap Press of Harvard University Press, 1972.

Arnold, Denis, ed. *The New Oxford Companion to Music.* New York: Oxford University Press, 1983.

Badura-Skoda, Eva and Paul. *Interpreting Mozart on the Keyboard.* New York: St. Martin's Press, 1962.

Benjamin, Thomas, Michael Horvit, and Robert Nelson. *Techniques and Materials of Music, Seventh Edition.* United States: Thompson/Schirmer, 2008.

Berry, Wallace. *Structural Functions in Music.* New Jersey: Prentice-Hall, Inc., 1976.

Cole, Richard and Ed Schwartz. *Virginia Tech Multimedia Dictionary.* http://www.music.vt.edu/musicdictionary, 1996-2006.

Foote, Arthur and Walter R. Spalding. *Modern Harmony in its Theory and Practice.* New York: The Arthur P. Schmidt Co., 1936.

Gehrkens, Karl W. *Music Notation and Terminology.* San Francisco: Laidlaw Brothers, 1914.

Goetschius, Percy. *Lessons in Music Form: A Manual of Analysis of All the Structural Factors and Designs.* Boston: Oliver Ditson Company, 1904.

Goodrich, A.J. *Complete Musical Analysis.* New York: The John Church Co., 1889.

Hindemith, Paul. *Traditional Harmony, Books 1 and 2.* New York: Schott Music Corporation, 1968.

Kohs, Ellis B. *Music Theory, Volume II.* New York: Oxford University Press, 1961.

Kostka, Stefan and Dorothy Payne. *Tonal Harmony, Fifth Edition.* San Francisco: McGraw Hill, 2004.

Lovelock, William. *The Rudiments of Music.* New York: St. Martin's Press, 1971.

McHose, Allen Irvine. *The Contrapuntal Harmonic Technique of the 18th Century.* New Jersey: Prentice-Hall, Inc., 1947.

Persichetti, Vincent. *Twentieth-Century Harmony.* New York: W.W. Norton & Company, Inc., 1961.

Piston, Walter. *Harmony, Third Edition.* New York: W.W. Norton & Company Inc., 1969.

Reed, Owen. *Basic Music.* New York: Mills Music, Inc., 1954.

Salzer, Felix. *Structural Hearing, Volumes One and Two.* New York: Dover Publications, Inc., 1962

Salzer, Felix, and Carl Schachter. *Counterpoint in Composition.* San Francisco: McGraw-Hill Book Company, 1969.

Soderlund, Gustave Fredric. *Direct Approach to Counterpoint in 16th Century Style.* New Jersey: Prentice-Hall, Inc., 1947.

Winold, Allen. *Elements of Musical Understanding.* New Jersey: Prentice Hall, 1966.

Printed music and audio files created with Finale music notation software

CD Example 172: String Quartet No. 6, SZ 114 by Bela Bartok. © Copyright 1941 by Hawkes & Son (London) Ltd.

Index

Accent, 140, 143, 150, 152, 289, 292-294, 296, 313, 318, 348

Accented passing tone, 140, 143, 150, 152

Accidentals, 19, 30, 33, 40-41, 43-44, 47-48, 86, 91, 95-96, 179, 229, 248

Aeolian mode, 40, 43, 45, 48, 50

Agogic accent, 292-294, 296

Alberti bass, 234, 240, 298, 300, 305, 307, 309, 326, 332, 349

Alto, 185, 187-191, 202, 211, 213-215, 218-219, 222, 225, 233, 235, 237, 239, 243, 310, 325, 330

Anacrusis, 288, 296

Antecedent, 127, 131, 136, 138, 282

Anticipation, 139, 143, 150, 152, 234, 252, 276

Antiphon, 270, 272-273

Antiphonal, 270, 274, 347

Appoggiatura, 139-140, 142-143, 150, 234, 282, 340

Arco, 313, 317, 350

Aria, 334, 336-338, 352

Arpeggiated, 51, 59, 240

Arpeggiating 6/4, 156-157, 162, 166, 346

Arpeggio, 240, 298, 332

Art song, 336-338, 352

Articulation, 313-314, 317, 350

Ascending, 11, 18-21, 111, 332

Assymetrical meter, 290

Augmentation, 117-120, 124, 126, 234, 241, 292, 294

Augmented intervals, 30-36, 113, 221, 280

Augmented triad, 51-52, 54, 59-60, 62-63, 73-74, 113, 198, 232, 246

Authentic cadence, 99-104, 107-110, 127, 129-130, 252, 332, 340

Auxiliary tone, 139, 141-142, 150, 234

Bar line, 285

Bass (vocal), 185, 187, 189-191, 202, 211, 213-214, 218-221, 225-226, 234, 236-237, 239-240, 243-244, 252, 276, 310-311, 320, 325-326, 330-331, 340, 346

Beat, 139-142, 150, 159, 163, 176, 285-290, 292-293, 295-296, 312, 348

Beat type, 285

Binary, 253-254, 256-257, 272, 347

Brass, 321-324, 326

Bridge, 343-344, 352

Cadence, 99-110, 114, 127, 129-130, 136, 150, 156, 158, 242, 252, 282, 332, 340, 344

Cadential 6/4, 156-158, 166, 197, 199, 201, 209, 234, 346

Cadential extension, 100, 106, 234, 340

Call and response, 270, 273

Cambiata, 139, 143, 149-150, 152

Canon, 240, 303, 306-307, 309, 349

Canonic, 303

Changing meter, 291, 296, 340

Changing notes, 139, 143

Changing tone, 139, 143

Chordal accompaniment, 300, 305, 307-309, 349

Chordal homophony, 276

Chordal texture, 299, 305-306

Chorus, 267, 273, 274, 338, 343-344, 347, 352

Chromatic, 18-21, 25-26, 28, 33, 111, 113, 140, 143, 221, 224, 332, 342

Circle of fifths, 11-12, 14, 158, 161-163, 166

Close position, 187-190, 243

Coda, 265-266, 273-274, 328, 340, 347

Codetta, 265, 273, 274, 340, 347

Common Practice Style, 63, 185, 193, 224, 238

Common tone, 168-169, 175-176, 178, 213, 217-218

Common tone modulation, 168-169, 175-176, 178

Compound beat, 285-286

Compound interval, 31, 33, 113, 180, 290

Concerto, 323, 327-329, 351

Conclusive cadence, 99, 107

Conjunct, 117, 120, 122, 213, 241, 346

Consequent, 127, 131, 136, 138, 234, 282

Consonance, consonant, 1, 180

Continuo, 227, 322, 324, 351

Contour, 116, 241

Contrapuntal, 302, 304, 307, 309

Contrary motion, 139, 214, 217

Contrasting period, 128-129, 132-134, 136, 138

Countermelody, 118-119, 124, 241, 281, 301, 305, 308-309, 349

Counterpoint, 302, 349

Crescendo, 314, 318, 350

Cross relation, 221, 224

Cross rhythm, 293, 295-296

Crossed voices, 215, 217-218

Deceptive cadence, 99-101, 103-104, 107-110, 130, 158, 252, 332

Deceptive progression, 158, 161, 163, 166

Descending, 18-21, 111, 332

Diatonic, 17, 26

Diminished intervals, 29-32, 34-36, 113, 195

Diminished seventh chord, 80-81, 85-86, 88-89, 96, 113, 228, 247, 250

Diminished triad, 51-52, 54, 59-60, 62-63, 73-74, 80, 85, 95-96, 113, 198, 232, 246

Diminished-diminished seventh chord, 80, 85

Diminished-minor seventh chord, 80

Diminuendo, 314, 317, 350

Diminution, 117-119, 123, 126, 234, 241, 292, 294

Direct fifths, 215, 217

Direct octaves, 215, 218

Disjunct, 117, 120, 213, 241, 346

Dissonance, dissonant, 1, 180, 141, 298

Dominant function, 153-154, 162-164, 242

Dominant seventh chord, 77-78, 85-86, 88-89, 91, 95-96, 113, 240, 247

Dominant, 68, 74, 77-78, 85-86, 88-91, 95-98, 113, 153-154, 156, 162-164, 197-198, 200, 203, 206, 222, 228, 234, 240, 242, 247, 254, 257-258, 263, 277, 320

Dorian mode, 39, 43, 45, 47-48, 50, 113

Dot, 118, 252, 285-286, 295

Dotted rhythm, 118, 252, 286

Double dot, 285, 295

Double neighbor, 139, 143

Double period, 129, 131-136, 138, 282, 298

Doubling, 187, 189-190, 193-202

Duple meter, 289-290, 295-296

Duplet, 287-288, 295

Duration, 285, 303

Dynamic accent, 292-294, 296

Dynamics, 314, 317, 350

Echappe, 139, 143, 149, 152, 240

Elision, 131, 133, 136

Embellishing tone, 139

Embellishment, 141, 150, 245, 298

Escape tone, 139, 143, 149-150, 152, 240

Extended version, 117, 119-120, 124, 126

False relation

Figured bass, 52-56, 59, 70, 72-74, 78-79, 82, 85, 91-92, 101, 187, 189, 227-232, 237-238, 244-245, 322

First inversion, 53-54, 56, 60, 69, 77-79, 85, 107, 227, 229-230, 249

Flatted fifth, 179, 184, 232, 146, 246-250

Forte (f), 314, 318

Fortissimo (ff), 314

Fragment, 116, 241

Fragmentation, 116, 119, 120-121, 124

Fragmented motive, 116, 120

Fugal imitation, 303, 306, 349

Fugue, 277-284, 303, 348

Function, 77, 153-154, 156, 162-166, 213, 240, 242-243, 254, 263

Genre, 301, 327-329, 351

Half cadence, 99-101, 103-104, 107-110, 127, 129-130, 252, 332, 340

Half step, 2, 6, 17-18, 29-30, 33-34, 39-40, 51-52, 77, 140, 179, 182, 217, 222, 229

Half-diminished seventh chord, 80, 85-86, 88, 96, 113-114, 247

Harmonic function, 153, 165-166, 243

Harmonic minor, 17, 19-21, 25-26, 28, 47, 63-64, 69, 77, 90, 111

Harmonic rhythm, 159-164

Hemiola, 293-294, 296

Heterophonic, 304

Heterophony, 304, 306-309, 349

Hidden fifths, 215

Hidden octaves, 215

Homophonic, 276, 299-301, 304, 306-307, 309, 349

Homophony, 299, 305, 307, 310, 326, 349

Homorhythmic, 299, 305-306, 349

Imitation, 116, 119-120, 124, 126, 241, 277, 302-303, 306-308, 310, 349

Imitative polyphony, 302-304, 306-308, 310, 349

Imperfect authentic cadence, 102-104, 107-108, 110, 130, 340

Inconclusive cadence, 99, 108

Instrumentation, 321, 324

Interlude, 327-329, 351

Internal expansion, 117, 119, 120, 124, 241

Interval, 29-34, 36-38, 43-44, 47-48, 52-53, 77, 79-80, 113-114, 117-118, 123, 180, 182, 195, 214, 217, 221, 229-230, 241, 247-248, 281, 320, 326, 346, 348

Introduction, 265, 273, 277, 302, 327, 332, 347, 348

Inversion of chords, 51-54, 56, 59, 60, 62, 69, 77-81, 85-86, 90-91, 107, 113, 156, 197, 209, 227-230, 234, 240, 245-246, 249-250, 252, 276, 311, 320, 326, 331, 340, 346

Inversion of melody, 117, 119, 120, 121, 124, 126, 241

Inverted interval, 35-36

Ionian mode, 39, 43, 45, 47-48, 50

Irregular meter, 285, 290, 295

Key signature, 1-3, 5-7, 12-14, 17, 19, 30, 32-33, 40-41, 43-44, 51, 56, 64, 66-67, 69, 78-79, 91, 111, 114, 227

Lead sheet, 245-246, 248-250

Leading tone, 17, 68, 74, 77, 89, 91, 95-97, 194-195, 197-198, 222, 224, 276

Legato, 313, 317-318, 350

Literal repetition, 116, 119, 121, 240-241, 298, 340

Locrian mode, 40, 43-45, 47, 50

Lower neighbor, 139, 143

Lydian mode, 39, 41, 43-45, 48, 50, 114

Lyrics, 327-328, 333, 337-338, 351

Major intervals, 29-36, 113

Major key/tonality, 1-6, 8, 11-16, 41, 43-44, 63, 68-69, 72, 74, 77-78, 89-96, 100-104, 111, 113-114, 118, 153, 167-168, 188-189, 193-199, 207, 227, 280, 346

Major seventh chord, 78-79, 85-86, 88-89, 113-114, 228, 247

Major triads (chords), 51-56, 59-60, 62-63, 69, 73, 77-78, 90-91, 96, 113-114, 158, 161, 179-181, 231-232, 246, 280

Major-major seventh chord, 78, 85

Major-minor seventh chord, 77-78, 85

Marcato, 313, 317, 350

Mediant, 68, 74, 198, 234

Melismatic, 333, 337-378, 352

Melodic inversion, 117, 119, 120, 121, 124, 126, 241

Melodic minor, 17-18, 20-21, 25-26, 28, 111

Melody with accompaniment, 245, 299, 304, 349

Melody, 116-119, 123, 125-126, 152, 165, 203, 205, 208-209, 213, 238, 241, 244-246, 254, 263, 267-270, 272-275, 281-282, 292, 299-304, 306, 340, 343-345, 347, 349, 352

Meter, 276, 285, 289-291, 293, 295-296, 298, 332, 340, 349

Metrical accent, 292, 294

Mezzo forte (mf), 314, 318, 350

Mezzo piano (mp), 314, 318, 350

Minor intervals, 29-36, 113

Minor key/tonality, 6-8, 11-17, 33, 51, 63-64, 68-69, 72-73, 90-91, 100, 103-104, 107, 111, 113-114, 180, 193-196, 200, 207, 276, 280, 346

Minor seventh chord, 77, 79-80, 86, 88-89, 96, 113, 247

Minor triads (chords), 51-52, 54, 60, 62-63, 73-74, 79, 96, 113, 158, 179, 181, 231-232, 246

Minor-minor seventh chord, 79, 85

Mixolydian mode, 39-40, 43-45, 47-48, 50

Modality, 29

Mode, 39-50, 111, 114

Modulation, 167-171, 175-178, 234, 276, 346

Monophonic, 299, 304, 307-310, 349

Monophony, 299

Motive, 115-117, 120-123, 136, 241-242, 258, 302, 320

Motivic transformation, 116, 120-121

Multimeter, 291, 296

Natural minor, 17-18, 20-21, 25-26, 28, 40, 47-48, 79, 111

Neighbor group, 139, 143, 149

Neighbor notes, 139, 141, 158

Neighboring 6/4, 156-157, 162, 166, 346

Neighboring chord, 156, 158, 160, 162-164, 166

Neighboring tone, 152

Nonharmonic tones, 139, 141, 143, 151-152, 241

Nonimitative polyphony, 304, 306, 308-310, 349

Note value, 241, 286

Obbligato, 323-324, 351

Objectionable parallels, 221

Oblique motion, 214, 217

Octave displacement, 118-120, 124, 126, 241

Open position, 189-190, 243

Opera, 327-329, 334, 338, 351

Ornament, 139, 141-143, 148-152, 234, 241, 304

Ostinato, 140, 143, 150, 152, 234, 240, 252, 282, 298, 300, 305, 307-309, 332, 349

Overlapping voices, 221, 224

Parallel fifths, 221, 224

Parallel intervals, 214, 221

Parallel keys, 6

Parallel major, 6

Parallel minor, 6, 13

Parallel motion, 214, 217

Parallel octaves, 221, 224

Parallel period, 128, 132-133, 135-136, 138

Passing tone, 140, 143, 149-150, 152, 234, 298

Pedal 6/4, 158, 162, 175, 346

Pedal point, 140, 143, 150, 152, 240, 252, 298, 332

Pentatonic, 18-19, 25-26, 28, 47, 73, 111, 113, 346

Percussion, 321-324, 326

Perfect authentic cadence, 102-104, 107-108, 110, 127, 129-130, 340

Perfect intervals, 11, 29-35, 43

Period (phrase structure), 127-129, 131-138, 141-142, 242, 282, 298

Phrase elision, 131, 133, 136

Phrase chain, 130, 131, 133

Phrase group, 130-138, 282

Phrase modulation, 168-169, 175-176, 178

Phrygian half cadence, 100-101, 103-104, 107, 109-110

Phrygian mode, 39-40, 43-45, 47, 50, 114

Pianissimo (pp), 314, 318, 350

Piano (p), 314, 318, 350

Picardy third, 180, 280

Pickup, 288, 296

Pivot chord modulation, 168-169, 175-176, 178

Pizzicato, 313, 317-318, 350

Plagal cadence, 99-101, 103-104, 107-110, 252, 332, 340

Polyphonic, 276, 302, 304, 306, 308-309, 349

Polyphony, 302-304, 306-310, 326, 349

Polyrhythm, 293, 295-296

Postlude, 327-329, 351

Pre-dominant function, 153-154, 162-164, 242

Prelude, 327-329, 351

Preparation, 141, 143, 152

Progression, 76, 97, 153, 158-161, 163, 166, 203, 206-210, 216, 244, 246, 282, 344

Pulse, 14, 285, 289-290, 293

Quadruple meter, 289-290, 295, 332

Quality, 30, 32, 35-36, 52, 56, 60, 62, 72-74, 85-86, 90-91, 96, 100, 158, 161, 193, 199, 227, 323, 351

Rate of harmonic change, 159-160, 164, 166

Realize, realization of figured bass, 227-229, 237, 244

Rearticulated suspension, 141, 143, 150

Refrain, 267, 273

Register, 333, 337-338, 352

Relative keys, 6

Relative major, 13, 14

Relative minor, 6, 13, 257

Repetition, 116, 119-120, 123, 126, 234, 302, 349

Resolution, 92, 98, 180, 182, 187, 216

Retardation, 141, 143

Retrograde, 117, 119-120, 123-124, 126, 241

Retrogression, 159, 162-163, 166, 282

Rhythm, 100, 115, 117-118, 122-123, 126, 159, 254, 263, 267, 269, 285, 287-288, 291-299, 301, 305-306, 312-313, 322-323, 326, 348-349

Rhythm section, 322-323

Rhythmic transformation, 118, 122, 126, 241

Roman numerals, 63-64, 66-68, 73, 78, 92, 98, 100-101, 104, 108, 114, 189, 203, 205, 207-209, 227, 230, 234, 237-238, 240, 244, 252, 276, 311, 320, 326, 331, 340, 346, 352

Root, 51-53, 55-56, 59, 62, 69, 77, 79-82, 86, 102, 156, 161, 189-190, 193-201, 213, 227, 247-249

Root position, 51-54, 60, 62, 77, 85, 102, 107, 193, 199-200, 227, 229-230, 240, 246-248

Rounded binary, 254, 256, 272, 347

Scale degrees, 39-40, 47, 63, 68, 74, 193, 198-199, 216, 234, 320, 340

Second inversion, 53-54, 60, 77-79, 85, 91, 156, 197, 227, 230, 249

Secondary dominant, 89-91, 95-98, 222, 254

Secondary leading tone chord, 89-91, 95-97

Semitone, 29, 33-34

Sequence, 116, 118-119, 123-124, 126, 240-241, 302

Sequential repetition, 116, 120

Seventh chords, 77-88, 190, 193, 197, 199-200, 228, 247

Shortened version, 118-120, 124

Similar motion, 139, 214-215, 217, 221, 224

Simple beat, 285-286

Slur, 313, 318, 350

Solo (Soli), 323-324, 326-328, 334, 343, 351

Sonata, 257-258, 263, 265, 272, 300, 327-328, 347, 351

Song, 206, 263, 268, 327-328, 333, 336-338, 343-344, 351-352

Song form, 343-344, 352

Soprano, 102, 185, 187-192, 196, 201-202, 211-215, 218-219, 221, 225-226, 233-234, 236-237, 239-240, 243, 252, 276, 310-311, 320, 325-326, 330-331, 340, 346

Staccato, 295, 313, 318, 350

Stanza, 267, 273-274, 347

String quartet, 327-329, 351

Strings, 313-314, 321-324, 326-327

Strophic, 268, 272-274, 347

Subdominant, 68, 74, 198, 204, 206, 234, 263, 320

Submediant, 68, 74, 198, 206, 320

Supertonic, 68, 74, 198, 206

Suspension chain, 141, 143, 152

Suspension, 141, 143, 150, 152, 179-184, 230, 240, 252

Swing rhythm, 293-296, 345

Syllabic, 333, 337-338, 352

Symphony, 327-328, 351

Syncopation, 293-295

Tempo, 14, 153, 155, 167, 170, 315-318, 320, 350

Tendency tone, 195, 216-217

Tenor, 185, 187-191, 200, 202, 211, 213-215, 218-219, 222, 225, 233, 235, 237, 239, 243, 310, 322, 325, 330

Tenuto, 313, 318, 350

Ternary, 256-257, 272, 347

Terraced dynamics, 314

Tessitura, 333, 337, 352

Tetrachord, 17, 26, 28

Thematic transformation, 115, 123, 268, 273-274, 347

Theme, 115-118, 123, 241, 258-259, 263, 265-266, 272-274, 277, 302-303, 347-349

393

Third inversion, 77-79, 85-86, 113

Tie, 263, 287

Timbre, 323-324, 351

Time signature, 14, 276, 285-287, 289-291, 293, 295, 349

Tonal, 1, 6, 13-14, 63, 277, 280-282, 348

Tonality, 1, 14, 114, 276, 346

Tonic, 68, 89, 102, 107, 153-154, 162-164, 198, 203, 216, 222, 234, 242, 258, 263, 277-278, 320

Tonic function, 153-154, 162-164, 242

Tonicization, 167, 172, 175, 177-178, 346

Transposition, 118-120, 122, 124, 241, 277, 282, 348

Triads, 46, 51-80, 85, 89, 95, 153, 196, 198

Triple meter, 289-290, 332

Triplet, 287-288, 293, 332

Tritone, 29-30, 34, 113-114, 221, 224

Truncation, 118-119, 124, 126, 234

Turnaround, 342, 344, 352

Tutti, 323-324, 351

Twelve-bar blues, 341, 344, 352

Unaccented passing tone, 140, 143

Unison, 29, 33-34, 113-114

Unresolved leading tone, 222, 224

Upbeat, 288, 296

Upper neighbor, 139, 143, 156

Voice exchange, 215, 218

Voice leading, 193, 213, 215-218, 221-222, 224, 238, 245

Walking bass, 301, 305, 306-308, 332

Whole step, 17, 29-30, 33-34, 182, 217

Whole tone, 18-21, 25-26, 28, 33, 41, 111, 113, 346

Woodwinds, 321-323, 326

Also Available from J. Johnson Music Publications

Basics of Keyboard Theory

Levels Preparatory through Ten

- Each level reviews old material and presents new concepts
- Excellent for transfer students; important reinforcement for returning students
- Clear, easy to understand explanation of skills with practice drills
- Analysis of new concepts in repertoire
- Multi-chapter reviews and final test include drills and analysis
- Successfully used and praised by hundreds of music teachers!

"Bravo! The books are excellent!"

"I love your theory books and am grateful that you have put them together in such an organized fashion."

"They are the clearest and most direct books I have seen."

Available at www.bktmusic.com, or ask your local music store

Instructions for MP3 CD

The CD, attached to the inside back cover, contains the Ear Training and Listening Examples. These files are in MP3 format, and may be loaded onto a computer. From the computer, they may be transferred to an MP3 player or burned onto four audio CD's.

To load the CD:

1. Place the CD into your computer's CD or DVD drive.
2. Select the CD or DVD Drive.
3. Copy and paste the files into your computer's music folder.
4. Follow the instructions in your media software to burn audio CD's if desired.

To purchase 4 audio CD's playable on traditional CD players, please email info@bktmusic.com.